THE BOOK OF INDIAN BIRDS

THE BOOK
OF
INDIAN BIRDS

SÁLIM ALI

With 74 plates in colour (depicting 296 species)
3 in line and 22 in half-tone

ELEVENTH EDITION

BOMBAY NATURAL HISTORY SOCIETY
OXFORD UNIVERSITY PRESS
BOMBAY DELHI CALCUTTA MADRAS

Oxford University Press

OXFORD NEW YORK

DELHI BOMBAY CALCUTTA MADRAS KARACHI PETALING JAYA SINGAPORE
HONG KONG TOKYO NAIROBI DAR ES SALAAM MELBOURNE AUCKLAND

and associates in

BERLIN IBADAN

First published, August 1941
Second edition, October 1942
Third edition, June 1944
Reprinted, December 1945
Fourth edition, October 1946
Fifth edition (Revised), 1955
Sixth edition (Revised and enlarged), 1961
Seventh edition (Revised), 1964
Eighth edition (Revised and enlarged), 1968
Ninth edition (Revised), 1972
Tenth edition (Revised and enlarged), 1977
Eleventh edition (Revised and enlarged), 1979
Reprinted, August 1984, *May* 1986, *June* 198
Reprinted, February 1990
Reprinted, 1992
Reprinted, 1993

SBN 19 562167 0

PRINTED IN INDIA BY BRO. PAULINUS JOHN AT ST. FRANCIS INDUSTRIAL
TRAINING INSTITUTE, MOUNT POINSUR, BORIVLI, BOMBAY 400 103 AND
PUBLISHED BY BOMBAY NATURAL HISTORY SOCIETY AND CO-PUBLISHED BY
S.K. MOOKERJEE, OXFORD UNIVERSITY PRESS, OXFORD HOUSE, APOLLO
BUNDER, BOMBAY 400 039

PREFACE

THE publication by the Bombay Natural History Society in 1961 of A SYNOPSIS OF THE BIRDS OF INDIA AND PAKISTAN by S. Dillon Ripley meant an upheaval for bird students in this country accustomed to the older order of classification. The latter had been followed in all important publications on Indian birds since the first edition of the Bird volumes in the FAUNA OF BRITISH INDIA series by Oates and Blanford (1889-1898), including the second edition of that work by E. C. Stuart Baker (1922-1930), POPULAR HANDBOOK OF INDIAN BIRDS by Hugh Whistler (1949), the fifth edition of THE BOOK OF INDIAN BIRDS, and others as well as in periodical literature. The change was bound to cause some inconvenience and confusion at first, but it had become essential in order to bring Indian ornithology in line with the system of classification which, with minor variations, has now come to be internationally accepted and adopted. Ripley's SYNOPSIS and all present-day publications on birds, including those pertaining to our neighbouring areas — the Palaearctic Region, Burma, Thailand, Malaysia, Sri Lanka and others — follow the modern system. Increasing use and familiarity with the new arrangement should soon dispel its initial disadvantages for Indian bird students. Therefore an attempt has been made to modernize the sequence of Orders and Families to accord with the prevailing 'fashion'. This has been largely achieved by appropriate shifting and rearrangement of the plates and text. Despite some remaining inconsistencies, due to the old illustrations having been specially prepared for the superseded classification, the result has been more satisfactory than was at first thought possible. Nevertheless the list showing the new sequence of Orders and Families has been retained from the 8th edition as a corrective where necessary.

The omission of a number of species commonly seen in certain parts of the plains, and likewise in the peninsular hills, was a source of inconvenience to users of the book. By the addition of eight new colour plates depicting 32 extra species and their descriptions it is sought to remove this lacuna in part. Thus the present edition embraces the entire subcontinent south of the Himalayas together with Sri Lanka—hills as well as plains. It now covers 296 birds illustrated in colour and fully described, in addition to several others briefly noticed. The species selected are amongst the more common and readily seen birds in the country, chiefly in the plains and foothills. They represent just under 15 per cent of the total avifauna of India as listed in SYNOPSIS and described and illustrated in the 10 volumes of HANDBOOK OF THE BIRDS OF INDIA AND PAKISTAN (including also those of Bangladesh, Nepal, Sikkim, Bhutan and Sri Lanka) by Sálim Ali & S. Dillon Ripley published between 1968 and 1974.

Hindi names of birds have been provided wherever available. I cannot vouch for their correctness in all cases or say how common or well understood they are in general. But it seems obvious, if bird study is to prosper and develop in India, that simple Hindi names should be standardized —if necessary coined or borrowed from other languages — and put into circulation as early as possible under the authority of some recognized central organization like the Bombay Natural History Society.

The standards of size employed in previous editions have been retained as they were on the whole found satisfactory in practice except in the case of complete strangers to the country and its birds. The size in inches given after each ' standard ' should help the latter up to a point.

A	Sparrow	6"	G	Crow	17"
B	Quail	7-8"	H	Kite	24"
C	Bulbul	8"	I	Duck	24"
D	Myna	9"	J	Village hen	18-30"
E	Pigeon	13"	K	Vulture	36"
F	Partridge	13"			

Minus and plus signs are used to indicate whether the bird is smaller or bigger than the standard.

October, 1979
S.A.

CONVERSION TABLE
(to metric system)

1 inch	=	2·54 centimetres
10 inches	=	25·4 cm
1 foot	=	30·48 cm
10 feet	=	304·8 cm or 3·048 metres
100 feet	=	30·48 m
1000 feet	=	304·8 m

CONTENTS

Black and White Plates

Diagrams

Maps

Order COLUMBIFORMES

Family PTEROCLIDIDAE: Sandgrouse
    ,,   COLUMBIDAE: Pigeons and Doves

Order PSITTACIFORMES

Family PSITTACIDAE: Parrots

Order CUCULIFORMES

Family CUCULIDAE: Cuckoos

Order STRIGIFORMES

Family STRIGIDAE
  Subfamily TYTONINAE: Barn Owls
        ,,   STRIGINAE: Owls

Order CAPRIMULGIFORMES

Family CAPRIMULGIDAE: Nightjars

Order APODIFORMES

Family APODIDAE
  Subfamily APODINAE: Swifts
        ,,   HEMIPROCNINAE: Crested Tree Swifts

Order TROGONIFORMES

Family TROGONIDAE: Trogons

Order CORACIIFORMES

Family ALCEDINIDAE: Kingfishers
    ,,   MEROPIDAE: Bee-eaters
    ,,   CORACIIDAE: Rollers
    ,,   UPUPIDAE: Hoopoes
    ,,   BUCEROTIDAE: Hornbills

Order PICIFORMES

Family CAPITONIDAE: Barbets
    ,,   PICIDAE: Woodpeckers

Order PASSERIFORMES

Family PITTIDAE: Pittas
    ,,   ALAUDIDAE: Larks
    ,,   HIRUNDINIDAE: Swallows
    ,,   I ANIIDAE: Shrikes
    ,,   ORIOLIDAE: Orioles
    ,,   DICRURIDAE: Drongos

CHANGES IN TERRITORIAL NAMES

Within recent years many areas of the subcontinent have changed their names and boundaries. The following note is provided to avoid confusion and enable users to keep up with the changes.

Andhra Pradesh: Until 1953 the northern half of Madras State, including the deltas of the Krishna and Godavari rivers and the arid hills of the Eastern Ghats. **Arunachal Pradesh:** 'The Province of the Dawn'. The Himalayas east of Bhutan, including the Dafla, Abor, Miri and Mishmi Hills; before 1972 this area was the North-East Frontier Agency (NEFA) comprising the Kameng, Subansiri, Siang and Luhit frontier divisions. **Assam:** Before 1947 this province included Arunachal Pradesh, Meghalaya, Mizoram and Nagaland (qq. v.); in 1972 it was restricted to the Brahmaputra Valley. **Bangladesh:** Constituted in 1971, formerly East Pakistan; besides the Brahmaputra plains it includes the Chittagong Hill Tracts in the south. **Bengal:** Prior to 1947 the Ganges-Brahmaputra delta area, later divided into Bangladesh (q.v.) and West Bengal. **Haryana:** The fertile plains area north and west of Delhi, formerly part of the Punjab (q.v.). **Himachal Pradesh:** 'The Snowy Province'. The Himalayan hill States were united under this name in 1948, and in 1966 the area was enlarged by the hill regions of the Punjab. **Karnataka:** The official name of Mysore since 1973. **Lakshadweep:** The official name of the Laccadive Islands since 1973. **Meghalaya:** 'Cloud-land'. The Garo, Jaintia, Khasi and Cachar hill districts, constituted a separate State in 1972. **Mizoram:** The Lushai or Mizo Hills area, constituted a separate State in 1972. **Nagaland:** The Naga Hills area, constituted a separate State in 1962. **NEFA:** Now Arunachal Pradesh (q.v.). **Oudh** (= Awadh): The eastern Gangetic plains, now part of Uttar Pradesh ('Northern Province'), the name given in 1950 to the United Provinces of Agra and Oudh. **Pakistan:** Sind, Baluchistan, Punjab (q.v.), the North-West Frontier Province and Bahawalpur, **Punjab:** Prior to 1947 the whole of the northern plains area watered by the Indus, and its five tributaries, namely Jhelum, Chenab, Ravi, Beas and Sutlej; divided in 1947 into West Punjab (Pakistan) and East Punjab (India). In 1966 East Punjab was further divided into Punjab, Haryana and Himachal Pradesh (qq. v.). **Saurashtra:** The union of Kathiawar States was merged with Bombay in 1956 and since 1960 has been part of Gujarat. **Sri Lanka:** The official name of Ceylon since May 1972. **Tamil Nadu:** The name given to Madras State in 1969.

INTRODUCTION

What is a Bird ?

A BIRD has been described as a ' Feathered Biped '. This description is apt and precise, and can apply to no other animal.

Birds are vertebrate warm-blooded animals, i.e. whose temperature remains more or less constant and independent of the surrounding temperature. This is in contradistinction to Reptiles, Amphibians and Fishes which are cold-blooded, i.e. of temperature that changes with the hotness or coldness of their surroundings.

To assist in maintaining an even temperature, the body of a bird is covered with non-conducting feathers — its chief characteristic — which in details of structure and arrangement reflect the mode of life of the group to which the bird belongs. Compare for example the thick, soft, well-greased covering on the underside of an aquatic bird like a Duck or Grebe with the peculiar, narrow, hairlike, ' double ' feathers of the Cassowary to be seen in any zoo. Except in the Flightless Birds such as the last named, the Ostrich and the Penguin (*Ratitae* and *Sphenici*) whose feathers grow more or less evenly over the entire surface of the body, the growth of feathers is restricted only to welldefined patches or tracts known as *pterylae* on various parts of the body, whence they fall over and evenly cover the adjoining naked interspaces or *apteria*. A study of the arrangement of the feather tracts (*pterylosis*) which varies in the different orders, families, and even species, is of great importance in determining the natural relationships of different birds.

The feathers covering the body of a bird fall into 3 classes: (1) the ordinary outside feathers known as Contour feathers or *pennae*, whether covering the body as a whole or specialised as pinions or flight feathers (remiges) or as tail feathers (rectrices) which serve as rudder and brake; (2) the fluffy Down feathers or *plumulae* hidden by the Contour feathers and comparable to flannel underclothing, whether confined to nestlings or persisting throughout life; (3) the hairlike Filo-plumes which are hardly seen until the other feathers have been plucked off. They are particularly noticeable, for instance, in a plucked pigeon.

The body temperature of birds, about 38°-44°C., is higher than that of most mammals. Assisted by their non-conducting covering of feathers birds are able to withstand great extremes of climate. As long as they can procure a sufficiency of food supply, or 'fuel' for the system, it makes little material difference to them whether the surrounding temperature is over 60°C. on the burning desert sands or 40°C. below zero in the icy frozen north. Their rate of metabolism is higher than that of mammals. They lack sweat-glands. The extra heat generated by their extreme activity which would, under torrid climatic conditions result in overheating, fever, and death, is eliminated through the lungs and air sacs as fast as it is produced. For one of the functions of the 'air sacs' — a feature peculiar to birds and found in various parts within the body — is to promote internal perspiration. Water vapour diffuses from the blood into these cavities and passes out by way of the lungs, with which they are indirectly connected.

In addition to these two cardinal attributes, warm-bloodedness and insulated feather covering, birds as a class possess certain well-marked characteristics which equip them pre-eminently for a life in the air. In India we have at present no indigenous flightless birds like the Ostrich or the Penguin, so these need not be considered here. The forelimbs of birds, which correspond to human arms or to the forelegs of quadrupeds, have been evolved to serve as perfect organs of propulsion through the air. Many of their larger bones are hollow and often have air sacs running into them which, as mentioned above, function principally as accessory respiratory organs. This makes for lightness without sacrificing strength, and is a special adaptation to facilitate aerial locomotion. Modifications in the structure of the breast bone, pectoral girdle and other parts of the skeleton, and the enormously developed breast muscles enable a bird to fly in the air. It has been estimated from analogy with birds that a man, to be able to lift himself off the ground by his own effort, would require breast muscles at least 4 feet deep! There is, moreover, a general tendency for various bones to fuse with each other, conducing to increased rigidity of the skeletal frame — also a factor of great importance in flight. As a whole the perfectly streamlined spindle-shaped body of a bird is designed to offer the minimum resistance to the wind. On account of their warm-bloodedness coupled with these peculiar facilities for locomotion with which Nature has endowed them, birds enjoy a wider distribution on the earth than any other class of animals. They cross ocean barriers and find their way to remote regions and isolated islands, and exist under physical conditions where their cold-blooded relatives must perish. It is also this power of swift and sustained flight that enables birds living in northern lands to migrate periodically over enormous distances in order to escape from the rigours of winter — shortening days and dwindling food supply — to warmer and more hospitable climes.

Birds are believed to have sprung from reptilian ancestors in bygone aeons. At first sight this appears a far-fetched notion, for on the face of it there seems little in common between the grovelling cold-blooded reptile and the graceful, soaring warm-blooded bird. But palaeontological evidence, supplied chiefly by the earliest fossil of an undoubted bird to which we have access — the *Archaeopteryx* — and modern researches on the skeletal and other characteristics of our present-day birds, tend in a great measure to support this belief. The method of articulation of the skull with the backbone, for instance, and the nucleated red blood corpuscles of the bird are distinctly reptilian in character. To this may be added the fact that birds lay eggs which in many cases closely resemble those of reptiles in appearance and composition, and that the development of the respective embryos up to a point is identical. In the majority of birds scales are present on the tarsus and toes which are identical with the scales of reptiles. In some birds, like sandgrouse and certain eagles and owls, the legs are covered with feathers, a fact which suggests that feathers are modified scales and that the two may be interchangeable. The outer covering of the bills of certain birds, for example the Puffin (*Fratercula arctica*), is shed annually after breeding in the same way as the slough in reptiles. The periodical moulting of birds is also essentially the same process as the sloughing of reptiles. In short, birds may reasonably be considered to be extremely modified reptiles, and according to the widely accepted classification of the great scientist T. H. Huxley, the two classes together form the division of vertebrates termed Sauropsida.

*   *   *

Of the senses, those of Sight and Hearing are most highly developed in birds; that of Taste is comparatively poor, while Smell is practically absent. In rapid accommodation of the eye, the bird surpasses all other creatures. The focus can be altered from a distant object to a near one almost instantaneously; as an American naturalist puts it, ' in a fraction of time it (the eye) can change itself from a telescope to a microscope '.

*   *   *

For the safety of their eggs and young, birds build nests which may range from a simple scrape in the ground, as of the Lapwing, to such elaborate structures as the compactly woven nest of the Weaver Bird. With rare exceptions they incubate the eggs with the heat of their own bodies and show considerable solicitude for the young until they are able to fend for themselves. Careful experiments suggest however, that in all the seemingly intelligent and purposeful actions of nesting birds, in the solicitude they display for the welfare of their young and in the tactics they employ when the latter are in danger, *instinct* and not intelligence is the primary operating factor. The power of reasoning and the ability to meet new situations and overcome obstacles beyond the simplest, are non-existent. It is good therefore always to bear this in mind when studying birds, and to remember that their actions and behaviour cannot be judged purely by comparison with human standards and emotions.

*　　　*　　　*

The total number of bird species known to science as inhabiting the earth to-day has been estimated as about 8600. If subspecies or geographical races are taken into account the figure would rise to nearly 30,000.

For its size, the erstwhile ' Indian Empire ' or ' British India ', in which, besides Pakistan and Burma it was customary for biological considerations to include Ceylon as well, contains one of the richest and most varied avifaunas on the face of the globe. Covering some 40 degrees of latitude and about the same of longitude, it encloses within its boundaries a vast diversity of climate and physical features. These range from the dry, scorching sandy deserts of Sind and Rajasthan and the humid evergreen rain forests of Assam and the southern Western Ghats, to the region of glaciers and eternal snow in the mighty Himalayas. Smooth wide spaces of depressed river basins, either sandy, dry and sun-scorched or cultivated, or waterlogged under a steamy moisture-laden atmosphere (the *terai*) lie along the base of the northern ramparts. The great central Indian and Deccan plateaux succeed the fertile alluvial Gangetic Plain and are flanked on tne west by the broken crags and castellated outlines of the ridges of the Western Ghats which overlook the Arabian Sea and continue southward in gentle, smoothly rounded slopes of green uplands — the Nilgiri and other hills of southern India.

This vast subcontinent — two-thirds of Europe in superficial area — with its extensive coastline, affords suitable living conditions to a great variety of feathered inhabitants. The second edition of the FAUNA OF BRITISH INDIA series on Birds enumerated some 2400 forms (species and subspecies). The latest checklist, A SYNOPSIS OF THE BIRDS OF INDIA AND PAKISTAN (which excludes Burma) lists 2061 forms of which over 300 are winter visitors, chiefly from the Palaearctic Region to the north.

The area as a whole falls into the zoogeographical division of the earth known as the Oriental Region. For the sake of convenience it

xvii

has been split up (Blanford, *Phil. Trans. of the Royal Soc.* Vol. 194, 1901, pp. 335-436) into 5 primary subdivisions as under:

(*a*) T h e I n d o - G a n g e t i c P l a i n extending across the whole of northern India from the Arabian Sea to the Bay of Bengal. Its boundaries run up the hill ranges from Karachi to Peshawar, thence along the outer spurs of the Himalayas to Bhutan, and thence roughly southward to east of the Sundarbans. The southern boundary takes a line from the Rann of Kutch to Delhi and from about Agra to Rajmahal whence it goes south to the Bay of Bengal.

(*b*) P e n i n s u l a r I n d i a, southward of the above area.

(*c*) C e y l o n.

(*d*) T h e H i m a l a y a s including the whole area of the mountain ranges from their foothills up to the limit of tree-growth.

(*e*) A s s a m (and B u r m a).

The Punjab, Sind and Rajasthan, however, have a fauna differing considerably from that of the other parts of India and resembling that found in W. Asia and N. Africa, whilst the animals of the Higher Himalayas (above the tree-line) and the Upper Indus Valley resemble those of central Asia. Both these areas belong to the zoogeographical region which extends over the greater part of Asia and all Europe, known as the Palaearctic.

A still further splitting of the fauna within these broad subdivisions on the basis of ecological or environmental factors is clearly desirable. A scrutiny shows that there is a close similarity between the fauna and flora of those regions in which the incidence of the Southwest Monsoon is heaviest, namely the Himalayas east of Sikkim and the hilly portions of Assam and Burma on the one hand, and the southwestern corner of the Indian peninsula, south of about Goa, together with the southwestern portions of Ceylon, on the other. On account of the similar physical configuration of all these areas and their geographical position relative to the strike of the SW. Monsoon currents, they are areas of heavy rainfall and excessive humidity. These, precisely, are two of the most important factors that regulate the character of the vegetation. Similarity in vegetation is a striking feature of these heavy-rainfall areas. As would be expected, this similarity extends to the insect forms dependent upon the plants, which in turn conduce to similarity in the birds predatory upon them. It has therefore been suggested that all these parallel areas, far-flung though they be, are perhaps better lumped together in one zoogeographical subdivision.

There are certain biological axioms of more or less universal application which are found to hold good in the case of our Indian avifauna also. They are of great importance, particularly in view of the modern practice of recognizing geographical variations and races. A cursory glance through any well-arranged museum collection, or through the description of geographical races in any up-to-date work on systematic ornithology reveals the fact that the largest race of a bird species — this is true of other warm-blooded animals as well — is, with rare exceptions, found inhabiting the cooler part of its distributional range while the smallest inhabits the warmer. Parallel with this axiom is the fact that in the Northern Hemisphere races occupying the cooler (northern) portions of the range of a species tend to lay larger clutches of eggs than those occupying warmer (southern) parts.

Furthermore, it is well known that of a given species the races that inhabit desert areas are always pale or sandy-coloured whereas those living under the influence of heavy rainfall, in well-wooded or humid tracts, tend to be darker in coloration. This is true not only of individual races and species, but also of the entire aspect of the avifauna of these tracts as a whole. What the precise factors are that bring about these changes in coloration, and the manner of their operation, we do not know. That humidity has to do with increased pigmentation is clear enough, and it has recently been suggested that the reduced force of ultraviolet rays due to water vapour suspended in the air may account for the darkening.

* * *

A few remarks with regard to the classification of birds seem called for in the interest of the beginner. It will be observed that after the English or trivial name of each species in the following pages, there appear two Latin names. The practice of employing a uniform Latin terminology is current throughout the modern scientific world. It is a boon to workers in different countries since it is more or less constant and enables the reader of one nation to understand what the writer of another is talking about. To take an example: What the Englishman calls Hoopoe is Wiedehopf to the German. A Pole knows the bird as something else — doubtless with a good many c's, z's s's and other consonants in bewildering juxta position—while the Russian has yet another equally fantastic looking name for it. A fair working knowledge of a language seldom implies a familiarity with popular names as of birds, for instance, many of which often are of purely local or colloquial application. Thus it is possible that while the Englishman may follow more or less all he reads in German about the Wiedehopf he may still be left in some doubt as to the exact identity of the bird. The international Latin name *Upupa epops* after the English or Polish or Russian name will leave no doubt as to what species is meant.

In the above combination the first name *Upupa* denotes the Genus of the bird corresponding roughly, in everyday human terms, to the surname. The second name *epops* indicates the Species and corresponds, so to say, to the Christian name. Modern trend of scientific usage has tended to split up the Species further into smaller units called Geographical Races or Subspecies. An example will clarify what this means: It will be admitted that all the peoples living in India are human and belong to one and the same human species. Yet a casual glance is enough to show that the Punjabi is a very different type in build and physiognomy from the dweller in Madras. The differences, though small, are too obvious to be overlooked. They are primarily the result of environment which includes not only climatic conditions of heat and cold, dampness and dryness, but also of diet and many other subtle factors working unceasingly upon the organism in direct or indirect ways. Thus while retaining all our inhabitants under the human species, when you talk of the Madrasi or the Punjabi you automatically recognize the sum total of the differences wrought in either by his particular environment.

A comparative study of birds reveals that there are similar minor but well-marked and readily recognizable differences in size, coloration and other details in those species which range over a wide area and live under diversified natural conditions, or which have been subjected to prolonged isolation as on oceanic islands, or through other causes. It is important for science that these differences should be duly recognized and catalogued since they facilitate the study of speciation and evolution. This recognition is signified by adding a third Latin name to the two already existing, to designate the Geographical Race or Subspecies. Thus, for example the House Crow, *Corvus splendens*, has been subdivided on the basis of constant differences in size and coloration brought about in the different portions of the ' Indian Empire ' it occupies as follows:

> *Corvus splendens splendens* (the nominate race), Common House Crow
> *Corvus splendens zugmayeri*, Sind House Crow
> *Corvus splendens insolens*, Burmese House Crow
> *Corvus splendens protegatus*, Ceylon House Crow

Barring restricted areas and particular groups of birds which still require careful collecting and working out, we can now claim to have a sufficiency of dead ornithological material from India in the great museums of the world to satisfy the needs of even an exacting taxonomist. Most bird lovers in this country possess neither the inclination, training, nor facilities for making any substantial additions to our knowledge of systematics. Speaking generally, therefore, Indian *systematic* ornithology is best left in the hands of the specialist or museum worker who has the necessary material and facilities at his command. Our greatest need to-day is for careful and rational field work on *living* birds in their natural environment, or what is known as Bird Ecology. It is a virgin field; both the serious student and the intelligent amateur can contribute towards building up this knowledge. A great many biological problems await solution by intensive ecological study. This is a line of field research that may be commended to workers in India; it will afford infinitely more pleasure and is capable of achieving results of much greater value and usefulness than the mere collecting and labelling of skins.

Among the questions which the ornithologist in India is constantly being asked are the following. I have had to face them so frequently, from such a variety of people and in such far-flung corners of the country that it might perhaps be as well to devote a little space to them here.

Q. What is the largest Indian bird, and what the smallest?

A. It is not easy to say which particular one is *the* largest, but amongst the upper ten are certainly the Sarus Crane (p. 37) and the Himalayan Bearded Vulture or Lämmergeier. The former stands the height of a man; the latter has a wing spread of over 8 feet. Amongst our smallest birds are the flowerpeckers, e.g. Tickell's Flowerpecker (p. 119) scarcely bigger than a normal thumb.

Q. What is our most beautiful bird?

A. Difficult to pick out any single species for the highest honour, and depends rather on individual tastes. A large number of birds of many different families, particularly those resident in areas of humid evergreen forest, possess extraordinarily brilliant plumage. As a family, the pheasants occupy a high place for colour and brilliancy of plumage and adornment possessed by the cocks of most species. At the bottom of the size ladder come the sunbirds — tiny creatures about half the size of the House Sparrow or less — whose glistening resplendent plumage scintillating in the bright sunshine as they flit from flower to flower, or dart from one forest glade to another, transforms them into living gems.

Q. What is our commonest bird, and what our rarest?

A. The answer depends largely on what part of the country you live in. But for India as a whole, perhaps the House Crow and the Sparrow would be hard to beat for commonness and abundance. They have followed Man everywhere — up in the hills and out in the desert — wherever his ingenuity has created liveable conditions for himself. Next in abundance come birds like Mynas and Bulbuls which though not wholly commensal on Man are yet quick to profit by his presence and activities.

Perhaps the three rarest birds in India at present are the Mountain Quail (*Ophrysia superciliosa*), Jerdon's Courser (*Cursorius bitorquatus*), and the Pinkheaded Duck (*Rhodonessa caryophyllacea*), all illustrated and described (pp. 19-20). The first has not been met with since 1876 and the second since 1900, and all attempts to re-discover them have ended in failure. The fate of the Pinkheaded Duck is also shrouded in mystery and to all appearances the species has become extinct. The last example shot was in 1935, and though it has since been reported off and on as seen by sportsmen, in all the cases investigated these reports have proved unreliable, the bird actually seen being the Redcrested Pochard (p. 19).

Q. Do birds have a language?

A. They certainly have, if by language is meant that they can communicate with and understand one another. It consists not of speech as we know it, but of simple sounds and actions and enables birds — especially the more sociable ones — to maintain contact amongst themselves and convey simple reactions such as those of pleasure, threat, alarm, invitation, and others. Several of these signals — vocal, behavioural, or a combination of the two — are understood not only by members of the same species but also by other birds generally, e.g. the alarm-notes and behaviour of many on the approach of a marauding hawk. To this extent Man can also claim to understand the language of birds; Solomon himself could hardly have done more. But the structure of a bird's brain suggests a comparatively low level of intelligence and precludes the possibility of their holding regular conversations or expressing views and opinions as we humans are usually so ready to do!

Q. What is our most accomplished songster? and talker?

A. Personally, for song I would give the palm to the Greywinged Blackbird (*Turdus boulboul*) of the Himalayas. A number of its close relations, members of the Thrush family, including the Malabar Whistling Thrush (p. 112) and the Shama (p. 109) follow close on its heels.

The best talker amongst our Indian birds is certainly the Hill Myna (p. 88) whose articulation of the human voice and speech is infinitely clearer and truer than that of the parakeets. The latter enjoy a wider reputation and are more generally kept as cage birds because more readily procured.

Q. How long does a bird live?

A. The age-potential, or the age to which a bird is capable of living, of course varies according to species and to the environment and conditions under which it lives. Reliable data concerning the life-span of wild birds in a state of nature are very difficult to obtain. It is only possible by the method of marking individual birds, particularly as nestlings. Most of the figures of age available are from birds in captivity and therefore living under somewhat unnatural conditions. It is known that within a group of related forms the larger the bird the longer its life, but outside related groups, size does not seem to matter a great deal. An ostrich in captivity has lived for 40 years; a raven to 69 and another to 50. Passerine birds of about Sparrow size have occasionally reached 25 years although normally their span is 5 to 8. A vulture attained 52, a horned owl 68, swan 25, pigeon 22 to 35, peacock 20. The longest lived wild birds in a natural state, as determined by the marking method, are: herring gull 36 years, oriole 8, pintail duck at least 13, grey heron about 16, blackbird 10, curlew $31\frac{1}{2}$, kite $25\frac{3}{4}$, and swallow $16 +$.

The common belief that crows are immortal is of course groundless, while there seems no proof for the popular assertion that vultures ' score centuries '.

Finally, to those desiring a closer acquaintance with birds in general, no better or more readable book can be recommended than THE BIOLOGY OF BIRDS by J. A. Thomson, but this is now out of print. Two other useful books on general ornithology, though largely using American examples, are NATURAL HISTORY OF BIRDS by Leonard W. Wing (The Ronald Press Co., New York) and AN INTRODUCTION TO ORNITHOLOGY by George J. Wallace (The Macmillan Co., New York). For India in particular, the excellent serial on ' The Study of Indian Birds ' by Hugh Whistler published in the *Journal of the Bombay Natural History Society*, and his POPULAR HANDBOOK OF INDIAN BIRDS are useful guides. Inglis and Fletcher's BIRDS OF AN INDIAN

GARDEN is good and describes and illustrates a number of the commoner species. Douglas Dewar's series of books on Indian birds will be found helpful, and no one should be without EHA's (E. H. Aitken) classic little COMMON BIRDS OF BOMBAY which, despite its title, covers a good many of the commoner birds found in India[1]. For masterly touch of matter and charm of style EHA is unapproachable. To the advanced student the 8 volumes of the 2nd edition of the FAUNA OF BRITISH INDIA series on Birds by Stuart Baker and the 4 companion volumes of his NIDIFICATION OF BIRDS OF THE INDIAN EMPIRE must remain indispensable for a long time to come. To these must now be added HANDBOOK OF THE BIRDS OF INDIA AND PAKISTAN in ten volumes, by Sálim Ali and S. Dillon Ripley (Oxford University Press). This work is, in effect, a revision and updating of Stuart Baker's FAUNA volumes and contains, in addition, colour illustrations and field identification clues for practically every bird found within our limits. It is thus comprehensive and of equal usefulness to the museum ornithologist as to the bird watcher. To facilitate cross reference to the HANDBOOK for more detailed information the relevant volume number has been indicated in the following pages under each species.

[1] A new edition of this was published in 1946 by Thacker & Co. Ltd., Bombay, under the title COMMON BIRDS OF INDIA with notes by Salim Ali and a biographical sketch of the author by W. T. Loke.

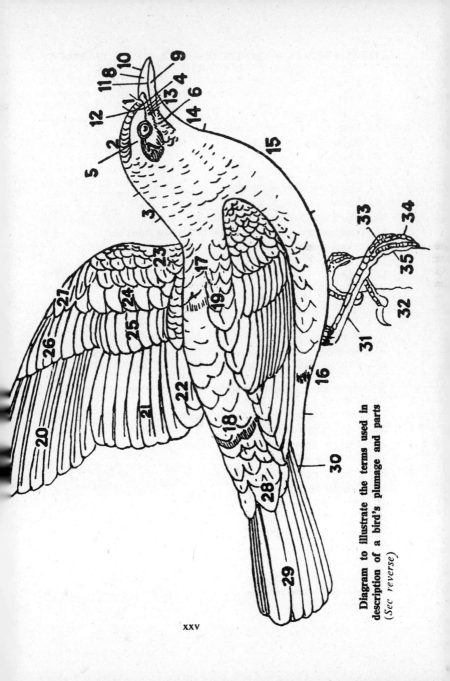

Diagram to illustrate the terms used in description of a bird's plumage and parts

(*See reverse*)

xxv

TERMS USED IN DESCRIPTION OF A BIRD'S PLUMAGE AND PARTS

1. Forehead
2. Crown
3. Nape or occiput
4. Lores (space in front of eye)
5. Supercilium
6. Cheeks
7. Ear-coverts
8. Upper mandible or maxilla
9. Lower mandible
10. Culmen or upper profile of maxilla
11. Commissure or line of junction of the two mandibles
12. Rictal bristles or vibrissae
13. Chin
14. Throat
15. Breast
16. Abdomen
17. Back
18. Rump
19. Scapulars
20. Primaries (the earlier or outermost 9 or 10 visible quills of the wing)
21. Outer secondaries (wing-quills springing from the radius and ulna)
22. Inner secondaries, tertiaries or tertials
23. Lesser wing-coverts
24. Median wing-coverts
25. Greater wing-coverts
26. Primary wing-coverts
27. Winglet or bastard wing
28. Upper tail-coverts
29. Tail feathers or rectrices
30. Under tail-coverts
31. Tarsus
32. Hind toe or first toe, or hallux
33. Inner or second toe
34. Middle or third toe
35. Outer or fourth toe

Types of Bills

1. *Cutting*

2. *Tearing and piercing flesh*

3. *Seed crushing*

4. *Flower probing*

5. *Wood chiselling*

6. *Mud probing*

7. *A sieve for straining mud*

8. *Tooth-edged for gripping fish*

1. Jungle Crow 2. Pariah Kite 3. House Sparrow 4. Purple Sunbird
5. Goldenbacked Woodpecker 6. Stilt 7. Flamingo 8. Cormorant

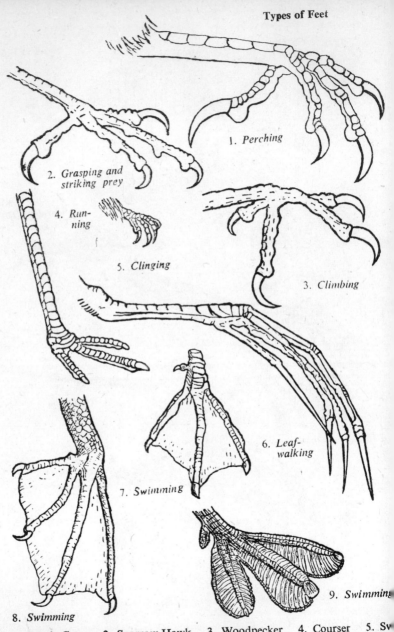

1. *Perching*

2. *Grasping and striking prey*

4. *Running*

5. *Clinging*

3. *Climbing*

6. *Leaf-walking*

7. *Swimming*

8. *Swimming*

9. *Swimming*

1. Jungle Crow 2. Sparrow-Hawk 3. Woodpecker 4. Courser 5. Sw
6. Jaçana 7. Gull 8. Cormorant 9. Dabchick or Grebe

HOW TO RECOGNIZE BIRDS IN THE FIELD

1. Birds with prominent Tails

Size *	Species	Length of Tail	Predominant colours of Bird	Page
A —	Indian Wren-Warbler (6e) ..	2″	Earthy brown.. ..	107
	Ashy Wren-Warbler ..	2″	Ashy slate, fulvous-white	108
	Tailor Bird ..	1½″-3½″	Olive-green, white ..	108
A	Grey Wagtail (5b)	4″ —	Grey, yellow	117
	White Wagtail ..	4″ —	White, grey, black ..	118
	Yellowheaded Wagtail (5b) ..	4″ —	Black, yellow, grey ..	117
	Common Swallow	3-5″	Steel blue, pinkish white, chestnut ..	82
	Wiretailed Swallow	7″ —	Steel blue, white, chestnut	81
	Redrumped Swallow	4″	Steel blue, fulvous, white	81
	Green Bee-eater (2, 5a)	5″	Green	70
C —	Crested Tree Swift (3, 6d)	5″ +	Blue-grey, whitish ..	62
C	Bluetailed Bee-eater (5a) ..	6″ —	Green	71
	Paradise Fly-catcher, *ad. male* (3, 6b)	10-15″	White, black	102
	Paradise Fly-catcher, *imm. male* (3, 6e) ..	10-15″	Chestnut, black, white	102
	Shama	6″	Black, chestnut, white	109
	Black Drongo (6a)	7″ —	Black..	85
	Whitebellied Drongo ..	6″	Indigo, whitish ..	85
	Common Babbler (6e)	5″	Streaked earthy brown	100
	Large Pied Wagtail (6c) ..	5″ —	Pied black & white ..	118
D	Tree Pie (6e) ..	12″	Chestnut brown, sooty black, grey	92
	Whitebellied Tree Pie (6e) ..	12″	Chestnut-bay, white ..	140
D	Racket-tailed Drongo (3, 6a)	15″	Black	86

* See Key on p. vii.

The numbers in brackets after name of species are to facilitate cross reference to these keys.

1. Birds with prominent Tails — contd.

Size *	Species	Length of Tail	Predominant colours of Bird	Page
D	Pied Crested Cuckoo (3, 6c)	7"	Pied black & white ..	59
	Grey Shrike (6d)	5"	Grey, black & white..	83
	Blossomheaded Parakeet (5a) ..	9"	Green, purplish plum	69
	Bluewinged Parakeet (5b) ..	10"	Green, blue	140
D +	Roseringed Parakeet (5a) ..	10"	Green	57
E —	Large Parakeet (5a)	12"	Green	57
	Common Sandgrouse (6e) ..	2½"	Sandy, black	36
F	Pheasant-tailed Jaçana (6c) ..	5" —	Chocolate-brown, white	42
G —	Koel, *male* (6a) ..	8"	Black	58
	Koel, *female* ..	8"	Brown, spotted and barred white	58
G +	Crow-Pheasant ..	11" —	Black, chestnut ..	58
	Little Cormorant (6a)	6"	Black	1
	Sirkeer Cuckoo (6e)	10" +	Earthy brown, rufous, (Bright cherry red & yellow bill)	61
H	Grey Hornbill (2, 6d) ..	12"	Slaty grey	74
H +	Malabar Pied Hornbill (2, 6c)	13" —	Pied black & white ..	62
I —	Darter or Snakebird (2, 6a) ..	9"	Black, brown, silver grey	2
J	Red Junglefowl, *cock* (5c) ..	13" —	Orange-red chestnut, black	35
	Grey Junglefowl, *cock* ..	18"	Grey, brownish yellow, black	35
K	Peafowl, *cock* (3, 5d)	36-48" (train)	Metallic blue, green, brown	36

* See Key on p. vii.

2. Birds with prominent Bills

Size*	Species	Shape, colour and length of Bill	Predominant colours of Bird	Page
A —	Purple Sunbird, *male* (6a)	Curved, black, 1″ —	Metallic purplish black	121
	Purplerumped Sunbird, *male*	Curved, black, 1″ —	Metallic green, purple, crimson, yellow	120
	Females of above two	Curved, black, 1″ —	Brown, pale yellow	120
A	Green Bee-eater (1, 5a)	Curved, black, 1½″ —	Green	70
	Small Blue Kingfisher (5d)	Straight, pointed, black, 2″	Blue, green, rusty	72
B +	Painted Snipe (4)	Straight, slender, brown, 2″	Metallic olive-green, white, buff, black	41
	Common or Fantail Snipe (6e)	Straight, slender, brown, 3″ —	Dark brown, black, rufous, buff ..	50
C	Bluetailed Bee-eater (1, 5a)	Curved, black, 2″ —	Green	71
C-D	Slatyheaded Scimitar Babbler (6e)	Curved, yellow, 1″ +	Dark brown, white	99
D	Hoopoe (3, 6e)	Curved, slender, dark brown, 2″ +	Fawn, black, white	68
D +	Goldenbacked Woodpecker	Straight, wedge-shaped, black, 1½″	Golden yellow, black, white, crimson ..	75
	Blackcapped Kingfisher (5d)	Straight, pointed, red, 3″	Deep blue, black, rusty white ..	73
D-E	Pied Kingfisher (6c)	Straight, pointed, black, 3″	Pied black & white	72
	Whitebreasted Kingfisher (5d)	Straight, pointed, red, 3″ —	Blue, chocolate-brown, white ..	73
E —	Brownheaded Storkbilled Kingfisher	Straight, pointed, compressed, blood-red, 4″ —	Pale blue, buffy brown	74
F	Blackwinged Stilt (4, 6c)	Straight, slender, black, 3″ —	White, grey-brown, black	47
F +	Avocet (6c)	Upcurved, slender, black, 3″ +	Pied black & white	47

* See Key on p. vii.

2. Birds with prominent Bills — *contd.*

Size*	Species	Shape, colour and length of Bill	Predominant colours of Bird	Page
F +	Oystercatcher (6c)	Straight, snipe-like, orange-red, 3″ ±	Pied black & white	30
	Indian Skimmer (6e)	Flat knife-blade-like, with upper mandible shorter; orange yellow, 4″ —	Pied black & white	132
H	G r e y Hornbill (1, 6d)	Curved, heavy, hornlike, black and white, 5″	Slaty grey ..	74
	Night H e r o n, *adult* (6d)	Straight, heavy, black & yellow, 4″ —	Ashy grey, black	6
	Night H e r o n, *immature* (6e)		Streaked brown	6
H +	Grey Heron (6d)	Straight, dagger-like, yellow, 6″	Ashy grey, white, black ..	4
	Openbilled Stork (6c) (standing 36″ —)	Reddish black with gap between mandibles, 7″	G r e y i s h white, black	10
	Malabar P i e d Hornbill (1, 6c)	Heavy, h o r n-shaped, yellow & black, 8″ —	Pied black & white	62
I —	Darter or Snake-bird (1, 6a)	Straight, dagger-l i k e, brown and yellow, 2″	B l a c k, brown, silver grey ..	2
I +	Spoonbill (6b)	Spatulate, brown and yellow, 8″	White	2
J —	Whimbrel (6e)	Curved, slender, brown, 3″+	Sandy b r o w n, streaked black & fulvous ..	48
	Blacktailed God-wit (6e)	Slender, straight, o r a n g e & black, 4″+	Brown	46

*See Key on p. vii.

2. Birds with prominent Bills — *contd.*

Size*	Species	Shape, colour and length of Bill	Predominant colours of Bird	Page
J —	Cattle Egret, *breeding* (6b)	Straight, pointed, yellow, 3″	G o l d e n yellow, white	4
	Cattle Egret, *non-breeding*		White	
	Reef Heron (6d)	Straight, pointed, brownish yellow, 4″	B l u i s h slaty, or white	3
	Pond Heron or Paddy Bird (6e)	Straight, pointed, brown, and yellow, 3″	E a r t h y brown, white	5
	Little Green Bittern	Dagger - l i k e, greenish yellow & black, 3″	Glistening greenish black, ash grey, white ..	5
	Chestnut Bittern (5c)	Dagger - l i k e, black, 3″ —	Chestnut, ochraceous	6
J	Curlew (6e)	Curved, slender, brown, 5-6″	S a n d y b r o w n streaked black and fulvous ..	48
	Black Ibis (6a)	Curved, slender, black, 6″ —	Black	8
	Little Egret (6b)	Straight, pointed, black, 4″	White	3
J +	White Ibis (4, 6b)	Curved, stout, black, 7″ —	White	8
K	White Stork (4, 6c) (standing 40″ high)	Straight heavy, red, 8″±	White, black ..	7
	Whitenecked Stork (4, 6c) (standing 36″ high)	Straight, heavy, black, 7″ —	Black, white ..	7
	Painted S t o r k (4, 6c) (standing 48″ high)	Heavy, yellow, decurved at tip, 10″	White, black, rose-pink	9

* See Key on p. vii.

3

2. Birds with prominent Bills — *contd.*

Size*	Species	Shape, colour and length of Bill	Predominant colours of Bird	Page
K +	Adjutant Stork (standing 48-60″ high) (4)	Heavy, yellow, 4-sided, wedge-shaped, 13″	Black, grey, white	10
	Blacknecked Stork (4, 6c)	Straight, heavy, black, 12″	Metallic black, white	9
	Sarus Crane (4, 6d) (standing, 48-60″ high)	Straight, heavy, pointed, greenish brown, 7″	Ashy grey ..	37
	Flamingo (standing about 4 ft) (4, 6b)	Red, h e a v y, down - curved (' broken '), sieve	Rosy white, crimson	11
	Spottedbilled or Grey Pelican	Long, flat, with elastic bag below	Brownish white ..	1

*See Key on p. vii.

Size*	Species	Principal colours	Associated colours	Page
A	Yellowcheeked Tit (5b)	Yellow, black	White	115
	Crested Bunting (6a)	Black, chestnut	.. ..	130
A +	Crested Lark (6e)	Brown ..	Whitish	79
C −	Crested Tree Swift (1, 6d)	Blue-grey ..	Whitish. (Chestnut throat in male)	62
C	Redvented Bulbul (6e)	Brown ..	Black, crimson ..	97
	Redwhiskered Bulbul (6e)	Brown ..	White, black, crimson ..	98
	Blackheaded Yellow Bulbul (5b)	Olive-yellow and bright yellow	Black	78
	Whitecheeked Bulbul (6e)	Brown ..	White, black, yellow	98
	Paradise Fly-catcher, *adult male* (1, 6b)	White	Black	102
	Paradise Fly-catcher, *adult female* and *immature male* (1, 6e)	Chestnut ..	Black, whitish ..	102
D −	Brahminy Myna (6e)	Reddish fawn	Grey, black ..	90
D	Racket-tailed Drongo (1, 6a)	Black	.. ..	86
	Rosecoloured Starling or Rosy Pastor	Pale pink, black	.. ..	88
	Hoopoe (2, 6e)	Fawn	Black, white ..	68
D +	Pied Crested Cuckoo (1, 6c)	Pied black & white ..	.. ..	59
H	Crested Serpent Eagle (6e)	Dark brown, fulvous	White	26
H +	Crested Hawk-Eagle	Umber brown, whitish	Blackish brown ..	25
K	Peacock (1, 5d)	Glistening blue and green ..	Brown	36
	Peahen (6e)	Variegated brown, white, glistening green	.. ..	36

*See Key on p. vii.

HOW TO RECOGNIZE BIRDS IN THE FIELD

4. Long-legged Birds

(Most with proportionately, or markedly long necks)

Size*	Species	Colour of Legs	Predominant colours of Bird	Associated colours	Bill	Page
B +	Painted Snipe (2) ..	Olive-green ..	Metallic olive-green	Buff, black ..	Greenish brown; slender	41
F –	Redshank	Orange-red ..	Greyish brown	White	Blackish; slender, straight, 2″	49
F	Indian Courser . ..	China white ..	Sandy brown	Chestnut, black ..	Black	51
	Golden Plover	Black	Brown, black, white	Gold and white (spangled)	Black; pigeon-like	45
	Whitebreasted Waterhen	Yellowish green..	Slaty grey	White	Green and red ..	39
	Indian Moorhen ..	Greenish yellow or greenish slate	Slaty grey	Brown, white ..	Green and red ..	39
	Bronzewinged Jaçana ..	Dull green ..	Metallic bronze-green	Black, chestnut-red	Greenish yellow and red	42
F +	Pheasant-tailed Jaçana ..	Dull green ..	White	Chocolate-brown	Yellowish brown ..	42
	Blackwinged Stilt (2, 6c)	Crimson-red ..	Black-and-white	.. .. ..	Black; slender ..	47
	Redwattled Lapwing ..	Yellow	Bronze-brown	White	Orange-red and black	43
	Avocet (2, 6c)	Bluish	Black-and-white	.. .. ..	Black; slender upturned	47
	Spurwinged Plover ..	Black	Brown, white, black	Vinous grey ..	Black, short, pigeon-like	45

HOW TO RECOGNIZE BIRDS IN THE FIELD

4. Long-legged Birds — contd.

(Most with proportionately, or markedly long necks)

Size*	Species	Colour of Legs	Predominant colours of Bird	Associated colours	Bill	Page
F +	Jerdon's or Double-banded Courser ..	Yellowish- or pinkish white	Pinkish sandy brown	Rufous, white ..	Pale yellow and blackish ..	20
	Stone Curlew ..	Yellow	Brown ..	Black, white ..	Black and yellow.. ..	51
H	Night Heron (2, 6d)	Dull green ..	Ashy grey ..	Greenish black ..	Black and greenish yellow; straight, pointed	6
I	Spoonbill (2, 6b) ..	Black	White ..	—	Black and yellow; spoon-shaped	2
	White Ibis (2, 6b) ..	Black	White ..	Black	Black; long, curved ..	8
	Black Ibis (2, 6a) ..	Dark brick-red ..	Black ..	—	Slaty green; long, curved	8
J —	Pond Heron (2, 6e)	Yellowish green	White ..	Brown ..	Yellowish brown; straight, pointed	5
	Reef Heron (2, 6d)	Greenish black ..	(1) White .. (2) Slaty grey	—	Yellowish brown; straight, pointed	3
J	Purple Moorhen ..	Red	Purplish blue	White	Red; heavy	40
	Lesser Florican ..	Yellowish ..	Black, brown ..	White	Yellowish brown	38
	Little Egret (2, 6b)	Black	White ..	—	Black; straight, pointed ..	3
	Cattle Egret (2, 6b)	Greenish black ..	White ..	—	Yellow; straight, pointed	4
K —	Demoiselle Crane ..	Black	Grey ..	Black	Red-tipped greenish ..	37

xxxvii

HOW TO RECOGNIZE BIRDS IN THE FIELD

4. Long-legged Birds — contd.

(Most with proportionately, or markedly long necks)

Size*	Species	Colour of Legs	Predominant colours of Bird	Associated colours	Bill	Page
K −	Whitenecked Stork (2, 6c)	Red	Black	White ..	Reddish black; heavy, pointed	7
	Openbilled Stork (2, 6c)	Dull pinkish	Greyish white	Black ..	Reddish black; pointed, with gap between mandibles ..	10
	Grey Heron (2, 6d) ..	Greenish brown..	Grey	White ..	Yellowish or brownish; dagger-shaped	4
K	White Stork (2, 6c) ..	Red	White and black	..	Red, heavy, pointed ..	7
	Painted Stork (2, 6c) ..	Yellowish or reddish brown	Black and white	Pink ..	Yellow; heavy, pointed, slightly bent down at tip	9
K +	Adjutant Stork (2) ..	Greyish white	Blackish grey ..	Dirty white	Yellowish; heavy, pointed	10
	Sarus Crane (2, 6d) ..	Red	Grey	White ..	Greenish; heavy, pointed ..	37
	Blacknecked Stork (2, 6c) ..	Coral-red ..	Black and white	..	Straight, heavy, black ..	9
	Flamingo (2, 6b) ..	Red	Rosy white ..	..	Red; heavy, down-curved ('broken'), sieve ..	11

*See Key on p. vii.

5. Bright coloured Birds
a. *Chiefly GREEN or BLUE*

Size *	Species	Associated colours	Page
A	Crimsonbreasted Barbet or Coppersmith	Yellow, crimson	60
	Lorikeet	Crimson	69
	Green Bee-eater (1, 2)	Rusty brown	70
C	Bluetailed Bee-eater (1, 2)	Chestnut, yellow, blue	71
	Goldfronted Chloropsis	Golden yellow, purple, black	95
	Goldmantled Chloropsis, *male*	Black, purple	97
	do. *female*	Bluish green	97
D	Blossomheaded Parakeet (1)	Plum colour, maroon, blue	69
	Bluewinged Parakeet (1)	Green, blue	140
	Bluethroated Barbet	Blue, crimson	60
D +	Roseringed Parakeet (1)	Black, rose-pink (in male)	57
	Large Green Barbet	Brown	60
	Fairy Bluebird	Ultramarine blue, black ♂	138
		Dull blue-green ♀	138
E	Large Indian Parakeet (1)	Black, rose-pink, maroon (in male)	57
	Common Green Pigeon	French grey, yellowish, dark brown	54

b. *Chiefly or largely YELLOW*

Size *	Species	Associated colours	Page
A −	White-eye	Olive-green	121
	Purplerumped Sunbird, *male*	Metallic green, crimson, purple	120
	Greyheaded Flycatcher	Greenish yellow, ashy grey	106
	Green Munia	Olive-green, yellow (Scarlet bill)	125
A	Yellowcheeked Tit (3)	Black, white	115
	Iora, *male*	Black, white	95
	do. *female*	Greenish yellow, dark brown	95
	Baya Weaver Bird, *male* (breeding)	Brown (streaked)	123
	Yellowheaded Wagtail	Black, grey	117
	Yellow Wagtail	A. Black	78
		B. Blue-grey	78
A +	Blackheaded Bunting, *male*	Brown, black	130
	Redheaded Bunting, *male*	Chestnut brown	130
	Grey Wagtail (breeding plumage) (1)	Grey, blackish	117
C	Scarlet Minivet, *female*	Ashy grey	94
	Blackheaded Yellow Bulbul (3)	Black	78
	Yellowbrowed Bulbul	Olive-yellow, lemon-yellow	139
D	Golden Oriole	Black	87
	Blackheaded Oriole	Black	87

* See Key on p. vii

5. Bright coloured Birds — *contd.*

c. *Chiefly or largely RED*

Size*	Species	Associated colours	Page
A —	Red Munia, *male (breeding)*	White (spots)	127
A	Small Minivet	Black, grey	94
	Hodgson's Rosefinch, *male*	Brown	128
C	Scarlet Minivet, *male* ..	Black	94
G +	Crow-Pheasant or Coucal	Black	58
J —	Chestnut Bittern (2) ..	Ochraceous	6
	Red Junglefowl, *cock* (1)	Black, orange	35

d. *Several BRIGHT colours in plumage*

Size*	Species	Associated colours	Page
A —	Firebreasted Flowerpecker	Greenish black, crimson buff	119
A	Small Blue Kingfisher (2)	Blue-green, rusty brown	72
	Blacknaped Blue Flycatcher	Bright blue, black, white	103
C	Blueheaded Rock Thrush	Cobalt blue, chestnut, black, white	111
D	Indian Pitta	Green, blue, brown, black, crimson, white	76
	Whitethroated Ground Thrush	Golden rufous, slaty blue, black, white	112
D +	Blackcapped Kingfisher (2)	Deep blue, black, rusty white	73
	Emerald Dove.. ..	Emerald bronze-green, bluish grey, vinous red	54
D-E	Whitebreasted Kingfisher (2)	Blue, chocolate-brown, white	73
E	Roller or Blue Jay ..	Oxford-and-Cambridge blue, rufous brown, lilac	70
K	Peacock (1, 3)	Metallic blue, green, brown, chestnut ..	36

6. Sober coloured Birds

a. *General effect more or less wholly BLACK*

Size*	Species	Page
A—	Purple Sunbird, *male (breeding)* (2)	121
	House Swift (6c)	67
A	Crested Bunting (3) (Chestnut wings)..	130

* See Key on p. vii.

a. General effect more or less wholly BLACK — contd.

Size *	Species	Page
A+	Indian Robin, *male*	110
C	Black Drongo (1)	85
D	Racket-tailed Drongo (1, 3)	86
D+	Hill Myna	88
D-E	Malabar Whistling Thrush	112
G —	Koel, *male* (1)	58
G	House Crow	91
G+	Jungle Crow	91
	Little Cormorant (1)	1
I —	Coot	41
	Darter or Snake-bird (1, 2)	2
I+	Pinkheaded Duck, *male*. (Bright rose-pink head and bill)	19
J+	Black Ibis (2)	8
K	King Vulture	21

b. General effect more or less wholly WHITE

Size *	Species	Page
C	Paradise Flycatcher, *adult male* (1, 3)	102
I+	Spoonbill (2)	2
J —	Cattle Egret (2)	4
J	Little Egret (2)	3
J+	White Ibis (2, 4)	8
K+	Flamingo (2, 4)	11

c. General effect PIED BLACK AND WHITE

Size *	Species	Page
A —	Whitebacked Munia	124
	House Swift (6a)	67
	Blackheaded Munia, (Upperparts chestnut)	128
A	Pied Bushchat, *male*	113
	Pied Flycatcher-Shrike	131
C	Magpie-Robin, *male*	109
	Pied or Mahratta Woodpecker	76
	Large Pied Wagtail (1)	118
D —	Pied Myna. (Orange bill and orbital skin)	126
D+	Pied Crested Cuckoo (1, 3)	59
D-E	Pied Kingfisher (2)	72
F	Pheasant-tailed Jaçana (1)	42
	Blackwinged Stilt (2, 4)	47
F+	Avocet (2)	47

* See Key on p. vii.

6. Sober coloured Birds — contd.

c. General effect PIED BLACK AND WHITE — contd.

Size *	Species	Page
F+	Oystercatcher (2). (Long, straight, snipe-like, orange-red bill)	30
	Indian Skimmer (2). (Orange-yellow bill; flat knife-blade-like with upper mandible shorter)	132
H+	Openbilled Stork (2)	10
	Malabar Pied Hornbill (1, 2). (Heavy, yellow and black bill)	62
I—	Tufted Pochard. (Leaden or greyish blue legs and bill)	18
K	White Stork (2, 4)	7
	Whitenecked Stork (2, 4)	7
	Painted Stork (2, 4)	9
K+	Blacknecked Stork (2, 4)	9

d. General effect largely ASHY GREY, BLUE-GREY or SLATY

Size *	Species	Associated colours	Page
A	Grey Tit	Black, white	92
	Chestnutbellied Nuthatch	Chestnut	115
	Tickell's Blue Flycatcher	Rusty brown, azure blue	101
	Whitebellied Blue Flycatcher	Indigo blue, white	137
	Nilgiri Verditer Flycatcher	Greenish blue, white	137
A+	Orphean Warbler	Slaty grey (above), buffy white (below), black (cap)	104
	Little Pratincole	Sandy grey, black, white	133
C—	Crested Tree Swift (1, 3)	Blue-grey, whitish	62
C	Blackheaded Cuckoo-Shrike	Black, white	93
	Blue Rock Thrush	Dark brown	111
	Black Bulbul	Slaty	139
C+	Rufousbacked Shrike	Rufous, black	84
	Plaintive Cuckoo	Dark grey, whitish	61
D—	Bank Myna	Blackish, white	89
D	Grey Shrike (1)	White, black	83
E—	Large Cuckoo-Shrike	White, black	93
	Ring Dove	Vinous, dark brown	56
	River Tern	White, black	52
E	Blue Rock Pigeon	Glistening purple and green, black	53

See Key on p. vii.

6. Sober coloured Birds — contd.

d. *General effect largely ASHY GREY, BLUE-GREY or SLATY — contd.*

Size *	Species	Associated colours	Page
E	Hawk-Cuckoo or Brainfever Bird	White, rusty brown ..	59
	Shikra	White, rusty brown ..	53
F —	Mountain Quail ..	Olive-tinged slaty grey-brown, black, white (coral-red bill) ..	20
G	Blackwinged Kite ..	White, black	23
G+	Blackheaded Gull ..	White, black	52
	Shahin Falcon	Slaty, black, white, ferruginous	29
H —	Pale Harrier, *male* ..	White, black	24
H	Night Heron (2, 4) ..	White, greenish black ..	6
	Grey Hornbill (1, 2) ..	Dark brown	74
H+	Grey Heron (2)	White, black	4
I	Mallard, *male*	Metallic green, chestnut, white, black; vermiculated. (Greenish bill, orange legs)	17
I +	Barheaded Goose ..	Brownish, white, black..	11
J —	Indian Reef Heron (2) ..	Dark brown	3
J	Little Green Bittern ..	Greenish black, ashy grey white	5
K —	Demoiselle Crane ..	Black, white	37
K+	Sarus Crane (2,4) ..	White, dark brown ..	37

e. *General effect more or less BROWN (all shades)*

Size *	Species	Associated colours	Page
A —	Rufousbellied Babbler ..	.. ..	99
	Streaked Fantail Warbler	.. ..	107
	Indian Wren-Warbler (1)	.. ..	107
	Whitethroated Munia ..	.. ..	124
	Spotted Munia	White	127
	Blackbellied Finch-Lark, *male*	White, black	122
	do. *female*	.. .. ..	122
	Purple Sunbird, *female*..	Pale yellow	121
	Purplerumped Sunbird, *female*	Pale yellow	120
	Tickell's Flowerpecker..	Whitish	119
	Palm Swift	Sooty grey	67
	Dusky Crag Martin ..	.. .. ..	82
	Redbreasted Flycatcher	Orange-chestnut (only male), black, white ..	105

* See Key on p. vii.

6. Sober coloured Birds — contd.

e. *General effect more or less BROWN (all shades — contd.)*

Size *	Species	Associated colours	Page
A —	Lesser Whitethroat ..	Earthy brown, grey white	103
	Thickbilled Flowerpecker	Ashy olive-brown, greyish white (stout bluish bill)	126
	Pigmy Woodpecker ..	Barred dark brown and white above; streaked dusky white below ..	77
A	Pied Bushchat, *female* ..	.. ..	113
	Collared Bushchat, *female*	.. ..	113
	Redstart, *female* ..	Rusty reddish	114
	Indian Robin, *female* ..	.. ..	110
	Whitespotted Fantail Flycatcher	White	102
	Hodgson's Rosefinch, *female*	.. ..	128
	House Sparrow, *male* ..	White, grey, black ..	129
	do. *female*..	.. ..	129
	Yellowthroated Sparrow	Sulphur yellow, white, chestnut	129
	Indian Pipit	.. ..	80
	Baya Weaver Bird ..	Golden yellow (only in male breeding plumage)	123
	Streaked Weaver Bird ..	Golden yellow (only in male breeding plumage)	123
	Blackbreasted Weaver Bird	Black, pale yellow. Golden yellow (cap) in male breeding plumage ..	125
	Little Stint	White	50
	Indian Small Skylark ..	.. ..	79
	Redwinged Bush Lark ..	Fulvous, rufous, chestnut	80
	Bluethroat	Blue (only male), white, chestnut	106
	Black-&-Orange Flycatcher	Orange-brown, black ..	138
A+	Crested Lark (3)	.. ..	79
	Redheaded Bunting, *female*	.. ..	130
	Blackheaded Bunting, *female*	.. ..	130
	Rufoustailed Finch-Lark	Rúfous	122
	Wryneck	Streaked silvery grey-brown above; dark-spotted whitish below	77
B —	Blackbreasted or Rain Quail	Buff, black	33

* See Key on p. vii.

6. Sober coloured Birds — *contd.*

e. *General effect more or less BROWN (all shades) — contd.*

Size *	Species	Associated colours	Page
B —	Jungle Bush Quail	Vinous, black	34
	Bluelegged Bustard-Quail	Buff, black	32
	Yellowlegged Button Quail	Greyish brown, buff, black, white, ferruginous red	40
	Painted Bush Quail	Olive-brown, chestnut, white	134
	Little Ringed Plover	White, black	44
B	Common or Grey Quail	Buff, black	33
	Spotted Sandpiper	White	48
B +	Common or Fantail Snipe (2)	Rufous, buff whitish	50
C —	Yelloweyed Babbler	White	100
	Quaker Babbler	Ashy	96
	Spotted Babbler	Chestnut, white	96
C	Common Babbler (1)		100
	Blue Rock Thrush, *female*	Whitish	111
	Paradise Flycatcher, *female (3) and young male (1, 3)*	Black, white	102
	Redvented Bulbul (3)	Black, crimson	97
	Redwhiskered Bulbul (3)	White, black, crimson	98
	Whitecheeked Bulbul (3)	White, black, yellow	98
C-D	Slatyheaded Scimitar Babbler (2)	White	99
C +	Alpine Swift	White	68
D —	Brahminy Myna (3)	Grey, black	90
D	Indian Myna	White (wing-patch)	90
	Jungle Myna	White (wing-patch), black, fulvous	104
	Rufous Woodpecker	Chestnut	75
	Whitebellied Tree Pie (1)	Chestnut-bay, white	140
	Tree Pie (1)	Sooty black, grey	92
	Jungle Babbler		116
	Large Grey Babbler	Grey, whitish	105
	Blackcapped Blackbird		110
	Little Brown Dove	Lilac, vinous, ashy grey, white	56
	Hoopoe, (2, 3)	Black, white	68
	Common Indian Nightjar	Grey, buff, black	64
	Collared Scops Owl	Rufescent, buff, black	65
	Spotted Owlet	White	65

* See Key on p. vii.

6. Sober coloured Birds — contd.
e. General effect more or less BROWN (all shades) — contd.

Size *	Species	Associated colours	Page
D	Barred Jungle Owlet ..	Olive-brown, rufous, chestnut, white ..	66
	Nilgiri Laughing Thrush	Olive-brown, rufous, (white supercilium) ..	135
	Kerala Laughing Thrush	Olive-brown, grey, rufous,(white supercilium)	135
	Wynaad Laughing Thrush	Chestnut-brown, ashy, white	136
	Rufous Babbler ..	Olive-brown, bright .. ferruginous	136
E —	Common Sandgrouse (1)	Black	36
	Painted Sandgrouse ..	Black, chocolate, white, buff, close-barred ..	30
E	Little Grebe or Dabchick	White	14
E +	Nilgiri Wood Pigeon ..	Reddish brown (with .. black-and-white chess-board' on hindneck) ..	133
E	Grey Partridge	Whitish	32
	Indian Courser	Black, rufous, white ..	51
	Yellow-wattled Lapwing	Black, white	43
	Ruff and Reeve ..	Grey-brown, blackish, (Scaly patterned above)..	46
	Painted Spurfowl ..	Chestnut, black, buff ..	134
F +	Stone Curlew	Buff, white	51
	Redwattled Lapwing ..	Black, white	43
	Jerdon's or Double-banded Courser (4)	Pinkish sandy brown, rufous, black, white ..	20
G +	Laggar Falcon	White	22
	White-eyed Buzzard ..		25
	Sirkeer Cuckoo (1) ..	Earthy brown, rufous, (Bright cherry red and yellow bill)	61
H	Common Pariah Kite ..	.. ..	23
	Brahminy Kite, immature	.. ..	24
	do. adult ..	White	24
	Brown Fish Owl ..	Buff, black	63
	Indian Great Horned Owl	.. ..	64
	Scavenger Vulture, immature	.. ..	22
	Night Heron, immature (2)	.. ..	6
H +	Tawny Eagle	.. ..	27
	Crested Serpent Eagle (3)	.. ..	26
	Ringtailed or Pallas's Fishing Eagle ..	White, greyish	26
	Whitebellied Sea Eagle	Ashy brown, white, black	29

* See Key on p. vii.

6. Sober coloured Birds — *contd.*

e. *General effect more or less BROWN (all shades) — contd.*

Size *	Species	Associated colours	Page
I —	Lesser Whistling Teal ..	Pale brown, chestnut ..	132
	Garganey Teal	Rufous-brown, ashy grey buff, white	16
	White-eyed Pochard ..	White	14
	Pintail, *male*	Umber brown, black, white, grey, buff ..	15
	Common Teal, *female* ..	.. ..	16
	Shoveller, *male* .. · ..	Green, black, bluish grey, white, buff, chestnut ..	13
	Wigeon, *male*	Chestnut, buff (forehead patch), black, white; vermiculated. (Blue bill)	18
	Gadwall, *male*	Dark brown, chestnut, grey, white, black; vermiculated. (Yellow legs)	17
I	Spotbill Duck	Black, white, metallic green and purple, fulvous	13
I +	Redcrested Pochard, *male*	Pale brown, black, white, chestnut-orange. (Crimson bill)	19
	Pinkheaded Duck, *male*	Brownish black. Bright rose-pink head, hind-neck and bill ..	19
J —	Pond Heron or Paddy Bird (2)	White	5
	Whimbrel (2)	Fulvous buff, black ..	48
	Blacktailed Godwit (2)..	White, black	46
J	Red Junglefowl, *hen* ..	.. ..	35
	Grey Junglefowl, *hen* ..	White	35
	Curlew (2) . ..	Fulvous, buff	48
K	Whitebacked or Bengal Vulture	White	21
	Peahen (3)	Metallic green	36
K +	Great Indian Bustard ..	White, black	38

* See Key on p. vii.

For Field Recognition tables for species 281-296
see Appendix.

1. **Spottedbilled** or **Grey Pelican.** *Pelecanus philippensis* Gmelin
HINDI NAMES : *Hāwāsil, Kūrēr*
Handbook Vol. 1

Size: Vulture $+$. **Field Characters:** A large squat water bird, chiefly grey and greyish white, with a brown nuchal crest. Short stout legs, large webbed feet and enormous heavy flattened bill, underhung throughout its length by an elastic bag of dull purplish skin. Large blue-black spots along edge of upper mandible, blackish wing quills and greyish brown tail diagnostic. Sexes alike. Flocks, at jheels etc.
Distribution : Well-watered tracts throughout the Indian Union; Bangladesh ; Pakistan; Ceylon ; Burma. Resident but capricious; also locally migratory. **Habits:** Flocks float buoyantly or rest on mudbanks preening themselves. They fish by cooperative effort, swimming in a semi-circle, driving the fish before them into the shallows with vigorous splashing of their great wings, and scooping them up in their pouch which acts like a landing net. Considering their size, the birds take off the water with little effort, and when once launched fly strongly with steady rhythmical wing beats, head drawn in between the shoulders. Frequently seen during midday soaring in circles at great heights in company with storks. **Nesting:** *Season* — November to April. *Nest* — a large stick platform in tall trees and palms, often far from water; several nests in the same tree, and the colony often covering large areas. *Eggs* — 3, chalky white, becoming considerably dirty as incubation proceeds.

2. **Little Cormorant.** *Phalacrocorax niger* (Vieillot)
HINDI NAMES : *Pān-kowwā, Gānhil*
Handbook Vol. 1

Size: Jungle Crow $+$. **Field Characters:** A glistening black duck-like water bird with a longish stiff tail, and slender, compressed bill sharply hooked at the tip. A small white patch on throat, and suggestion of a crest at back of head. Sexes alike. Singly, or gregariously, at tanks, jheels, etc.

The LARGE CORMORANT (*P. carbo*) and the INDIAN SHAG (*P. fuscicollis*) are often found associated with it. The former is the size of the domestic duck, black, but in the breeding season with some white in head and neck, and a large white patch on either flank conspicuous in flight. The Shag is intermediate in size and easily confused except in breeding dress when white feather tufts behind eyes and white speckles on head and neck distinguish it.
Distribution: Throughout the Indian Union; Bangladesh; Pakistan; Ceylon; Burma. **Habits:** Found on all inland waters; also brackish lagoons and tidal creeks. Lives exclusively on fish which it chases and captures under water, being an expert diver and submarine swimmer. Flocks occasionally hunt in concert like pelicans. When satiated, perches upright on a rock or stake near water, drying itself with outstretched wings. **Nesting:** *Season* — in N. India chiefly July to September; S. India November to February. *Nest* — a shallow twig platform, like a crow's, in trees usually in mixed colonies of egrets, storks, etc., both near and away from water. *Eggs* — 4 or 5, pale bluish green, with a chalky surface.

1

3. Darter or Snake-bird. *Anhinga rufa* (Daudin)
HINDI NAMES: *Pān dūbbi, Bănbé*

Handbook Vol. 1

Size: Kite ± . **Field Characters:** A black cormorant-like water bird with silvery grey streaks on the back, and velvety brown head and neck. Chin and throat whitish; tail long, stiff, wedge-shaped. The slender, snake-like neck, narrow head, and pointed dagger bill are diagnostic features. Sexes alike. Singly, or loose parties, on tanks and jheels. **Distribution:** Throughout the Indian Union; Bangladesh; Pakistan; Ceylon; Burma. **Habits:** Very like the cormorants' except that it is more individualistic, less gregarious and does not hunt in cooperative flocks. When swimming the body remains submerged; only the slender, snake-like neck shows above the surface, swaying and turning this way and that, aptly suggestive of the bird's name. Its staple food is fish. The Darter chases them below the surface with speed, wings held half open and head and neck swaying back and forth like a javelin-thrower poising his missile. A special contrivance in the neck bones enables the bird to shoot out its bill at the quarry as by a powerful spring. When suddenly come upon, resting in a tree overhanging water, the birds flop plumb down, ' dragging ' through the intervening branches as if shot dead; they dive and scatter in all directions, surfacing again a safe distance away. **Nesting:** *Season* — N. India June-August; S. India November-February. *Nest* — a twig platform, similar to the cormorant's, built gregariously in trees amongst a mixed heronry, usually near water. *Eggs* — 3 or 4, elongated, pale greenish blue.

4. Spoonbill. *Platalea leucorodia* Linnaeus
HINDI NAMES: *Chămăch bāzā, Chămchā, Dābil*

Handbook Vol. 1

Size: Domestic duck + . **Field Characters:** A long-necked, long-legged snow-white marsh bird with black legs and a distinctive, large, flat, black-and-yellow spoon-shaped bill. A pale yellowish brown patch on foreneck. A long, full nuchal crest in the breeding season. Sexes alike. Individually, or flocks, at jheels etc. **Distribution:** Throughout the Indian Union; Bangladesh; Pakistan; Ceylon; Burma. Only the one race *major* concerns us. **Habits:** Affects marshes and jheels, mudbanks in rivers, and also estuarine mudflats. Feeds actively in the mornings and evenings. A flock wades into shallow water, and with outstretched necks and obliquely held partly open bills the birds move forward sweeping in a half circle from side to side and raking up the bottom mud with the tip of the lower mandible. **Food:** Tadpoles, frogs, molluscs, insects and vegetable matter. Flight rather slow, with steady wing beats, neck and legs extended. Flocks fly in V-formation or in diagonal single lines. A low grunt and a clattering of the mandibles are the only sounds uttered. **Nesting:** *Season* — between July and November, later in S. India, varying with monsoon conditions. *Nest* — rather massive stick platforms amongst a mixed heronry on trees standing in or near water. *Eggs* — 4, sullied white, sparingly spotted and blotched with deep reddish brown.

2

PLATE 1

PLATE 2

6

7

5

8

INS

5. Little Egret. *Egretta garzetta* (Linnaeus)
HINDI NAMES : *Kilchiā* or *Kărchiā băglā*
Handbook Vol. 1

Size: Village hen; longer neck and legs. **Field Characters:** A lanky snow-white marsh bird differentiated from the very similar Cattle Egret (8) in non-breeding plumage by its *black* bill and parti-coloured black and yellow feet. A long drooping crest of two narrow plumes acquired in the breeding season; also dainty filamentous ornamental feathers (' aigrettes ') on both back and breast. Sexes alike. Flocks on marshland and jheels etc.

The solitary LARGE EGRET (*A. alba*) and the more sociable MEDIAN EGRET (*E. intermedia*), both pure white, are found in the same habitat and often in association with it. In breeding plumage the Large Egret (heron size) has flimsy ornamental dorsal plumes (' aigrettes ') falling over beyond the tail. In the slightly smaller *intermedia* these plumes are present on both breast and back as in 5, but the crest is lacking.

Distribution: Throughout the Indian Union; Bangladesh; Pakistan; Ceylon; Burma. **Habits:** Gregarious. Affects marshes, jheels and rivers; also tidal mudflats. Flies with steady wing beats, neck pulled in like a heron; roosts in trees. **Food:** Insects, frogs and small reptiles. In former years ' aigrettes ' were in great demand in western countries for millinery purposes. The trade is now illegal. **Nesting:** *Season* — principally July/August in N. India; November to February in the south. *Nest* — a shallow twig platform, like a crow's, lined with straw, leaves, etc. Built in trees, amongst mixed heronries, often near a village. *Eggs* — 4, pale bluish green.

6. Indian Reef Heron. *Egretta gularis* (Bosc)
HINDI NAME : *Kālā băglā*
Handbook Vol. 1

Size: Little Egret + . **Field Characters:** General effect of the Little Egret but has two colour phases: (1) pure white, (2) bluish slaty with a white patch on throat. Some examples parti-coloured. A backwardly drooping crest of two narrow plumes is acquired in the breeding season. White phase difficult to differentiate from the Small Egret, but its seashore habitat is suggestive. Sexes alike. Singly, on rocky seashore, mangrove swamps, etc. **Distribution:** The coast of western India; Pakistan; Ceylon. Only the race *schistacea* concerns us.

The allied EASTERN REEF HERON (*E. sacra*) with a bushy crest, occurs in Burma and Andaman Islands.

Habits: Not appreciably different from other egrets and herons, except that it is essentially a bird of the seacoast, seldom found far inland above tidal influence. **Food:** Mainly crustaceans, molluscs and fish, especially the mud-crawler (*Periophthalmus*). Wades into the shallow surf or in a rock pool left by the receding tide, crouching forward on flexed legs, ' freezing ' with poised neck and bill and jabbing at quarry blundering within range. **Nesting:** *Season* — March to July, varying with locality. *Nest* — a twig platform like that of other egrets, commonly built in colonies on mangrove trees in a tidal swamp, or in a large peepul or jambul, often in association with other egrets, paddy birds, etc. *Eggs* — 3 or 4, pale sea-green or blue-green, unmarked.

3

7. Grey Heron. *Ardea cinerea* Linnaeus
HINDI NAMES: *Nāri, Kābūd, Ănjăn*

Handbook Vol. 1

Size: Openbilled Stork ± . **Field Characters:** A lanky stork-like bird, ashy grey above with white crown and neck; greyish white below, with long slender S-shaped neck, narrow head, and pointed dagger bill. A long black occipital crest, and elongated white feathers on the breast with some black streaks. A conspicuous black dotted line down middle of foreneck. Female similar, but crest and pectoral plumes less developed. Solitary, at reedy jheels, rivers, etc.

The PURPLE HERON (*A. purpurea*), somewhat smaller but of the same general habits, is also seen in similar habitats. Bluish grey above with rufous head and neck; black and chestnut below.

Distribution: Throughout the Indian Union up to 5000 ft in the Kashmir Valley; Bangladesh; Pakistan; Ceylon; Burma. Resident and locally migratory. **Habits:** Somewhat crepuscular. Wades circumspectly into shallow water with neck craned and bill poised, or stands hunched up but alert waiting for a frog or fish to blunder within striking range. Flies with steady wing beats, neck folded back and head drawn in between the shoulders, the long legs trailing behind. **Call:** A deep harsh croak uttered in flight. **Nesting:** *Season* — mainly July to September in N. India; November to March in the south and in Ceylon. *Nest* — a twig platform with the central depression lined with grass etc. Built gregariously in trees, often amongst mixed heronries. *Eggs* — 3 to 6, deep sea-green. Both sexes share all domestic duties.

8. Cattle Egret. *Bubulcus ibis* (Linnaeus)
HINDI NAMES: *Sūrkhiā băglā, Găi-băglā*

Handbook Vol. 1

Size: Little Egret. **Field Characters:** In non-breeding pure white plumage distinguished from the Little Egret by colour of bill which is *yellow*, not black. The orange-buff head, neck, and back of the breeding plumage render it unmistakable. Sexes alike. Parties, attending on grazing cattle. **Distribution:** Throughout the Indian Union; Bangladesh; Pakistan; Ceylon; Burma. Only the race *coromandus* concerns us. **Habits:** Gregarious. Mostly seen with grazing cattle, stalking energetically alongside the animals, running in and out between their legs or riding upon their backs, and lunging out to seize insects disturbed by their movements amongst the grass. **Food:** Chiefly grasshoppers, bluebottle flies and other insects; also frogs, lizards, etc. Roosts at night in favourite trees, sharing these with crows, mynas and other birds. **Nesting:** *Season* — chiefly June to August in N. India; November to March in the south and in Ceylon, varying according to monsoon conditions. *Nest* — an untidy twig platform like a crow's. In mixed colonies with cormorants, paddy birds, etc., in large leafy trees, not necessarily near water and often in the midst of a noisy town. *Eggs* — 3 to 5, pale skim-milk blue.

4

9. Little Green Bittern. *Butorides striatus* (Linnaeus)

HINDI NAME : *Kanchā bǎglā*

Handbook Vol. 1

Size: Paddy Bird ± . **Field Characters:** Like the Paddy Bird in general effect, but largely blackish grey, glossy dark green and bronze-green above; ashy grey below. Crown and long occipital crest glossy greenish black. Chin and throat white. Sexes alike. Solitary, in brushwood at water's edge. **Distribution:** Throughout the Indian Union; Bangladesh; Pakistan; Ceylon; Burma. Several races. **Habits:** Largely crepuscular, but also active in daytime, particularly in cloudy overcast weather or in shady spots with bushes bordering water. Affects streams and inland waters as well as mangrove swamps and tidal creeks. **Food:** Crabs, shrimps, mud-fish, etc. Flight and general behaviour similar to the Paddy Bird's but is less common and more secretive. Silent. **Nesting:** *Season* — overall March to August, varying locally. *Nest* — a rough stick platform up in a small tree on the edge of water, or in a mangrove swamp. Built singly, not in colonies. *Eggs* — 3 to 5, very like the Paddy Bird's, pale greenish blue.

10. Paddy Bird or Pond Heron. *Ardeola grayii* (Sykes)

HINDI NAMES : *Āndhā bǎglā, Bōgli*

Handbook Vol. 1

Size: Cattle Egret — . **Field Characters:** An egret-like marsh bird chiefly earthy brown when at rest, but with the glistening white wings, tail and rump flashing into prominence immediately it flies. In breeding season acquires maroon hair-like plumes on back, and long white occipital crest. Sexes alike. Singly, or loose parties, at jheels, ponds, etc. **Distribution:** Throughout the Indian Union; Bangladesh; Pakistan; Ceylon; Burma. Plains and up to about 3000 ft elevation. **Habits:** Found wherever there is water; river, jheel, roadside ditch, *kutcha* well, or temple pond, often even in the midst of populous towns. Also on the seacoast in mangrove swamps, tidal mudflats, etc. Its normal method of feeding is to stand hunched up at the water's edge watching patiently for movement and jabbing at the quarry when opportunity offers. Sometimes it wades into the shallows, moving forward stealthily and with circumspection, neck craned and bill poised in readiness. **Food:** Frogs, fish, crabs and insects. Flight typically heron — steady wing beats with neck pulled in. Roosts in large leafy trees in mixed congregations of crows and other birds. **Call:** a harsh croak uttered when flying off. A low conversational note, *wāku*, and a variety of peculiar mumblings is produced by nesting pairs. **Nesting:** *Season* — chiefly May to September (SW. monsoon); November to January in S. India. *Nest* — an untidy twig platform like a crow's up in large mango, tamarind and such-like trees, shared with other egrets. Frequently within town limits; not necessarily near water. *Eggs* — 3 to 5, pale greenish blue.

11. Night Heron. *Nycticorax nycticorax* (Linnaeus)
HINDI NAMES : *Wāk, Kwāk, Kokrai*
Handbook Vol. 1

Size: Paddy Bird ± ; Kite. **Field Characters:** General effect of a stocky Paddy Bird, with stouter bill. Ashy grey above with glistening black back and scapulars; white below. Crown, nape and long occipital crest black; the last with some white plumes intermixed. Young birds streaked brown, rather like Paddy Bird. Sexes alike. Gregarious. Flying at dusk with loud, raucous *kwaark*. **Distribution:** Throughout the Indian Union; Bangladesh; Pakistan; Ceylon; Burma. Resident and locally migratory. **Habits:** Largely crepuscular and nocturnal. Affects jheels and other inland waters as well as tidal creeks and mangrove swamps. Colonies spend the daytime resting in some clump of leafy trees, often far from water, and fly out to their accustomed feeding grounds at dusk in straggling ones and twos uttering a distinctive *kwaark* from time to time. Flight like the Paddy Bird's — steady flapping, neck pulled in; in silhouette resembles both the flying fox's and the gull's. The same communal roosts and nesting trees are occupied year after year. **Food:** Crabs, fish, frogs, aquatic insects, etc. More actively procured and not usually in the 'wait and strike' manner of herons. **Nesting:** *Season* — between April and September in N. India; December to February in the south. *Nest* — the usual twig structure of egrets. Built in colonies in canopy of large leafy trees or screwpine brakes, near or removed from water. *Eggs* — 4 or 5, pale sea-green. Both sexes share all domestic duties.

12. Chestnut Bittern. *Ixobrychus cinnamomeus* (Gmelin)
HINDI NAME : *Lāl băglā*
Handbook Vol. 1

Size: Paddy Bird — . **Field Characters:** An unmistakable cousin of the Paddy Bird. Upperparts chestnut-cinnamon; chin and throat whitish with a dark median stripe down foreneck. Upper breast chestnut and black; rest of underparts pale chestnut. Female duller with brown-streaked rufous-buff underparts. Solitary, in and about reedy marshes etc.

The YELLOW BITTERN (*I. sinensis*) is another locally common species of similar size and habits, also found in the same marshy habitats. Upperparts chiefly yellowish brown; crown and crest black. Upper breast blackish with buff streaks; rest of underparts pale yellowish buff.

Distribution: The greater part of the Indian Union; Bangladesh; Pakistan; Ceylon; Burma. Resident and locally migratory. **Habits:** Very similar to those of the Little Green Bittern (9). When surprised on its nest or cornered, it assumes the characteristic attitude of its tribe (the bitterns), aptly termed the 'On Guard'. The neck is stretched perpendicularly, bill pointing skyward, while the bird 'freezes', becoming astonishingly obliterated amongst its reedy environment. **Nesting:** *Season* — July to September (SW. monsoon). *Nest* — a small twig platform among reeds in a swamp, or in bushes at the edge of a monsoon-filled pond. *Eggs* — 4 or 5, white.

9

10

12

11

PLATE 4

13. Whitenecked Stork. *Ciconia episcopus* (Boddaert)
HINDI NAMES : *Mānik-jōr, Lăglăg*
Handbook Vol. 1

Size: White Stork — ; about 3 ft high. Field Characters: A glistening
black stork with conspicuous white neck and black ' skull cap '.
Abdomen and vent white. Long red legs; heavy blackish bill. Sexes
alike. Pairs, or parties, on or near marshland. Distribution: Practically
throughout the Indian Union up to about 3000 ft in the Himalayas;
Pakistan (rare); Bangladesh; Ceylon; Burma. Resident and locally
migratory. Habits: Affects well-watered plains country. Partial to
water-logged ground, and the environs of rivers, jheels and ponds
especially where the latter are in the process of desiccation leaving
fish and frogs high and dry. Soaring aloft and other habits similar to
those of the White Stork. Food: Fish, frogs, reptiles, crabs, molluscs,
large insects, etc. Nesting: *Season* — practically all year, varying
locally. *Nest* — a large stick platform with a central depression lined
with grass and rubbish; high up in a Silk Cotton (*Salmalia*) or similar
tall tree, usually near water and often also close to a village. *Eggs* — 3
or 4, white, obtuse ovals.

14. White Stork. *Ciconia ciconia* (Linnaeus)
HINDI NAME : *Lăglăg*
Handbook Vol. 1

Size: Vulture ± ; standing about 3½ ft high. Field Characters: A
long-legged, long-necked egret-like bird, pure white except for the
black wings. Legs and heavy, pointed bill red. Sexes alike. Singly,
pairs or parties on and about marshland. Distribution: Winter visitor
in small numbers. Practically throughout the Indian Union (rare south
of the Deccan); Bangladesh; Pakistan; Ceylon (straggler); Burma. Two
races : the European-W. Asiatic *ciconia*, and the E. Asiatic *boyciana*.
Habits: Keeps in pairs or small parties, collecting into large flocks
for the northward migration in spring. A young stork ringed in
Germany was recovered in Bikaner, about 4000 miles distant. Flight
seemingly leisurely, but swift, and strong — rapid wing beats punctuated with short glides. Much given to soaring and circling on thermal
currents high up in the air along with vultures etc. Food: Frogs,
lizards and large insects. Takes heavy toll of locusts and their eggs.
Lacks voice muscles; the only sound produced is a loud clattering of
the mandibles, especially during the breeding season, with the neck
bent right over so that the crown touches the back. The gular pouch,
puffed out, serves as a resonating organ. Nesting: *Season* — in W. Asia
and C. Europe May to July. *Nest* — a large stick platform on chim-
neys, tops of buildings, tall trees, etc. *Eggs* — 3 to 5, pure white.

15. Black Ibis. *Pseudibis papillosa* (Temminck)

HINDI NAMES : *Bāzā, Kālā bāzā, Kărānkūl*

Handbook Vol. 1

Size: White Ibis — . **Field Characters:** A largish black bird with long curlew-like downcurved bill, a conspicuous white patch near the shoulder, and brick red legs. Naked black head with a triangular patch of crimson warts on the crown. Sexes alike. Pairs, or scattered parties, on the open countryside.

The rather similar but smaller GLOSSY IBIS (*Plegadis falcinellus*) is found at marshes. Glistening blackish and chestnut, with slenderer bill and feathered head.

Distribution: The drier portions of the Indian Union (excepting the western seaboard) south to Mysore; Pakistan; Bangladesh (rare). Not Ceylon. The closely allied species *P. davisoni* occurs in Burma. **Habits:** Though often found in the neighbourhood of rivers and jheels it is by no means so dependent on water as the White Ibis, usually feeding around the dry margin higher up and in the surrounding stubbles and fallow land. Keeps to favoured localities, and roosts in accustomed trees. Parties fly in V-formation by steady wing beats alternated with short glides. **Food:** Insects, grain and small reptiles. **Call:** A loud, nasal screaming cry of 2 or 3 notes reminiscent of the Ruddy Sheldrake (29), uttered mostly on the wing. **Nesting:** *Season* — ill-defined. March to October in N. India; November/ December in south. *Nest* — large, cup-shaped, of twigs, lined with straw, feathers, etc. High up in a tree, generally away from water; built singly and not in colonies or amongst mixed heronries. Old eagle's or vulture's nest sometimes utilised. *Eggs* — 2 to 4, bright pale green, either unmarked or with spots and streaks of brown.

16. White Ibis. *Threskiornis aethiopica* (Latham)

HINDI NAMES : *Mūndā, Săfed bāzā, Mūndūkh*

Handbook Vol. 1

Size: Village hen + . **Field Characters:** A large white marsh bird with naked black head and neck, and long, stout, black, downcurved curlew-like bill. In breeding plumage some slaty grey on scapulars and in wings, and ornamental plumes at base of neck. Sexes alike. Parties, on marshy land. **Distribution:** Throughout the Indian Union; Bangladesh; Pakistan; Ceylon; Burma. Resident and locally migratory. **Habits:** A close relation of the Spoonbill (4) and very like it in habits and habitat. Walks about actively on marshy land probing with its bill into the soft mud, mandibles partly open like forceps. Often feeds in shallow water with the head momentarily submerged. Like storks and the spoonbill, it lacks true voice-producing mechanism and is silent except for peculiar ventriloquial grunts uttered when nesting. **Nesting:** *Season* — in N. India June to August; in the south November to February. *Nest* — a platform of twigs in trees standing in or near water, frequently on village outskirts, and usually amongst mixed heronries. *Eggs* — 2 to 4, bluish or greenish white, sometimes with delicate spots of yellowish brown.

8

17. Blacknecked Stork. *Ephippiorhynchus asiaticus* (Latham)

HINDI NAMES: *Loharjang, Loha sarang*
Handbook Vol. 1

Size: White Stork + ; about 4 ft high. **Field Characters:** The large size, enormous black bill, glistening black head and neck, white underparts, and pied black and white wings readily identify this stork. Sexes alike but iris brown in male, lemon yellow in female. Solitary, on marshland and jheels. **Distribution:** Throughout the Indian Union; Bangladesh; Pakistan; Ceylon; Burma. **Habits:** Confined to rivers, jheels and marshes. Usually met with as a solitary bird wading in shallow water. It is more of a fish eater than other storks, but also eats frogs, reptiles, crabs, etc. Though widely distributed, the species is nowhere common or abundant. **Nesting:** *Season* — between August and January, varying locally. *Nest* — an enormous deep platform of twigs with a depression in the centre lined with leaves and grass. Placed near the top of a large peepul or similar tree standing near water or amidst cultivation. *Eggs* — 3 or 4, white, like those of other storks.

18. Painted Stork. *Mycteria leucocephala* (Pennant)

HINDI NAMES: *Jānghil, Dōkh, Kănkāri, Jhingri*
Handbook Vol. 1

Size: White Stork ⊥ . **Field Characters:** A typical large stork with long, heavy, yellow bill slightly decurved near tip, and unfeathered waxy yellow face. Plumage white, closely barred and marked with glistening greenish black above, and with a black band across breast. Delicate rose pink about the shoulders and on wing. Sexes alike. Pairs, parties or large congregations at jheels, and marshes. **Distribution:** Throughout the Indian Union; Bangladesh; Pakistan; Ceylon; Burma. Resident and locally migratory. **Habits:** In general similar to those of other storks. Spends the day standing ' hunched up ' and inert or sauntering about sedately on grassy marshland in quest of fish and frogs. Also wades into shallow water moving forward with neck craned down, bill immersed and partly open swaying from side to side with a scythe-like action. **Nesting:** *Season* — between August and January, varying with local conditions. *Nest* — a large stick platform with a shallow depression in the middle lined with leaves, straw, etc. Built on trees standing in or near water, often 10 to 20 nests in a single tree and almost touching one another. Breeds in enormous heronries, often sharing these with cormorants, egrets, openbilled storks, white ibises, etc. *Eggs* — 3 to 5, dull sullied white, occasionally with sparse brown spots and streaks. Both sexes share all the domestic duties.

19. Openbilled Stork. *Anastomus oscitans* (Boddaert)
HINDI NAMES: *Gūnglā, Ghonghila, Ghūngil*

Handbook Vol. 1

Size: White Stork — ; about 2½ ft high. **Field Characters:** A small white or greyish white stork, with black in the wings. In the distance rather like the White Stork, but the peculiar reddish black bill with arching mandibles leaving a narrow open gap between them is diagnostic. Sexes alike. Twos and threes, or flocks, at jheels and marshes. Occasionally also tidal mudflats. **Distribution:** Throughout the Indian Union; Bangladesh; Pakistan; Ceylon; Burma. Resident and locally migratory. **Habits:** One of our commonest storks with a wide and general distribution. General habits typical of the storks. The precise significance and function of the curiously shaped bill is obscure and calls for special investigation. It may have to do with opening the thick shells of the large *Ampullaria* snails found on marshes, the soft body and viscera of which form a large proportion of its food in due season. It also eats frogs, crabs, large insects and other small living things. **Nesting:** *Season* — mostly between July and September in N. India; November to March in the south and in Ceylon. Breeds in colonies amongst mixed heronries of cormorants, egrets, painted storks, etc. *Nest* — a circular platform of twigs with the central depression lined with leaves. *Eggs* — 2 to 4, white, close textured.

20. Adjutant Stork. *Leptoptilos dubius* (Gmelin)
HINDI NAMES: *Hargila, Garūr, Dhēnk*

Handbook Vol. 1

Size: Vulture + ; standing about 4 ft high. **Field Characters:** A large, sad coloured black, grey and dirty white stork with an enormous yellow wedge-shaped bill, and naked head and neck. The long naked ruddy pouch pendent from the chest is diagnostic. Sexes alike. Singly, or parties, on marshes.

The SMALLER ADJUTANT (*L. javanicus*) occurs sparingly in well-watered tracts over the greater part of our area, including Malabar and Ceylon. It is smaller — chiefly glossy metallic black above, white below — and lacks the hanging pouch.

Distribution: Northern India and Assam; Bangladesh; Burma. Local migrant. **Habits:** A close relation of the African Marabou; called Adjutant from its measured martial gait as it paces up and down. An efficient scavenger, often consorting with kites and vultures to feed at carcases and garbage dumps on outskirts of villages. Also eats frogs, fish, reptiles, large insects, etc. Heavy in the take-off, but flies strongly with noisy rhythmical flaps when once properly air-borne, and also circles aloft gracefully on motionless wings as most other storks do. A loud clattering of the mandibles is the only sound normally produced. **Nesting:** Scattered colonies in N. India, Assam, and the Sundarbans. Its real breeding grounds lie in S. Burma where enormous colonies mixed with pelicans and Smaller Adjutants, are active between October and December. *Nest* — an immense stick platform on rock pinnacles or lofty forest trees. *Eggs* — 3 or 4, white.

PLATE 5

17

18

19

20

PLATE 6

INS:

23

21

22

24

INS

21. Flamingo. *Phoenicopterus roseus* Pallas
HINDI NAMES : *Bog-hăns, Rāj-hăns, hănj, Chărăj băggo*
Handbook Vol. 1

Size: Domestic goose; standing about 4 ft high. Field Characters: A long-legged, long-necked rosy white stork-like bird, with a heavy pink bill turned down at an angle (' broken ') from about half its length. Sexes alike. In flight the long outstretched legs and neck, and the black-bordered brilliant scarlet wings are diagnostic. Parties, or flocks, at shallow jheels, tidal mudflats, etc. Distribution: Capriciously throughout the Indian Union; Bangladesh; Pakistan; Ceylon. Not Burma. Resident, sporadic and locally migratory. Habits: Affects jheels, lagoons, salt pans, estuaries, etc. Feeds in shallow water with the slender neck bent down between the legs and head completely submerged. The curious bill is inverted so that the ridge of the culmen scrapes the ground. The upper mandible thus forms a hollow scoop into which the churned up liquid bottom mud is collected and strained by means of the lamellae and the fleshy tongue, sifting the minute food particles. Food: Crustaceans, worms, insect larvae, seeds of marsh plants, and organic ooze. Call: A loud goose-like *honk;* a constant babbling uttered while feeding in company. Flocks fly in V-formation, in diagonal wavy ribbons, or in single file. Nesting: *Season —* in the Great Rann of Kutch depending upon the requisite shallowness of water on the nesting ground; September/October, February to April. *Nest —* a truncated conical mound of hard sun-baked mud 6 to 12 inches in height with a slight pan-like depression at top. Built in hundreds close to one another in a compact, expansive ' city '. *Eggs —* 1 or 2, white with a faint bluish tinge.

22. Barheaded Goose. *Anser indicus* (Latham)
HINDI NAMES : *Hăns, Rājhăns, Birwā, Săwān*
Handbook Vol. 1

Size: Domestic goose $\pm$. Field Characters: A grey, brownish and white goose, with white head and sides of neck, and two distinctive broad black bars across nape. Sexes alike. Gaggles, on rivers and jheels, and about young winter cultivation.

The GREYLAG GOOSE (*Anser anser*) believed to be the ancestor of all our domestic breeds, is also a common winter visitor. Size and general effect that of the normal brown phase of the domestic goose. The grey rump and white nail to the flesh pink bill are leading clues to its identity. Keeps more to jheels than to rivers.

Distribution: In winter throughout northern India and Assam; rare in central India, straggling as far south as Mysore. Bangladesh; Pakistan; Burma. Habits: Arrives about October; departs by mid March. Rather crepuscular and nocturnal. Congregates in large gaggles when grazing in young gram fields, or when resting during the daytime on sandbanks in the middle of large rivers. Usually excessively wary and difficult to circumvent. Skeins flight in V-formation or in straight ribbons over a wide front to and from their feeding grounds. Food: Chiefly green shoots of winter crops such as wheat or gram. Call: A musical *aang, aang*. Produced in varying keys by skein after skein going over, it is one of the most unforgettable and exhilarating sounds to the wildfowler. Nesting: *Season —* in the nearest breeding localities to us, Ladakh and Tibet, April to June. *Nest —* a depression in lush herbage bordering the high altitude lakes, thickly lined with down and feathers. *Eggs —* 3 or 4, ivory white.

23. Cotton Teal. *Nettapus coromandelianus* (Gmelin)
HINDI NAMES: *Girriā, Gurgūrrā*

Handbook Vol. 1

Size: Pigeon + . **Field Characters:** The smallest of our wild ducks, white predominating in plumage. Bill short, deep at base, and goose-like. *Male* glossy blackish above, with white head, neck, and under-parts; a prominent black collar and white wing-bar. *Female* paler, without either. In non-breeding plumage male resembles female except for his white wing-bar. Flocks on jheels etc. **Distribution:** Practically throughout the Indian Union; Pakistan (patchy and rare); Bangladesh; Ceylon; Burma. Resident and locally migratory. **Habits:** Found on all inland waters — jheels, rain-filled ditches, inundated paddy fields, irrigation tanks, etc. Becomes very tame on village tanks wherever it is unmolested and has become inured to human proximity. Swift on the wing, and can dive creditably on occasion. **Call:** A peculiar clucking, uttered in flight. **Food:** Chiefly vegetable matter; also insects, crustaceans, etc. **Nesting:** *Season* — July to September (SW. monsoon). *Nest* — a natural hollow in a tree-trunk standing in or near water, sometimes lined with grass, rubbish and feathers. *Eggs* — 6 to 12, ivory white.

24. Nakta or Comb Duck. *Sarkidiornis melanotos* (Pennant)
HINDI NAME: *Năktā*

Handbook Vol. 1

Size: Domestic duck + . **Field Characters:** A large duck, black above glossed with blue and green; white below. Head and neck speckled with black. The swollen knob at base of drake's bill, much enlarged during breeding season, is diagnostic. *Female* similar but much smaller, and minus comb. Small flocks on reedy jheels. **Distribution:** Through-out the Indian Union; Pakistan (patchy and rare); Bangladesh; Ceylon; Burma. Resident and locally migratory. **Habits:** Affects jheels with reeds and floating vegetation interspersed with patches of open water. Walks and dives well and perches freely on boughs of trees. **Food:** Chiefly grain and shoots or wild and cultivated rice, and other vegetable matter. Procured chiefly by grazing in squelchy inundated fields or by ' up-ending ' in shallow water. Occasionally frogs, aquatic insects, etc. **Call:** A low, grating croak (drake); also a loud *honk* in the breeding season. **Nesting:** *Season* — mainly July to September (SW. monsoon). *Nest* — a natural hollow in a tree-trunk standing in water, sometimes with a scanty lining of sticks, grass and leaves. *Eggs* — 8 to 12, pale cream coloured with the texture and appearance of polished ivory. Evidently the female alone incu-bates.

25. Spotbill or Grey Duck. *Anas poecilorhyncha* Forster
HINDI NAMES: *Gărm-pāi, Gugral, Lăddim*
Handbook Vol. 1

Size: Domestic duck. Field Characters: The large size, scaly patterned
light and dark brown plumage, and the white and metallic green wing-
bar or speculum are leading pointers. Bright orange-red legs, yellow-
tipped dark bill with 2 orange-red spots at its base (one on either side
of the forehead), confirm the diagnosis. Sexes alike. Pairs, or small
flocks on jheels. Distribution: Throughout the Indian Union; Bangladesh; Pakistan; Ceylon (rare); Burma. Resident and locally migratory.
Three races, of which the typical *poecilorhyncha* mainly concerns us.
Habits: One of our most widely distributed resident ducks, but nowhere really abundant. It is among the species that seem fully conscious of their good qualities as sporting and edible birds, and one
of the first to make itself scarce when gunfire commences on a jheel.
Food: Chiefly vegetable matter. A surface feeder, obtaining its food
chiefly by tipping or ' up-ending' in shallow water. When reaching
down for food thus, the tail end of the bird sticks out comically above
the surface, the vertical stance being maintained by a kicking of the
legs. Call: A hoarse wheezy note by the drake, and a loud quack by
the duck, particularly when suddenly alarmed. Very silent on the
whole. Nesting: *Season* — not rigidly defined; chiefly July to September (SW. monsoon). *Nest* — a pad of grass and weeds amongst herbage
on marshy margins of tanks. *Eggs* — 6 to 12, greyish buff or greenish
white.

26. Shoveller. *Anas clypeata* Linnaeus
HINDI NAMES: *Tidāri, Punana, Ghirah, Khōkhār, Sănkhār*
Handbook Vol. 1

Size: Domestic duck — . Field Characters: *Drake:* head and neck
glossy dark green; breast white, rest of underparts mostly chestnut.
Pale blue on forewing, with a white bar between it and the metallic
green speculum. *Duck:* mottled dark brown and buff, with greyish
blue on wings, green speculum, and conspicuous bright orange bill
(at base). Broadened shovel-shaped bill and orange legs diagnostic in
both sexes. Parties, and small flocks, on jheels, irrigation reservoirs,
village tanks, etc. Distribution: In winter throughout the Indian
Union; Bangladesh; Pakistan; Ceylon; Burma. Habits: Another of the
more common migratory ducks visiting us in winter, and amongst
the last to leave. The peculiar spatulate bill is adapted to its special
method of feeding. Swims with neck and bill stretched rigidly in
front, the lower mandible immersed and furrowing the water while
the upper is exposed and skims flat along the surface. The minute
food particles so collected are strained out by means of the comb-
tooth edges of the bill. Occasionally also tips or ' up-ends ' in shallow
water. Food: Largely animal matter. It is not exacting in its food
preferences, and therefore its flesh is usually rank and unpalatable.
But in flight and other respects it is a good sporting bird. Nesting:
Season — in the Palaearctic Region (N. Europe etc.) April to June.
Nest — a pad of grass and rushes, on marshes etc. *Eggs* — 7 to 16
pale stone or buff, sometimes with a greenish tinge.

13

27. White-eyed Pochard. *Aythya nyroca* (Güldenstädt)
HINDI NAMES : *Kurchiyā, Măjithā*
Handbook Vol. 1

Size: Domestic duck — . **Field Characters:** In general aspect rufous brown and blackish brown, with a whitish wing-bar conspicuous in flight. When overhead, the abdomen seen as an oval white patch is diagnostic. *Female* duller coloured. Iris white in adult male; brown in female and young male. Flocks on jheels, irrigation tanks, coastal lagoons, etc. **Distribution:** In winter practically throughout the Indian Union and Pakistan.

The allied BAER'S POCHARD (*A. baeri*) uncommonly winters in W. Bengal, Assam, Bangladesh, Burma.

Habits: Perhaps the most widespread and abundant of our migratory ducks. Frequents every type of water. Rests during the day in the middle of open irrigation tanks etc., or on the sea beyond the surf zone, safe from human molestation, and flights inland after dusk to feed in inundated paddy fields and on grassy tank margins. Also obtains much of its food by diving. **Food:** Vegetable matter, insects, molluscs, small fish, etc. Swift on the wing and a good sporting bird, but on the whole poor eating. **Call:** A harsh *koor-ker-ker*. **Nesting:** *Season* — in Kashmir, the only breeding locality within Indian limits, May/June. *Nest* — a pad of rushes lined with finer grasses and a thick layer of down feathers. Built amongst reeds close to water. *Eggs* — 6 to 10 pale buff.

28. Little Grebe or Dabchick. *Podiceps ruficollis* (Pallas)
HINDI NAMES : *Pāndūbi, Dūbdūbi, Laokri*
Handbook Vol. 1

Size: Pigeon $\pm$; squat and tailless. **Field Characters:** A drab coloured, plump and squat little water bird with silky white underparts, short pointed bill, and no tail. In breeding plumage head and neck dark brown and chestnut, upper plumage slightly paler. Yellow swollen gape then conspicuous. Sexes alike. Pairs or parties, on jheels, village tanks, rain-filled ditches and ponds, etc. **Distribution:** Throughout the Indian Union; Bangladesh; Pakistan; Ceylon; Burma. Plains and up to about 7000 ft. elevation. The only race that concerns us is *capensis*. **Habits:** A good swimmer and expert diver. Vanishes below the surface with astounding rapidity, leaving scarcely a ripple behind. When fired at with a shot gun, the bird has often dived before the charge can reach it! Normally sedentary, but is capable of flying strongly and for long distances on its diminutive wings when forced by drought to change its habitation. **Call:** A sharp tittering heard chiefly when the birds are disporting themselves of an evening, pattering along the water, half running half swimming, with rapid vibrations of their stumpy wings and chasing one another around. **Food:** Aquatic insects and larvae, tadpoles, frogs, crustaceans, etc. procured by diving and under-water pursuit. **Nesting:** *Season* — ranging principally between April and October. *Nest* — a rough pad of sodden weeds and rushes on floating vegetation or a raft of debris, often half submerged. *Eggs* — 3 to 5, white but soon becoming brown-stained through contact with the sodden weeds with which the bird usually covers them up before leaving the nest in alarm or to feed.

PLATE 7

INS

28

25

27

26

Plate 8

29

31

32

30

JPIrani '84

29. **The Ruddy Sheldrake** or **Brahminy Duck.** *Tadorna ferruginea*
(Pallas). HINDI NAMES : *Chăkwā-chăkwi, Sŭrkhāb*
Handbook Vol. 1

Size: Domestic duck +. **Field Characters:** A large orange-brown duck
with paler head and neck and sometimes a faint black collar at its base.
Wings white, black, and glistening green. Tail black. *Female* similar,
but lacking the black collar and with much paler (almost whitish)
head. Pairs or parties, at open tanks and on shingle banks in rivers.
Distribution: In winter throughout the Indian Union; rare in extreme
S. India; Bangladesh; Pakistan; Ceylon (straggler); Burma. **Habits:**
Oftener seen on mudspits and sandbanks than actually on water. Walks
well and with ease, and grazes like a goose at water's edge. **Food:** Vegetable matter, molluscs, crustaceans, aquatic insects, fish and reptiles.
Occasionally said also to eat carrion in company with vultures. Seldom
shot by sportsmen, but nevertheless is amongst the wariest and most
vigilant of our ducks. **Call:** A nasal *aang, aang*, rather like a Bar-
headed Goose's honking in the distance, and also reminiscent of the
cries of the Black Ibis. **Nesting:** *Season* — in Ladakh and Tibet, its
nearest nesting grounds, April to June. *Nest* — a thick pad of down
feathers in holes in cliffs or even in a building, often at a considerable
distance and height from water. *Eggs* — 6 to 10, pearly white, smooth
textured.

(See also LESSER WHISTLING TEAL, p. 132)

30. **Pintail.** *Anas acuta* Linnaeus
HINDI NAMES : *Seenkh-păr, Dighōnch*
Handbook Vol. 1

Size: Domestic duck —. **Field Characters:** *Drake:* Upper plumage
pencilled grey. Head chocolate, with a white band on either side
running down into the white neck and underparts. Long, pointed
pin-like feathers projecting well beyond the tail, usually sufficiently
diagnostic. *Duck:* mottled brown and buff with characteristic elongated body and tapering tail, but without the pins. Differs from female
Gadwall by absence of white in the wing; from female Mallard in
lacking the bright wing-speculum. Pairs, or flocks, on reed-fringed
vegetation-covered jheels. **Distribution:** In winter throughout the
Indian Union; Bangladesh; Pakistan; Ceylon; Burma. **Habits:** One of
our commonest migrant ducks. Amongst the first species to rise out of
gunshot after shooting has commenced on a jheel, as if conscious of
the esteem it enjoys as a sporting and table bird. Largely vegetarian
in its food preferences. Grubs in squelchy mud in inundated cultivation and on grassy tank margins. Also ' up-ends ' in shallow water.
Nesting: *Season* — in the Palaearctic Region (Europe, N. and C. Asia)
May to July. *Nest* — a depression in grass in open marshy grassland,
compactly lined with rushes and down feathers. *Eggs* — 7 to 12, pale
sea-green with a buffish tinge.

31. Common Teal. *Anas crecca* Linnaeus
HINDI NAMES : *Chhōti mūrghābi, Kerra*
Handbook Vol. 1

Size: Domestic duck — ; Cotton Teal (23) + . **Field Characters:** *Male* pencilled greyish, with chestnut head and a broad metallic green band running backward from eye to nape, bordered above and below by whitish lines. A tricoloured wing speculum — black, green, and buff — particularly conspicuous in flight. *Female* mottled dark and light brown, with pale underparts and black and green speculum. Flocks on tanks, jheels and marshes, etc. **Distribution:** In winter throughout the Indian Union; Bangladesh; Pakistan; Ceylon; Burma. **Habits:** Perhaps our commonest migratory duck, and an excellent sporting bird, swift on the wing and good for the table. Largely vegetarian in its diet, grubbing for grain and tender shoots of rice and marsh plants in the squelchy mud of inundated paddy fields and grassy tank margins. Also ' up-ends ' in shallow water. **Call:** A low toned *krit* uttered by the drake, and a subdued wheezy quack by the duck. **Nesting:** *Season* — in the Palaearctic Region (northern Europe to E. Siberia) April to June. *Nest* — of reeds, rushes, etc. lined with down, on the edge of swamps. *Eggs* — 7 to 10, cream coloured, with a glossy texture.

32. Garganey or Bluewinged Teal. *Anas querquedula* Linnaeus
HINDI NAMES : *Chytā, Khirā*
Handbook Vol. 1

Size: Domestic duck — ; Common Teal + . **Field Characters:** *Drake* recognisable by his pink-brown white-speckled head, with conspicuous broad white eyebrows, and bluish grey on wing and shoulders. *Duck* closely resembles female Teal (31) but is paler. In flight, her very indistinct speculum as compared with the Teal's is suggestive. At close range the pure white throat (instead of brown-speckled) and the prominent superciliary stripe distinguish her. Flocks on grassy jheels etc. **Distribution:** In winter throughout the Indian Union; Bangladesh; Pakistan; Ceylon; Burma. **Habits:** Along with the Common Teal, one of our earliest migrants, commencing to arrive by August. Very similar to it in habits. Also a swift flier and a good sporting and table bird. **Food:** Largely vegetarian. **Nesting:** *Season* — in the Palaearctic Region (N. Europe to E. Siberia), May/June. *Nest* — a depression in the grass in wet meadows, sometimes lined with a layer of finer grasses but always with plenty of down feathers. *Eggs* — 6 to 12, buffy white with a glossy texture.

33. Mallard. *Anas platyrhynchos* Linnaeus
HINDI NAMES : *Nīl-sīr, Nīr-rugi, Līlgeh*
Handbook Vol. 1

Size: Domestic duck. **Field Characters:** *Drake* largely grey above and below, finely pencilled and vermiculated with black. Glistening dark green head and neck separated from chestnut breast by narrow white collar. Rump, tail-coverts, and two upcurled central tail feathers black. Metallic purplish blue ' mirror ' on wing bordered in front and behind by black and white lines, conspicuous in flight. Yellowish green bill; orange legs. *Duck* (and drake in eclipse plumage): brown and buff, streaked and spotted with black. Orange legs. Distinguished from the very similar female Shoveller (26), also orange-legged, by bill shape and *purple* speculum (as against green). Parties or flocks on reedy shallow jheels. **Distribution:** Winter visitor. Common in Pakistan and NW. India; less common or rare east to Assam, south to Bombay. Breeds in the Palaearctic Region; sparingly in Kashmir. **Habits:** A typical surface-feeding or dabbling duck, the ancestor of all our domestic breeds; largely vegetarian. Dabbles for food as it walks about on a marsh, or tips (' up-ends ') in water with forepart of body submerged, tail sticking comically skyward. A fast flier, excellent for the table, and much sought after by sportsmen. **Call:** Of drake normally a wheezy murmur; of duck a loud *quack-quack*, especially when alarmed and rising, almost vertically, off the water. **Nesting:** *Season* — in Kashmir, May/June. *Nest* — a pad of rushes and weeds thickly lined with down, under a bush or grass clump near edge of lake. *Eggs* — 6 to 10, greenish grey to yellowish stone.

34. Gadwall. *Anas strepera* Linnaeus
HINDI NAMES : *Myle, Bhuār, Beykhur*
Handbook Vol. 1

Size: Domestic duck — . **Field Characters:** General effect of *drake* dark brown and grey, with whitish belly and very black tail end. A glistening white patch on trailing edge of wing, broadly bordered in front with black, conspicuous in flight. At rest a chestnut patch in front of this black-and-white speculum is a good pointer. *Duck* dark brown mottled with buff, a duller and slightly smaller edition of the Mallard, also with yellow legs. Diagnosed in flight by white wing mirror as in drake, though at rest this usually concealed. Parties and flocks on shallow, reedy jheels and marshes. **Distribution:** Winter visitor. Perhaps one of our commonest and locally abundant migratory wildfowl, particularly in Pakistan and N. India. Less common in peninsular India; vagrant in Ceylon. Breeds in sub-arctic northern Europe and Asia. **Habits:** Keeps in parties or flocks in association with other ducks on suitable waters. A mixed surface feeder like the Mallard, largely vegetarian, and also possessing the same good qualities as a sporting bird and for the table. A number of call notes have been described, but it is a very silent bird in its winter quarters.

17

35. Wigeon. *Anas penelope* Linnaeus
HINDI NAMES : *Peasan, Patari, Pharia, Chhota lāl-sīr*
Handbook Vol. 1

Size: Domestic duck — ; about same as Gadwall. **Field Characters:**
General aspect of *drake* grey. The chestnut head with cream coloured
patch on forecrown, brownish pink breast, black tail-coverts, large
horizontal white patch on closed wing, and small narrow blue-grey
bill, are diagnostic points. In flight a broad white shoulder-patch near
leading edge of wing, and the whitish ' bald ' forecrown, are conspicuous. *Duck* like female gadwall but with speculum of different
pattern (not contrasty black-and-white), and small blue bill like drake's.
Flocks on shallow, reedy jheels and marshes. **Distribution:** Winter
visitor. Common in Pakistan and N. India; locally abundant in
some years. Less common in peninsular and eastern India and in
Burma; sparse and irregular in Ceylon. Breeds in the northern
Palaearctic Region. **Habits:** Frequents shallow grassy jheels and
marshes. A mixed surface feeder, largely vegetarian. Besides up-
ending in shallow water for food, is often seen walking about on
marshes grazing on grass shoots and aquatic weeds in the manner of
geese. A swift and powerful flier, with a peculiar rustling sound of
wings. Like other coveted sporting ducks, e.g. mallard, pintail and
gadwall, is usually amongst the first species to climb high and get
well out of gunshot soon after firing has commenced on a jheel.
A shrill pipe or whistle is uttered in flight as well as on the ground and
when swimming.

36. Tufted Pochard. *Aythya fuligula* (Linnaeus)
HINDI NAMES : *Dubāru, Åblăk, Rahwāra*
Handbook Vol. 1

Size: Domestic duck — ; about same as Gadwall. **Field Characters:**
The boldly contrasting black-and-white plumage of the *drake*, and the
limp occipital tuft, prominent when seen in profile, simplify identification at rest. In flight a broad white band along trailing edge of wing, in
both sexes, provides a further clue. *Duck* dark brown where drake
black, with no tuft and less white in lower plumage. Parties or small
flocks on reed-fringed jheels and open irrigation tanks. **Disfribution:**
Winter visitor to practically all India; Bangladesh; Pakistan; Burma.
Rare vagrant in Ceylon. Breeds in Europe, N. and C. Asia. **Habits:**
Along with White-eyed Pochard (27) one of our commonest migratory
diving ducks, a group distinguished by the possession of a broadly
lobed hind-toe. Legs set far back in the body, ill-adapted for walking
but admirably suited for diving and swimming both above and below
the surface. Feeds in deep water by diving; hence oftener seen on open
expanses in the middle of jheels and irrigation reservoirs. It can
remain submerged for considerable periods, and wounded birds are
hard to retrieve, especially from vegetation covered tanks where they
hold on to weeds below the surface. **Food:** Molluscs, crustaceans,
water insects, etc. Also water weeds.

18

PLATE 9

37. Pinkheaded Duck. *Rhodonessa caryophyllacea* (Latham)
HINDI NAME : *Gūlāb-sīr*

Handbook Vol. 1

Size: Domestic duck ± . **Field Characters:** *Drake:* blackish brown above and below with a light pinkish buff speculum prominent in flight. Partially tufted bright pink head, and bill — the colour of new blotting paper. Underside of wings pale shell pink. *Duck:* above and below dull brown with pale brownish buff speculum. Head suffused with bright pink but the pink area not sharply demarcated as in drake. Long thin neck and gradual slope of forehead rather reminiscent of Whistling Teal (263). Pairs and small flocks ' from 8 to 30 or even 40 ' on wooded jheels. **Distribution:** The swampy jungles of the Himalayan terai and duars from Nepal to Assam; Manipur; Bangladesh; Burma (?). Obtained as far south as Nellore (Andhra) and Jalna (Maharashtra). Last authentic record from Darbhanga district, Bihar, June 1935. Apparently never common or abundant, but was occasionally seen amongst sportsmen's bags of wildfowl. Reduction in numbers noticed as early as 1878, although until about 1890 a half dozen or so still turned up in Calcutta bird market every season. Since 1956 its killing or capturing is totally banned by law, but possibly the bird is already extinct. **Habits:** Resident and local wanderer. In captivity, observed to behave like dabbling ducks, not diving for its food. **Nesting:** Formerly bred in swampy dense forests amongst tall grass areas. *Season* — recorded as May to July. *Nest* — a round pad of grass on ground, well concealed. *Eggs* — 5 to 10, roundish, smooth, ivory white.

38. Redcrested Pochard. *Netta rufina* (Pallas)
HINDI NAMES : *Lāl-chōnch, Lāl-sīr, Doommer*

Handbook Vol. 1

Size: Domestic duck ± . **Field Characters:** *Drake:* Head and fluffy, full, mop-like crest rich chestnut and golden orange, with bright crimson bill. Upperparts light brown with white patches on shoulders, and white wing-mirror. Lower plumage black; flanks white. In flight, red head and bill, black body, white flanks, white underside of wing and the broad white bar on its trailing edge above, provide satisfactory identification. *Duck:* dull sooty brown above, largely whitish below, with dark brown crown and nape sharply demarcated from whitish face and foreneck. A whitish speculum. Identifying unaccompanied female needs practice. Flocks on vegetation-covered tanks and jheels. **Distribution:** Winter visitor. Common and locally abundant in Pakistan and N. India, decreasingly so in the Peninsula. Not found south of Madras or in Ceylon. Sparingly in Burma. Breeds in the southern Palaearctic Region, nearest in Baluchistan. **Habits:** A diving duck though commonly feeding on the surface, dabbling and up-ending like the Gadwall or Mallard. **Food:** Shoots and roots of water plants, molluscs, crustaceans, insects, etc. Very silent in its winter quarters, and on the whole wary.

Since this species is often mistaken for and reported as the rare and virtually extinct Pinkheaded Duck particular attention is invited from birdwatchers and sportsmen to the diagnoses of the two.

39. Mountain Quail. *Ophrysia superciliosa* (Gray)

HINDI NAME :

Handbook Vol. 2

Size: Between Quail and Partridge. **Field Characters:** *Male:* slaty grey-brown above tinged with olive. Forehead and prominent broad supercilium white, bordered above and below with black. Crown greyish brown with black streaks. Chin, throat, and face black, the last patterned with white. Under tail-coverts black with broad white terminal bars. Short, stout coral-red bill (shaped rather like bush quail's), red legs, and relatively long tail for partridge make it unconfusable with any other game bird. *Female:* cinnamon-brown above, paler below, spotted and broadly streaked with black. Face pinkish grey; bill and legs duller red than in male. **Distribution:** Known only from the western Himalayas between 6000 and 7000 ft altitude, in the neighbourhoods of Mussooree and Naini Tal. Last specimen procured near latter place in 1876. **Habits:** Was found in patches of long grass and brushwood on steep hillsides, in small coveys of 5 or 6. Flew reluctantly almost when trampled on, heavily and for short distances, soon pitching into the grass again. **Call:** A shrill whistle.

Less than a dozen specimens exist in museums, and nothing is known about its biology. All recent efforts to re-discover the bird have failed.

40. Jerdon's or Doublebanded Courser. *Cursorius bitorquatus* (Blyth)

HINDI NAME :

Handbook Vol. 3

Size: Partridge $\pm$. **Field Characters:** An unmistakable first cousin of the Indian Courser (102). Upper parts pinkish sandy brown. Crown and hindneck dark brown with broad whitish supercilium from lores to nape. Chin and throat whitish. Foreneck rufous, separated from brown breast by a white band. A second white band across lower breast. Rest of underparts whitish. Tail white and black. A white wing-bar prominent in flight. Sexes alike. **Distribution:** Indigenous to peninsular India though its nearest relations are African. Only known from the Godavari Valley in Andhra — Nellore, Cuddapah, Sironcha, Bhadrachalam, and Anantpur neighbourhoods. First discovered in 1848; last authentic record in 1900 since when, in spite of careful search, it has not been found again in the same localities or elsewhere. **Habits:** Apparently not very different from those of the common Indian Courser except that it is (or was) found in broken forested and scrub country instead of open wasteland; in pairs. **Nesting:** *Eggs*, very similar in coloration and markings to the Indian Courser's, are anonymously claimed to have been taken once on bare ground in thin scrub jungle. That was in 1895 since when further information is lacking.

(See also INDIAN COURSER, p. 51.)

Black or **King Vulture:** *Sarcogyps calvus* (Scopoli)
HINDI NAME : *Rāj gidh*
Handbook Vol. 1

Size: Peacock ± minus the train. **Field Characters:** A huge, black turkey-like vulture with deep scarlet naked head, neck and legs. In overhead flight a whitish band on underside of wings prominent; also white patches on upper thighs and at base of neck. In sailing, wings held above plane of body in a wide V. Sexes alike. Singly on the countryside. **Distribution:** Throughout the Indian Union, up to about 5000 ft in the Himalayas; Bangladesh; Pakistan; Burma. Not Ceylon. **Habits:** A carrion-feeder, usually present singly or in twos and threes among all vulture gatherings at animal carcases. Far less gregarious than 42. It has a false reputation for boldness and audacity and for monopolising a carcase until it has had its fill of the choicest tit-bits. Actually it is timid and cowardly, keeping deferentially aloof of the scrimmage, sneaking in and hurriedly withdrawing with a gobbet of flesh only when the pressure of the other feasters has momentarily eased. **Nesting:** *Season* — December to April. *Nest* — a massive platform of twigs in the top of a large tree 30 or 40 ft up, often close to a village. *Egg* — a singleton, white, fine textured roundish oval.

42. **Whitebacked** or **Bengal Vulture.** *Gyps bengalensis* (Gmelin)
HINDI NAME : *Gidh*
Handbook Vol. 1

Size: Peacock ± minus train. **Field Characters:** A heavy, dirty blackish brown vulture with scrawny, naked head and neck. At rest, and while banking in the air, the white back is diagnostic. In overhead flight a whitish band stretching along underside of wings, broken in the middle by the brown body, also helps identification. Sexes alike. Sub-adult birds brown, without white back and easily confused with LONGBILLED VULTURE *(Gyps indicus)*, another common Indian species. **Distribution:** Throughout the Indian Union; Bangladesh; Pakistan; Burma. Not Ceylon. **Habits:** Our commonest vulture. A carrion-feeder and useful scavenger on the countryside and in the environs of towns and villages. Large gatherings collect at animal carcases with astonishing promptness and demolish them with incredible speed. The obsequies are attended by a great deal of harsh screeching and hissing as the birds strive to elbow themselves into advantageous positions, or prance around with open wings, two birds tugging at a morsel from opposite ends. Though a repulsive creature at close quarters, a vulture gliding effortlessly in the sky is the very embodiment of graceful motion. **Nesting:** *Season* — October to March. *Nest* — a large untidy platform of sticks in the top of a banyan, tamarind or similar tree, often along roadsides or near villages. *Egg* — a singleton, white, occasionally speckled and spotted with reddish brown.

43. White Scavenger Vulture or Pharaoh's Chicken.
Neophron percnopterus (Linnaeus)
HINDI NAMES : *Săfēd gidh, Gōbăr gidh*
Handbook Vol. 1

Size: Pariah Kite. **Field Characters:** A dirty-white kite-like vulture with black wing quills, and naked yellow head and bill. Immature birds brown, rather like the kite, but the *wedge-shaped* (not forked) tail diagnostic. Sexes alike. Singly, or twos and threes, in open country about human habitations. **Distribution:** The Indian Union with the exception of Assam; Pakistan; Ceylon (rarely). Not Bangladesh or Burma. Two races, on size and coloration details. **Habits:** A useful scavenger. Affects open country, invariably in the neighbourhood of human habitations — town or village environs, rural homesteads or nomadic herdsmen's encampments. Stalks about on the ground with a high-stepping, waddling gait — reminiscent of the German 'goose-step' — picking up offal and human excrement which form a considerable proportion of its diet. Sometimes associates with kites, crows and other vultures to feed on wayside animal carcases. **Nesting:** *Season* — principally February to April. *Nest* — a large shabby mass of twigs, filthy rags, hair and rubbish on a ledge of rock or niche in ruined fortifications, ancient crumbling mosques, tombs and the like. Sometimes in the fork of a large banyan or similar tree. *Eggs* — 2, varying from white to pale brick red, blotched with reddish brown or blackish, heavily at the broad end; very handsome. Both sexes share all the domestic duties.

44. Laggar Falcon. *Falco biarmicus jugger* Gray
HINDI NAME : *Lăggăr*
Handbook Vol. 1

Size: Jungle Crow $\pm$. **Field Characters:** An ashy brown falcon with brown-streaked white underparts, and narrow brown moustachial stripes running down from in front and below the eyes. In overhead flight, white breast and brown-and-white pattern on underside of the long, pointed wings are suggestive clues. Immature birds brown underneath. Sexes alike, but male smaller. Pairs, in open country, about cultivation and habitations. **Distribution:** The Indian Union from about 2500 ft in the Himalayas; rare in Assam and extreme south India. Pakistan. Not in Ceylon or Burma. **Habits:** One of our commonest falcons. Affects open scrub country, thin jungle and neighbourhood of cultivation. Avoids humid forest tracts. Pairs work in concert, stooping on and chasing down winged prey. Is capable of sustained pursuit at great speed. In addition to pigeons which form the chief food item in urban areas, other small birds as well as field rats, lizards, locusts and dragonflies are also eaten. **Call:** A shrill prolonged *whi-ee-ee*. Before decline in vogue of falconry was trained to hunt birds as large as florican. **Nesting:** *Season* — principally January to April. *Nest* — a twig platform lined with straw, leaves, etc., high up in a tree, on ledge of cliff, or in a disused or ruined tower. Usually an old nest of crow or other bird. *Eggs* — 3 to 5, pale stone or pinkish cream, densely blotched and smudged with reddish brown. Both sexes share in all the domestic duties.

PLATE 11

41

42

43

44

PLATE 12

48

47

46

45

IN

45. Blackwinged Kite. *Elanus caeruleus* (Desfontaines)
HINDI NAMES : *Kăpāssi, Masunwa*

Handbook Vol. 1

Size: Jungle Crow. **Field Characters:** A dainty hawk, ashy grey above, white below, with a black line above the eyes and black patches on shoulders, conspicuous at rest as well as in flight. When closed, the wing tips extend beyond the short, square, white tail. **Distribution:** Patchily throughout the Indian Union from the base of the Himalayas; Bangladesh; Pakistan; Ceylon; Burma. Resident and locally migratory. **Habits:** Rather crepuscular, but also active in daytime. Inhabits well-wooded country and cultivation; also thin deciduous forest and grassland. Avoids dense jungle as well as arid plains. Keeps to a favoured locality, perched on the same pole or tree-top from day to day, whence to keep a lookout and pounce upon crawling prey. Cocks tail from time to time, jerking it up and down between the drooping wings. Also hovers in mid-air to scan the ground, and parachutes down in steps with motionless wings raised vertically above the body till when only a few feet above closes them and drops on the quarry, bearing it away in its claws. **Food:** Locusts, crickets, mice, lizards, etc. Flight sluggish; slow deliberate wing strokes alternated with short glides. **Call:** A shrill squeal, seldom heard. **Nesting:** *Season* — practically all year. *Nest* — loose, untidy, crowlike, of twigs sometimes lined with roots and grass, in small trees. *Eggs* — 3 or 4, yellowish white, densely blotched with brownish red. Both sexes share in the domestic duties.

46. Common Pariah Kite. *Milvus migrans* (Boddaert)
HINDI NAME : *Cheel*

Handbook Vol. 1

Size: Vulture ⚊ ; about 24″. **Field Characters:** A large brown hawk, distinguished from all similar birds by its forked tail, particularly in overhead flight. Sexes alike. Singly or gregariously, scavenging in towns and villages. **Distribution:** Throughout the Indian Union to about 8000 ft in the Himalayas; Bangladesh; Pakistan; Ceylon; Burma. A resident and a winter migratory race, the latter with a white patch on underside of wings. **Habits:** Our commonest raptor. A confirmed commensal of man and usually found in the neighbourhood of human habitations, whether populated city or outlying hamlet. Remarkably adroit on the wing, turning and twisting, banking and stooping to scoop up scraps from a traffic-congested thoroughfare and avoiding tangles of overhead telephone and electric wires with masterful ease. **Food:** Offal and garbage, earthworms, winged termites, lizards, mice, disabled or young birds, and almost anything else that can be procured. **Call:** A shrill, almost musical whistling *ewe-wir-wir-wir* uttered from a perch as well as on the wing. **Nesting:** *Season* — September to April, varying locally. *Nest* — an untidy platform of twigs, iron wire, tow, rags and rubbish of every description, up in a large tree or on roof or cornice of a building. *Eggs* — 2 to 4, dirty pinkish white, lightly spotted and blotched with reddish brown. Both sexes share in the domestic duties.

47. The Brahminy Kite. *Haliastur indus* (Boddaert)
HINDI NAMES : *Brāhmăni cheel, Dhōbiā cheel, Khēmkărni*

Handbook Vol. 1

Size: Pariah Kite $\pm$. **Field Characters:** A distinguished-looking raptor, bright rusty red above with white head, neck and breast down to abdomen. Immature birds chocolate-brown; separable from both kite and young Scavenger Vulture by shape of tail which is rounded, not forked or wedged. Sexes alike. Singly, by water — river, jheel or seacoast. **Distribution:** Throughout the Indian Union up to about 6000 ft in the Himalayas; Pakistan (part); Bangladesh; Ceylon; Burma. Resident and locally migratory. **Habits:** Keeps invariably to the neighbourhood of rivers, jheels, inundated paddy fields, and fishing villages and harbours on the seacoast. Spreads inland during monsoon for land crabs and frogs in water-logged country. Largely a scavenger in sea ports, picking up scraps and garbage cast overboard ships. **Food:** Offal, fish, frogs, small snakes, etc. Winged termites emerging from rain-sodden ground are hawked in the air. **Call:** A hoarse, wheezy squeal as of a pariah kite suffering from sore throat. **Nesting:** *Season* — principally December to April. *Nest* — a loose platform of twigs, lined with green leaves etc., built up in a large peepul, banyan or similar tree growing near water. *Eggs* — 2, greyish white, speckled and blotched with dingy reddish brown. Both sexes share in the domestic duties.

48. The Pale Harrier. *Circus macrourus* (S. G. Gmelin)
HINDI NAMES : *Dastmal, Girgit-mār*

Handbook Vol. 1

Size: Pariah Kite — ; much slenderer. **Field Characters:** A slender, pale ashy grey hawk with black tips to its long, narrow, pointed wings, especially conspicuous in flight. Relatively long white tail cross-barred with grey. *Female* umber brown with a buff-coloured owl-like ruff round head. Singly, sailing gracefully over standing crops and grassland.

Another common winter visitor, seen at jheels etc., is the MARSH HARRIER (*Circus aeruginosus*). Adult male chiefly rufous brown with silver grey wings and tail. Female, and young male, like a slim Pariah Kite with rounded tail and creamy buff cap on the head.

Distribution: In winter practically throughout the Indian Union; Bangladesh; Pakistan; Ceylon; Burma. **Habits:** Keeps to cultivated and scrub country, and rolling grassland. Perches on ground in preference to bush or tree. Quarters the countryside tirelessly on outspread motionless wings, skimming over the standing crops and grass, checking itself dead in mid-air when quarry is sighted on the ground, and wheeling sharply, almost in reverse gear, to pounce upon it. **Food:** Lizards, frogs, grasshoppers, nestling or disabled birds, etc. **Nesting:** Not within Indian limits; in eastern Europe and central Asia, April to June. *Nest* — a bed of leaves and grass on the ground in a corn field. *Eggs* — 4 or 5, white, spotted and blotched with reddish brown.

(See also SHIKRA, p. 53; PIED HARRIER, p. 142)

49. White-eyed Buzzard. *Butastur teesa* (Franklin)
HINDI NAME : *Teesā*

Handbook Vol. 1

Size: Jungle Crow ± . **Field Characters:** A small greyish brown hawk with white throat, two dark cheek stripes, brown and white underparts, and orange-yellow cere. Eyes, white or yellowish white, conspicuous at close quarters. A whitish nuchal patch and buffish wing shoulders provide additional clues to its identity. Sexes alike. Singly, in open scrub country. **Distribution:** The drier parts throughout the Indian Union up to about 3000 ft in the Himalayas (scarce in the southern peninsula); Pakistan; Burma. Not Ceylon. Resident, but also moves locally. **Habits:** Affects dry open country and thin deciduous forest; avoids humid and densely-wooded tracts. Rather sluggish. Perches on dry trees, telegraph posts, etc., and swoops down on its prey. **Food:** Locusts, grasshoppers, crickets and other large insects as well as mice, lizards and frogs. A beneficial species, quite wrongly accused of destroying game birds. **Call:** A not unpleasant, plaintive mewing, usually uttered when pairs soar in circles high up in the air, often in company with larger birds of prey. Silhouette of the rounded wings reminiscent of the Shikra. **Nesting:** *Season* — principally February to May. *Nest* — a loose, unlined cup of twigs like a crow's, up in the fork of a thickly foliaged tree such as mango, preferably one in a grove. *Eggs* — 3, greenish white broad ovals of a fairly smooth texture. Both sexes share nest-building and feeding young; female alone incubates.

50. Crested Hawk-Eagle. *Spizaetus cirrhatus* (Gmelin)
HINDI NAME : *Shāhbāz*

Handbook Vol. 1

Size: Pariah Kite + . **Field Characters:** A slender forest eagle in various confusing colour phases. Normally brown above; white below with black longitudinal streaks on throat and chocolate streaks on breast. Long narrow crest projecting behind head. In overhead flight, comparatively rounded wings (upturned at tip), longish tail, white body (spotted with brown) and grey underside of wings (streaked and spotted) are leading pointers. Sexes alike; female larger. Singly, in well-wooded country. **Distribution:** Practically the entire Indian Union; Bangladesh; Ceylon; Burma. Several races and closely allied species, differing in size and other details. **Habits:** Keeps a sharp lookout, perched bolt upright on a bough amongst the foliage canopy of some high tree standing near a forest clearing, for junglefowl, pheasants, hares and other small animals coming out into the open. Swoops down with a terrific rush, strikes and bears them away in its talons. **Call:** A loud, high-pitched *ki-ki-ki-ki-ki-ki-ki-kee*, beginning short, rising in crescendo and ending in a scream. **Nesting:** *Season* — December to April. *Nest* — a large stick platform lined with green leaves, high up in a forest tree. *Egg* — a singleton, greyish white, unmarked or with faint specks and blotches of light reddish at the broad end.

25

51. Pallas's or Ringtailed Fishing Eagle. *Haliaeetus leucoryphus* (Pallas). HINDI NAMES: *Machhmanga, Dhenk, Machharang*
Handbook Vol. 1

Size: Pariah Kite + . **Field Characters:** A large dark brown eagle with pale golden brown head and a broad white band across tail, particularly conspicuous in flight. Sexes alike; female larger. Pairs, at jheels and rivers. **Distribution:** North India including Bengal and Assam; Bangladesh; Pakistan; Burma. **Habits:** Inseparable from large rivers and jheels. Captures fish in the manner of the osprey, by hurling itself on the quarry from the air and seizing it in its talons; but it does not hover in the air. **Food:** Fish, snakes, rats, crabs and even carrion. Lives largely by piracy — attacking ospreys and other birds with determination, and depriving them of their legitimate prize. Occasionally it also kills coots and other water birds, or decamps with wildfowl falling to a sportsman's gun. **Call:** Loud, raucous screams very like the creaking of an unoiled wooden pulley of a village well. **Nesting:** *Season* — November to March. *Nest* — a massive stick platform at the top of some large isolated tree standing near water. *Eggs* — 3, white, broad ovals. Both sexes share all the domestic duties.

(See also OSPREY, p. 66)

52. Crested Serpent Eagle. *Spilornis cheela* (Latham)
HINDI NAME: *Dōgra cheel*
Handbook Vol. 1

Size: Pariah Kite + . **Field Characters:** A dark brown raptor with a prominent black-and-white nuchal crest, very full when erected. Underparts fulvous brown, ocellated and finely barred with black and white. In overhead flight a white bar across the tail (which is seldom fanned out as in a true eagle) and two similar bars on each of the broad, rounded wings, are suggestive clues. Sexes alike. Singly, or pairs, soaring over wooded country with peculiar shrill screaming calls. **Distribution:** The better-wooded parts throughout the Indian Union up to about 7000 ft in the Himalayas; Bangladesh; Pakistan; Ceylon; Burma. Resident and locally migratory. Three races concern us, differing in size and coloration details. **Habits:** An inhabitant of well-watered country and forested tracts, hill and plain. Keeps a lookout for prey from a branch high up in some lofty tree, preferably one commanding a clear view of the surrounding country. Commonly seen in pairs soaring in wide circles high up in the heavens, calling. **Call:** A penetrating high-pitched screaming whistle of 3 or 4 notes *kek-kek-kek-keee*. **Food:** Frogs, lizards, rats, snakes, etc. Rarely also takes junglefowl and peafowl. **Nesting:** *Season* — overall December to March. *Nest* — a large stick platform, lined with green leaves, high up in a lofty forest tree, preferably near streams or clearings. *Egg* — single, creamy or yellowish white boldly blotched with reddish brown.

PLATE 13

INS

PLATE 14

53. Tawny Eagle. *Aquila rapax* (Temminck)
HINDI NAME : *Okāb*
Handbook Vol. 1

Size: Pariah Kite + . Field Characters: A heavy, variably coloured raptor ranging from dark umber brown to dirty buff, with typical flat eagle's head, powerful hooked bill and fully feathered legs. Tail rounded like vulture's but relatively longer. Wings long, reaching almost to tip of tail when at rest; broad and ending in ' splayed fingers ', like vulture's, in flight. *Female* larger than male. Singly or pairs, in open country; perched on trees or soaring. Distribution: Practically throughout the drier portions of the Indian Union up to about 4000 ft in the Himalayas, Pakistan; Burma (part). Not Ceylon. Habits: Our commonest eagle. Affects dry open plains and scrub country, often in the neighbourhood of villages and cultivation. Largely a scavenger and pirate, feeding at carcases or by robbing other hawks of prey they have secured. Rarely also catches hares and other small rodents, and sick or disabled birds. Becomes a troublesome marauder of the poultry yard when it has nest-young to feed. Utters a variety of loud, raucous cackles. Nesting: *Season* — November to April. *Nest* — a large platform of sticks, thinly lined with grass and leaves, up at the top of a solitary thorny babool or similar tree, often near a village. *Eggs* — 2 or 3, white, with a few reddish brown spots and specks. Both sexes share in nest-building and feeding the young, but evidently the female alone incubates.

54. Short-toed Eagle. *Circaetus gallicus* (Gmelin)
HINDI NAME : *Sāmpmār*
Handbook Vol. 1

Size: Pariah Kite + . Field Characters: A brown, thick-set eagle with underparts below breast white, broadly barred with dark brown. Head large and owl-like. In overhead flight, general aspect silvery grey with darker head, and dark bars (usually 3) across tail. On close view, unfeathered legs and upwardly directed bristly feathers of face suggest identity. Immature birds brown and often confusing. Sexes alike, but female larger. Singly, in open country.

The CRESTED HONEY BUZZARD (*Pernis ptilorhynchus*) is rather like it on the wing, but slenderer, longer in the neck, and with smaller head. Seen from below its silvery grey underside has more dark markings, and usually only two blackish bands in the tail.

Distribution: Practically throughout the Indian Union except Assam; Pakistan. Absent in Bangladesh, Ceylon and Burma. Habits: Affects dry plains and foothills, as well as cultivated land. Method of hunting rather like the kestrel's. Frequently hovers in mid-air to scan the ground for prey, but its movements thus are cumbrous and ungainly. Food: Principally snakes and lizards, but also small or sickly rodents and birds. Call: A loud, screaming, plaintive *pieeou, pieeou* chiefly during the breeding season, when also a pair will indulge in remarkable aerial tumbling and darting displays. Nesting: *Season* — overall December to May. *Nest* — a rough, untidy platform of twigs, sometimes lined with green leaves and grass, on a medium-sized tree preferably standing by itself in open scrub jungle. *Egg* — a singleton, white or bluish white, broad oval.

27

55. Redheaded Merlin. *Falco chicquera* Daudin
HINDI NAME : *Turūmti*
Handbook Vol. 1

Size: Pigeon ± . **Field Characters:** An elegant little falcon, bluish grey above, white below closely barred with blackish on abdomen and flanks. In flight the narrow white edging to end of tail, preceded by a broad black band are useful clues. The conspicuous chestnut head is diagnostic. Sexes alike, but female larger. Singly or pairs, in open thinly-wooded country. **Distribution:** The drier parts of the Indian Union; Pakistan. Absent in eastern Assam, Bangladesh (?), Ceylon and Burma. **Habits:** Affects open plains and scrub country interspersed with villages and cultivation. Avoids humid forest tracts. Male and female frequently hunt in concert, one driving and heading off the quarry while the other pursues and strikes it down. Flight straight and swift attained by rapid and regular wing beats as in Sparrow-Hawk. **Food:** Small birds, rats, mice, lizards and insects; occasionally also bats. **Call:** A high-pitched squeal. **Nesting:** *Season —* principally January to May. *Nest —* a fairly well-made cup or platform of twigs lined with grass and roots, concealed up in a densely foliaged branch of large mango or similar tree. Usually old twig nests of other birds. *Eggs —* 3 or 4, pale reddish white thickly speckled with reddish brown. Bold and truculent while nesting, attacking and putting to flight much larger birds blundering into the vicinity of the nest-tree.

56. Kestrel. *Falco tinnunculus* Linnaeus
HINDI NAME : *Koruttia*
Handbook Vol. 1

Size: Pigeon ± . **Field Characters:** A small slender falcon, brick red above with grey head; light buff below with brown spearhead spots. In flight the pointed black wings and rounded grey tail with broad black terminal band are useful clues to identification. *Female* rufous above, including head, cross-barred with blackish. Singly, in open country, perched on stak^ or hovering. **Distribution:** Winter visitor from the Himalayas and beyond throughout the Indian Union, Bangladesh, Pakistan, Ceylon, Burma; two races. A third race, *objurgatus*, smaller and darker, resident in S. India and Ceylon. **Habits:** Chiefly distinguished for its spectacular method of hunting. Checks itself in flight now and again and remains poised stationary in mid-air on rapidly hovering wing tips for many seconds, intently scanning the ground below for crawling prey. If the quarry is sighted, the kestrel pounces upon it silently and bears it away in its talons. **Food:** Field mice, lizards, locusts and other large insects. **Call:** A sharp *ki-ki-ki* or *tit . . . wee* uttered on the wing; sometimes when hovering. **Nesting:** *Season —* Himalayas April-June; S. India February-April. *Nest —* a sketchy affair of twigs, roots, rags and rubbish in hole or crevice, or on ledge, of cliff. Occasionally in trees and on ruined buildings. *Eggs —* 3 to 6, pale pinkish or yellowish stone, profusely speckled and blotched with various shades of red. Both sexes share all the domestic duties.

57. **Whitebellied Sea Eagle.** *Haliaeetus leucogaster* (Gmelin)
HINDI NAME : *Kohassa*
Handbook Vol. 1

Size: Pariah Kite + . **Field Characters:** A large handsome eagle, ashy
brown above with pure white head, neck, and underparts and terminal
third of tail. In overhead flight the broad blackish border to white
underside of wings, and the wedge-shaped tail are diagnostic features.
When sailing, the wings are held above the line of the back in a wide
V. Sexes alike. Singly or pairs, by the sea coast. **Distribution:** The
seaboard of India from about Bombay south, and up the eastern side;
Ceylon; Burma; Malaysia to Australia. **Habits:** Keeps to the sea
coast and tidal estuaries. Where undisturbed, pairs occupy the same
localities for many years in succession, almost traditionally. **Call:**
A distinctive loud, nasal cackling *kenk-kenk-kenk* etc., quickly repeated. **Food:** Fish and, principally, sea snakes scooped up in its
talons from near the surface of the water. It does not dive after them
like the Osprey. **Nesting:** *Season* — October to June. *Nest* — a huge
platform of sticks lined with green leaves, high up in a casuarina or
other lofty tree near the seashore. Also on rocky offshore islets.
Usually the traditional nest is renovated from year to year. *Eggs* — 2,
white, unmarked.

(See also GREYHEADED FISHING EAGLE, p. 142.)

58. **Shahin Falcon.** *Falco peregrinus peregrinator* Sundevall
HINDI NAMES : *Shāhiñ* (female), *Kohi* or *Koela* (male)
Handbook Vol. 1

Size: Jungle Crow. **Field Characters:** A powerful, alert, broad-
shouldered falcon, slaty above with black head, nape, and conspicuous
moustachial stripes. Throat and breast white; rest of underparts
ferruginous. Young birds vary but are blacker above, striped on
breast and heavily barred on flanks. *Female* larger. Solitary, or pairs,
on cliffs, rock pinnacles, about hill forts, etc. **Distribution:** Resident
practically throughout the hilly portions of India; Bangladesh;
Ceylon; Burma. The north Asian race of the Peregrine (*F. p. japonensis*)
— paler above, almost white below — is a winter visitor. **Habits:** A
typical falcon with pointed wings. Flight swift and powerful, on
rapidly beating wings interspersed with long glides. Lives largely on
birds like duck, partridges, pigeons, and parakeets stooping on them
with tremendous velocity, striking in mid-air with its powerful hind
claw, and bearing them away to its favourite perch on a crag to be
devoured. In the breeding season pairs indulge in a spectacular aerial
display, stooping at each other, looping, turning, and twisting with
phenomenal speed. **Nesting:** *Season* — March to May. *Nest* — a platform of twigs, grass, etc. on a ledge on a cliff-face. *Eggs* — 2 or 3,
variable, pinkish buff to pinkish red marked lightly or heavily with
dark brick-red or purplish.

59. Painted Sandgrouse. *Pterocles indicus* (Gmelin)
HINDI NAMES : *Pāhāri bhăt-teetăr, Bhăt-ban, Handeri*
Handbook Vol. 3

Size: Between Myna and Pigeon. **Field Characters:** Smaller than the Common Sandgrouse (72), with close-barred plumage and no pin feathers in tail. White forecrown cut across by a black band, tricoloured gorget on breast (chestnut, buff, and black), and close-barred underparts diagnostic of male. *Female* finely barred above and below with chocolate, black, and buff. Pairs or small parties in dry, stony scrub country, and open forest. **Distribution:** Peculiar to India. Resident over the greater part of peninsular and central India and NW. Pakistan; locally migratory in rainy season. Not in Assam, Bangladesh, or Ceylon. **Habits:** Terrestrial; usually pairs, seldom flocks. Walks and runs better than Common Sandgrouse. Extraordinarily well camouflaged when squatted. Rises suddenly when almost trampled on, with a clucking *yek-yek-yek* and noisy clapping of wings. Has swift flapping flight. Partly crepuscular. Large numbers concentrate to drink at a favourite water-hole at dusk, arriving in small parties, and continuing, till almost quite dark. Said to drink in the morning also well before sunrise. When flying to and from water, utters a distinctive *chirik-chirik* which in the dark is often the only indication of the traffic. **Food:** Grain, seeds and shoots. **Nesting:** *Season* — Practically throughout the year, chiefly March to June. *Nest* — a scrape on stony ground under protection of a bush or grass clump. *Eggs* — 3, cream to salmon pink, sparsely spotted and blotched with purplish red or reddish grey.

60. Oystercatcher. *Haematopus ostralegus* Linnaeus
HINDI NAME :
Handbook Vol. 2

Size: Partridge +. **Field Characters:** A striking black-and-white shore bird with stoutish bare red legs and long, straight, compressed orange-red bill, snipe-like but blunt or truncated at tip. In flight the broad white band across the black wings, white lower back and underparts contrasting with the black head, breast, and tail, are diagnostic points. Sexes alike. Pairs or parties on sea coast. **Distribution:** Practically world-wide. Winter visitor to India, Bangladesh and Pakistan; in two races: NW.-Asiatic *ostralegus*, NE.-Asiatic *osculans*. The latter form (presumably) has recently been discovered breeding in the Sundarbans. **Habits:** Keeps to rocky seashores and tidal estuaries where it runs about and feeds at low tide. **Food:** Chiefly oysters and mussels, the shells being prised open and contents chiselled out with the specially adapted bill. Also small crabs and marine worms probed out of the wet sand. **Call:** A shrill, plaintive piping, reminiscent of the Whistling Teal. **Nesting:** Only once recorded within Indo-Bangladesh limits (Khulna Sundarbans), in April. *Nest* — a scrape on an open sandbank paved with shells and pebbles. *Eggs* — 3 or 4, brownish buff spotted with black and dark grey, somewhat more heavily at the broad end.

PLATE 15

57

58

59

60

Scholz

PLATE 16

63

61

62

64

IN

61. **Black Partridge.** *Francolinus francolinus* (Linnaeus)

HINDI NAME : *Kālā teetar*

Handbook Vol. 2

Size: Half-grown village hen $\pm$. **Field Characters:** A plump, stub-tailed game bird chiefly black, spotted and barred with white and fulvous. The glistening white cheek-patches and chestnut collar of the cock are diagnostic. *Hen* considerably paler, mottled and speckled black and white, with a chestnut patch on nape. Singly or pairs, in well-watered and cultivated country. **Distribution:** Northern India and Assam (commonly up to 5000 ft in the W. Himalayas) south roughly to a curve from Kutch through Gwalior to Chilka Lake (Orissa). Also Pakistan. Three races, differing in details of coloration. **Habits:** Restricted to well-watered scrub, tamarisk and tall grass jungle. Millet and sugar cane fields in riverain or canal-irrigated country are favourite haunts, as well as tea gardens and their environs in the Outer Himalayas. Enters crops to feed in the mornings and evenings. An exceedingly swift runner, relying on its legs for escape unless driven or suddenly come upon. Flight strong and direct with rapid whirring wing beats. **Food:** Grain, grass seeds, green shoots, white ants and other insects. **Call:** A cheerful, ringing, high-pitched *chik-cheek-cheek-keraykek* with a peculiar ventriloquistic and far-reaching quality. Wholesale unregulated netting is causing serious depletion in its numbers in many areas. **Nesting:** *Season* — April to July. *Nest* — a shallow scrape lined with grass in tamarisk scrub, millet or cane fields. *Eggs* — 6 to 8, pale olive-brown to almost chocolate-brown.

62. **Painted Partridge.** *Francolinus pictus* (Jardine & Selby)

HINDI NAME : *Kālā teetar*

Handbook Vol. 2

Size: Grey Partridge. **Field Characters:** Brownish black profusely spotted and barred with white, with some ferruginous-red in the head and wings. General aspect that of female Black Partridge but without the chestnut nape-patch. When flying away from observer the blackish under tail-coverts showing on either side of tail, and the chestnut in wings are leading clues. Female differs in colour details, usually having the throat white. Singly or pairs, in grass-and-scrub country and cultivation, never far from water. **Distribution:** Peninsular India south of the range of the Black Partridge, excepting the Malabar coast; Ceylon. Absent in Bangladesh, Pakistan, and Burma. The Ceylon race *watsoni* is darker than the Indian *pictus*. **Habits:** Very similar in every way to those of the Black Partridge. Perhaps frequents somewhat drier country and perhaps is also more arboreal, not only roosting in trees at night but mounting into them in daytime and calling thence, particularly during the breeding season. **Call:** Almost indistinguishable from that of 61, the same harsh high-pitched *chik-cheek-cheek-keray*, rendered in Hindustani as *Sūbhan teri qūdrat*. Female also said to call, but this needs confirmation. **Nesting:** *Season* — SW. monsoon, June to September. *Nest* — similar to that of the Black Partridge, frequently under a bush on grassy *bunds* separating inundated paddy fields. *Eggs* — 4 to 8, very like those of 61 but much paler, being various shades of cream colour.

31

63. Grey Partridge. *Francolinus pondicerianus* (Gmelin)
HINDI NAMES : *Teetăr, Săfed teetăr*

Handbook Vol. 2

Size: Half-grown domestic hen; *c.* 13 inches. **Field Characters:** A plump, stub-tailed greyish brown game bird with chestnut blotching above and fine wavy black and buff vermiculations, and chestnut tail. Throat rufous-buff circumscribed by a broken blackish line. Sexes alike, but cock with a pointed spur on each leg. Pairs or coveys, in dry scrub country and cultivation. **Distribution:** The drier portions of the entire Indian Union (excepting Assam) up to 1500 ft in the Himalayas; Ceylon; Pakistan. Three races, differing in coloration details. **Habits:** Affects dry, open grass and thorn-scrub country. Avoids heavy forest and humid tracts. Commonly found in the neighbourhood of villages and cultivation. Coveys scratch the ground or cattle dung for food: grain, seeds, termites, beetle larvae, etc. Largely terrestrial, but roosts in babul and similar trees. When flushed, rises with a loud whir of wings. Flight swift and ' gamey ' consisting of a few rapid beats of the rounded wings, followed by a short glide. Usually trusts to its legs for escape, being a very fast runner. **Call:** A ringing, high-pitched, musical *kateetar, kateetar* or *pateela, pateela* quickly repeated. The female has a less challenging *pela, pela, pela*, etc. **Nesting:** *Season* — practically all year, varying locally. *Nest* — a grass-lined scrape in scrub jungle, ploughed field or grassland. *Eggs* — 4 to 8, cream coloured or *café au lait*.

64. Common or Bluelegged Bustard-Quail. *Turnix suscitator*
(Gmelin). HINDI NAMES : *Gulu, Gŭndră*

Handbook Vol. 2

Size: Rain Quail — . **Field Characters:** A typical little quail, rufous brown above, rusty and buff below. Chin, throat and breast closely barred with black. Female larger and more richly coloured, with throat and middle of breast black. The blue-grey bill and legs, and yellowish white eyes are diagnostic, as are also the pale buff shoulder-patches on the wings when in flight. Absence of hind toe distinguishes Bustard-and Button Quails from true quails. Pairs, in scrub and grassland. **Distribution:** The entire Indian Union up to about 8000 ft in the Himalayas; Ceylon; Bangladesh; Burma. Seven geographical races differing in colour details. **Habits:** Found in every type of country excepting dense forest and desert. Partial to scrub jungle, light deciduous forest, and neighbourhood of cultivation. Differs from true quails chiefly in the female being polyandrous. She fights with other females for the possession of a cock, uttering a loud drumming *drr-r-r-r-r* as a challenge to rival hens and also to announce herself to a cock. Eggs when laid are left to be incubated by the cock who also tends the young. The hen goes off to acquire another husband, and perhaps yet another, and so on, evidently only one at a time. **Nesting:** *Season* — practically throughout the year, varying locally. *Nest* — a grass-lined scrape or depression in scrub jungle or crops, often arched over by surrounding grass. *Eggs* — 3 or 4, greyish white profusely speckled with reddish brown or blackish purple.

32

65. Blackbreasted or Rain Quail. *Coturnix coromandelica* (Gmelin). HINDI NAMES: *China băteya* (or *băter?*), *Chănăk*
Handbook Vol. 2

Size: Grey Quail — . **Field Characters:** Similar to 66 but with upper breast black, and frequently also centre of abdomen. *Female* very like that of 66 but both sexes distinguishable from Grey Quail by absence of buff and brown cross-bars on the primaries. Pairs or small parties, on ground, in cultivation and grassland. **Distribution:** Throughout the Indian Union, up to about 6000 ft in the Himalayas; Bangladesh; Pakistan; North Burma. Rare in Ceylon. Resident but locally migratory. **Habits:** Differ little from those of Grey Quail. Moves about a great deal locally with the seasons, particularly during the monsoon when otherwise bare tracts become transformed into luxuriant grassland and provide both food and cover. There is, however still much to be learnt concerning its seasonal movements. **Call:** A disyllabic musical whistle *which-which*, *which-which*, etc., constantly repeated mornings and evenings, and in the breeding season also during the night. It is distinct and unmistakable with the call of the Grey Quail. **Nesting:** *Season* — overall March to October, but chiefly after the break of the SW. monsoon in June. *Nest* and site same as in the Grey Quail. Sometimes the scrape is in the open under an *Euphorbia* or similar bush. *Eggs* — 6 to 8, resembling those of 66 but smaller. Only the female incubates.

(See also MOUNTAIN QUAIL, p. 20.)

66. Common or Grey Quail. *Coturnix coturnix* (Linnaeus)
HINDI NAMES: *Băter*, *Ghăgus băter*
Handbook Vol. 2

Size: Dove minus tail; *c.* 7 inches. **Field Characters:** A plump, squat, almost tailless partridge-like bird, buffish brown with pale streaks and irregular blotches and bars of reddish brown and black above. *Female* lacks the black anchor mark on throat. Differentiated from Rain Quail (65) by presence of buff bars on outer webs of primaries. Pairs or gregariously, on ground in cultivation and grassland. **Distribution:** Practically the entire Indian Union; Pakistan; Burma. Not Ceylon. Two races differing in coloration details. Resident as well as winter visitor. **Habits:** Affects open country with standing crops, and grassland. Our resident population is vastly augmented during winter by immigrants from W. and C. Asia. Usually keeps in pairs, but large numbers concentrate in fields where food is plentiful. When such a field is walked up, the birds do not rise in a flock or all at once, but in twos and threes, and offer excellent sport with gun. Flight swift and direct; attained by rapid, vibrating wingstrokes. After flying a couple of hundred yards the bird drops into the grass again. **Call:** A loud whistling note followed rapidly by two short ones, described as ' a liquid *wet-mi-lips* '. **Food:** Grain and grass seeds, termites, etc. Quails are excellent eating, and are netted in very large numbers all along their migration routes. **Nesting:** *Season* — overall February to October; mainly March to May. *Nest* — a shallow scrape, sparsely lined with grass, well concealed in grass or standing crops. *Eggs* — 6 to 14, reddish or yellow buff, speckled and blotched with dark brown.

33

67. **Jungle Bush Quail.** *Perdicula asiatica* (Latham)
HINDI NAME : *Lowwā*
Handbook Vol. 2

Size: Rain Quail. **Field Characters:** *Male* fulvous-brown above, streaked and mottled with black and buff; white below, closely barred with black. *Female*: lower parts pale pinkish rufous. Both sexes have a prominent buff-and-chestnut superciliary stripe from forehead backward and down sides of the neck, and a bright chestnut throat-patch. Coveys, in scrub country.

The Rock Bush Quail (*P. argoondah*) frequently found side by side with this, has the chin and throat-patch dull brick red instead of chestnut in the male. The hen has a whitish chin and no throat patch.

Distribution: Locally throughout the Indian Union (excepting Assam), plains and hills up to 4000 ft, also Ceylon. Absent in Bangladesh, Pakistan and Burma. Four races concern us. **Habits:** Affects fairly open deciduous forest and dry stony grass and scrub jungle. Lives in coveys of 5 to 20 which rest bunched together and ' explode ' or rise suddenly with a whir of wings when almost trodden on, dispersing in all directions but soon reuniting. **Call:** A whistling *whi-whi-whi-whi* which brings the scattered members together. Breeding males are pugnacious and challenge rivals by harsh grating calls similar to the ' argueing ' of Black Drongos at the onset of their breeding. **Food:** Grass seeds, grain and tender shoots; also termites. **Nesting:** *Season* — not well defined; ranges between August and April. *Nest* — a scrape at base of a grass tussock in scrub jungle, lined with grass. *Eggs* — 4 to 8, creamy white. The hen alone incubates. It is not certain if the cock is monogamous.

(See also PAINTED BUSH QUAIL, p. 134.)

68. **Red Spurfowl.** *Galloperdix spadicea* (Gmelin)
HINDI NAMES : *Chhōti jāngli mūrghi, Chǎkōtri*
Handbook Vol. 2

Size: Threequarters-grown village hen. **Field Characters:** Hen differs from cock (illustrated) in being rufous-brown above with fine black bars and freckles. Breast pale chestnut-rufous with black spots. Cock has 2 to 4 pointed spurs on each leg; female 1 or 2. In both sexes a naked brick-red patch around eye. Pairs or family parties, on ground in stony overgrown nullahs etc.

Distribution: Wide but patchy; practically the entire Indian Union excepting Assam. Three races, differing in coloration details. Absent in Bangladesh, Pakistan, and Burma. Represented in Ceylon by the species *G. bicalcarata*. **Habits:** Affects deciduous scrub country, particularly where cut up by dry ravines etc. Overgrown ruins enveloped in jungle are favourite haunts. Scratches amongst the mulch and dry leaves for food. A great skulker; scuttles away through the thickets on the least alarm. **Food:** Seeds, berries and insects. **Call:** Of the cock, a peculiar chuckle-like crow — a quick-repeated rattling *krrr-kwek, krr-kwek, krr-kwek*, reminiscent of the guinea fowl. **Nesting:** *Season* — principally January to June, varying locally. *Nest* — a shallow scrape in scrub or bamboo jungle, sometimes sparsely lined with grass and leaves. *Eggs* — 3 to 5, buff coloured, like small eggs of the domestic fowl.

(See also PAINTED SPURFOWL, p. 134.)

PLATE 17

INS

PLATE 18

69. Grey Junglefowl. *Gallus sonneratii* (Temminck)
HINDI NAME : *Jăngli mŭrghi*
Handbook Vol. 2

Size: Village hen. **Field Characters:** General effect of the cock
streaked grey, with a metallic black sickle-shaped tail. Hen distinguishable from that of Red Junglefowl by her white (not rufous-
brown) breast with blackish borders to the feathers producing a scaly
pattern. Singly or small parties, in forest and scrub jungle. **Distribution:** Peninsular India north to a line roughly from Mount Abu to the
mouth of the Godavari river. On the borderline where the two species
meet they often hybridize. **Habits:** Inhabits deciduous as well as
evergreen forest, plain and hill. Particularly fond of lantana and
other scrub growing on the site of abandoned forest clearings. Very
shy and wary. Scuttles into cover on the least suspicion, neck outstretched and tail drooping. Roosts up in trees or bamboo clumps.
Food: Grain, shoots and tubers, berries, termites and other insects.
Call: A harsh crow *kuk-kaya-kaya-kuk*. When agitated or alarmed,
an angry-sounding *kăghak*, *kăghak* is uttered rapidly. **Nesting:**
Season — undefined: principally February to May. *Nest* and site
similar to the Red Junglefowl's. *Eggs* — 4 to 7, pale fawn to warm
buff, similar to the domestic fowl's and also to those of 70. In both
species the hen alone incubates.

70. Red Junglefowl. *Gallus gallus* Linnaeus
HINDI NAME : *Jăngli mŭrghi*
Handbook Vol. 2

Size: Village hen. **Field Characters:** Hen differs from cock (illustrated)
in being plain streaked brown with rufous-brown underparts. Both
sexes very like the 'Game Bantam' domestic breed. Pairs or parties, in
scrub and Sāl jungle. **Distribution:** Northern India, especially the
Himalayan foothills country to eastern Assam; south to the Godavari
river in eastern Madhya Pradesh; Burma. Almost completely overlaps distribution of Sāl tree (*Shorea robusta*) and Swamp Deer (*Cervus
duvauceli*). The Indian race *murghi* differs from the Burmese *spadiceus*
in details of coloration.

Represented in Ceylon by the allied species *G. lafayettii* with breast
of cock reddish orange instead of black.

Habits: The ancestor of all domestic breeds of fowl. Parties of
perhaps a cock and 3 or 4 hens come out in the early mornings and
afternoons to feed in stubble fields at the edge of forest, or on forest
roads and firelines, etc. Very shy. Roosts up in trees or bamboo
clumps. **Food:** Grain, vegetable shoots, insects, lizards, etc. **Call:** A
crow like that of the domestic Bantam, somewhat shriller and ending
more abruptly; uttered mostly in the morning and again before
turning in to roost, but also sporadically throughout the day. **Nesting:**
Season — principally March to May. *Nest* — a shallow scrape in dense
undergrowth, lined with dry leaves. *Eggs* — 5 or 6, like the domestic
fowl's. Cock apparently monogamous.

71. Common Peafowl. *Pavo cristatus* Linnaeus
HINDI NAMES : *Mōr, Măyūră*
Handbook Vol. 2

Size: Vulture. **Field Characters:** The gorgeous ocellated ' tail ' of the adult cock, 3 to 4 ft long, is in reality the abnormally lengthened upper tail-coverts. Hen, also crested like cock, but smaller; mottled brown with some metallic green on lower neck, and lacking the ornamental train. Parties or droves, in deciduous forest. Also locally semi-domesticated about villages and cultivation, where protected by religious sentiment. **Distribution:** Throughout the Indian Union, locally up to 5000 ft in the Himalayas; Ceylon; Bangladesh. Replaced in Burma by the species *P: muticus* with a pointed crest. **Habits:** Inhabits dense scrub and deciduous jungle — plain and foot-hill — preferably in the neighbourhood of rivers and streams. Poly-gamous; usually parties of one cock with 4 or 5 hens, but seasonally of the sexes separately. Always excessively shy and alert. Slinks away through the undergrowth on its legs, and flies only when suddenly come upon, or to cross a ravine or open river bed. Roosts at night in large trees. **Food:** Grain, vegetable shoots, insects, lizards, snakes, etc. **Call:** A loud harsh, screaming *may-awe*, and short gasping shrieks *ka-aan, ka-aan* repeated rapidly 6 to 8 times with a pumping action of head and neck. Cock displays before his bevy of hens erecting and fanning out his showy train, and strutting and posturing to the accompaniment of paroxysms of quivering. **Nesting:** *Season* — January to October. *Nest* — a shallow scrape in the ground in a dense thicket, lined with sticks and leaves. *Eggs* — 3 to 5, glossy pale cream or *café-au-lait* colour.

72. Common Sandgrouse. *Pterocles exustus* Temminck
HINDI NAME : *Bhăt teetăr*
Handbook Vol. 3

Size: Pigeon — . **Field Characters:** A yellowish sandy brown pin-tailed pigeon-like ground bird with a narrow black band across the breast, and brownish black belly. Cheeks, chin and throat dull yellow. *Female* streaked, spotted and barred with black all over except the chin; also with a black band across breast. When overhead, the dark underside with pointed tail and wings, and swift, direct flight ac-companied by the characteristic double note, proclaim its identity. Flocks of up to a dozen or more, on dry fallow land. **Distribution:** Dry areas throughout the Indian Union except Assam; Pakistan. Not Bangladesh, Ceylon or Burma. Only the one race *erlangeri* concerns us. **Habits:** Affects barren plains, stubble fields, and fallow land. Shuffles along the ground on its short legs, gleaning weed- and grass seeds supplemented by grit. Its remarkably obliterative colora-tion makes the bird completely invisible while it remains squatted still. Flocks and parties regularly travel long distances to drink at favourite spots soon after sunrise and again before sunset, and offer good sport for the gun as they fly to or from the water. **Call:** A penetrating far-reaching double note *kut-ro*, constantly uttered in flight. **Nesting:** *Season* — undefined; chiefly January to May. *Nest* — a shallow unlined scrape in open stony scrub country. *Eggs* — 3, pale greyish or yellowish stone colour, spotted and speckled with brown. Both sexes share in incubation.

(See also PAINTED SANDGROUSE, p. 30)

73. Sarus Crane. *Grus antigone* (Linnaeus)
HINDI NAME : *Sārǎs*
Handbook Vol. 2

Size: Vulture +; standing 4 to 5 ft. **Field Characters:** A large, tall grey bird with long bare red legs, and naked red head and upper neck. Sexes alike. Pairs, about cultivation and marshland. **Distribution:** Northern and central India; Bangladesh; Pakistan; Assam; Burma. Two races, the Burmese *sharpii* being darker than Indian *antigone*. **Habits:** Essentially a dweller of open, well-watered plains. Normally seen in pairs, occasionally accompanied by one or two young. Said to pair for life, and conjugal devotion has won for the species popular reverence and protection resulting in tameness and lack of fear of man. Flight attained by slow rhythmical wing strokes, neck outstretched in front, legs trailing behind; swifter than it appears and seldom high up in the air. **Call:** A loud, sonorous, far-reaching trumpeting, uttered from ground as well as on wing. During breeding season pairs indulge in ludicrous and spectacular dancing displays, bowing mutually, prancing with outspread wings and leaping round each other. **Food:** Grain, shoots and other vegetable matter, insects, reptiles, etc. **Nesting:** *Season* — July to December. *Nest* — a huge mass of reed- and rush stems and straw, in the midst of a flooded paddy field or a marsh. *Eggs* — 2, pale greenish or pinkish white, sometimes spotted and blotched with brown or purple. Both birds are vigilant in guarding the nest, boldly attacking dogs and cattle encroaching in its neighbourhood.

74. Demoiselle Crane. *Anthropoides virgo* (Linnaeus)
HINDI NAMES : *Kǎrkǎrā, Koonj*
Handbook Vol. 2

Size: Duck + ; *c.* 3 ft high. **Field Characters:** A dainty little grey crane with black head and neck. Feathers of lower neck long and lanceolate, and falling over breast. Conspicuous white ear-tufts behind eyes. Sexes alike. Large flocks in young gram and wheat fields, and on tank margins. **Distribution:** Winter visitor to the Indian Union south to Mysore. Pakistan; Burma.

The COMMON CRANE (*Grus grus lilfordi*) also visits us in enormous numbers, often associating with the Demoiselle. It is larger, with a naked black crown, distinctive red patch across nape, and no white tufts behind eyes.

Habits: One of our most prominent and well-known winter immigrants. Affects open cultivated country, feeding largely on tender shoots of young gram and wheat. Flocks rest on sandbanks in rivers or margins of jheels during the midday heat, or soar in circles at great heights. A fine sporting bird, exceedingly wary and difficult to circumvent and eagerly sought by sportsmen. **Call:** A loud, musical, high-pitched trumpet of far-reaching quality. The din of a great concourse of *koonj* taking off the ground, with their *kurr, kurr* calls uttered in varying keys, has been aptly likened to ,the distant roaring of the sea. **Food:** Besides shoots and grain, insects and small reptiles. Cranes fly in broad V formation, neck and legs fully extended. **Nesting:** In S. Europe, N. Africa and N. & C. Asia east to Mongolia. *Nest* — similar to the Sarus's. *Eggs* — 2, yellowish grey, blotched with reddish brown and grey.

75. Great Indian Bustard. *Choriotis nigriceps* (Vigors)
HINDI NAMES : *Tūqdār, Hūknā*
Handbook Vol. 2

Size: Vulture + ; standing *c.* 3 ft to top of head; weighing up to 40 lb. **Field Characters:** A heavy ground bird reminiscent of a young ostrich. Deep buff above finely vermiculated with black; white below with broad black gorget on lower breast. Conspicuous black-crested crown. In flight the white outstretched neck and underparts, black crown and gorget, and a large whitish patch near tip of wings prominent. Sexes alike; female smaller. Pairs, or parties, on open plains and about cultivation. **Distribution:** Locally throughout the Indian Union (excepting Bengal and Assam) south to Mysore; Pakistan. Resident and local migrant. **Habits:** Affects open sparse grass and scrub plains country interspersed with cultivation. Usually 3 or 4 loosely together, but scattered droves of 25 to 30 recorded. Is a good runner and heavy in take-off, but once launched flies strongly with steady rhythmical flapping of the broad wings. Persecution by shikaris and narrowing of its habitat due to spread of cultivation has reduced the species to near extinction. It is now totally protected by law. **Food:** Grain and shoots of various crops, locusts, beetles, centipedes, lizards, etc. **Call:** A bark or bellow — something like *hook*. Cock polygamous. When in puffed-out strutting display with drooping wings before his hens, utters a deep, far-reaching moaning call. **Nesting:** *Season* — undefined, chiefly March to September. *Eggs* — a singleton, rarely two, drab or pale olive-brown, faintly blotched with deep brown. Laid in a shallow depression at base of a bush. Only the female incubates.

76. Lesser Florican. *Sypheotides indica* (J. F. Miller)
HINDI NAMES : *Likh, Khăr mŏr*
Handbook Vol. 2

Size: Village hen; longer neck and legs. **Field Characters:** Hen sandy buff, mottled and streaked with blackish. Cock in non-breeding plumage like hen and minus the upwardly curled head plumes. He retains a good deal of the white in the wings. Singly, or widely separated pairs in tall grassland. **Distribution:** The greater part of the Indian plains, excluding Assam. Pakistan (part). Resident and locally migratory, chiefly during the rains. **Habits:** Affects tall grass country and standing fields of cotton, millets, etc. Not gregarious. Flight like bustard's but the more rapid wing strokes produce resemblance to a lapwing in silhouette. **Food:** Green shoots, grain, seeds, beetles, etc. Is good eating and much persecuted by shikaris during breeding season, when displaying cock particularly vulnerable. The cock's nuptial display consists of constantly jumping or springing up above cover of long grass or crops. This believed to advertise his presence to hens and to warn off rival cocks. A short guttural croak accompanies each jump, and the performer floats down perpendicularly with tail spread out, vaguely reminiscent of the male Iora's aerial display. **Nesting:** *Season* — July to October (SW. monsoon). *Eggs* — 3 or 4, some shade of olive-brown, mottled and streaked with brown. Laid on bare ground in a grass field or crops. The female alone incubates and tends the young.

PLATE 19

74

75

73

76

PLATE 20

77

79

78

80

INS

IN

77. Indian Moorhen. *Gallinula chloropus* (Linnaeus)
HINDI NAMES : *Jăl mŭrghi, Bōdăr*
Handbook Vol. 2

Size: Partridge ± . **Field Characters:** On land a typical waterhen, on water like a small duck. A slaty grey and brown marsh bird with white edges to the closed wings, and conspicuous white under tail-coverts. Forehead (frontal shield) and base of greenish bill bright red. Longish green legs and large ungainly feet. Pairs, or gregariously, amongst partially submerged rushes, swimming or skulking about. **Distribution:** Throughout the Indian Union up to 6000 ft elevation and higher; Bangladesh; Pakistan; Ceylon; Burma. Only the one race *indica* concerns us. **Habits:** Typical of the rails. Very like the Whitebreasted Waterhen except that it swims a great deal more. On water its progress is attended by the same characteristic jerky bobbing of head and flicking up of tail when the white under tail-coverts flash prominently. Flight laboured — usually low over the water with rapid wing beats, neck stretched in front and legs trailing behind. **Call:** A sharp loud and abrupt *kirrik-crek-rek-rek* uttered from within a reed-bed, principally in the mornings and evenings. **Food:** As of 78. **Nesting:** *Season* — June to September (SW. monsoon). *Nest* — bulky, of sedges and weeds on ground amongst aquatic herbage, or up in a low shrub near water. *Eggs* — 5 to 12, pale yellowish to warm buff stone colour, blotched with dark reddish brown.

78. Whitebreasted Waterhen. *Amaurornis phoenicurus* (Pennant)
HINDI NAMES : *Dāhŭk, Jăl mŭrghi*
Handbook Vol. 2

Size: Partridge ± . **Field Characters:** A familiar slaty grey stub-tailed, long-legged marsh bird with prominent white face and breast, and bright rusty red under the tail. Sexes alike. Singly or pairs, near reeds and thickets on marshy ground. **Distribution:** Throughout the Indian Union up to the base of the Himalayas; Bangladesh; Pakistan; Ceylon; Burma; Andamans; Nicobars. Three races. **Habits:** Affects moist ground overgrown with tangles of bushes, *Pandanus* brakes, etc., on the margins of jheels and ponds. Wanders considerably afield in the monsoon when low-lying tracts become water-logged. The stumpy tail, carried erect as the bird stalks or skulks along, is constantly jerked up flashing the chestnut colour underneath into prominence. Ordinarily shy and silent, but exceedingly noisy during the rainy season when it breeds. Clambers up for calling into the top of a bush whence it can command a good view of its surroundings, without exposing itself. **Call:** Beginning with loud, hoarse grunts, croaks and chuckles, settles down to a monotonous, metallic *krr-kwak-kwak, krr-kwak-kwak,* etc. or just *kook-kook-kook,* rather like the Crimson-breasted Barbet's but higher in key and faster in tempo. Heard chiefly on cloudy overcast days and often all through the night. **Food:** Insects, worms, molluscs, grain and shoots of paddy and marsh plants. **Nesting:** *Season* — June to October (SW. monsoon). *Nest* — a shallow cup of twigs, creeper stems and flags of bulrushes, up in a bush near water. *Eggs* — 6 or 7, cream or pinkish white, streaked and blotched with reddish brown.

79. Purple Moorhen. *Porphyrio porphyrio* (Linnaeus)
HINDI NAMES : *Kaim, Kharim, Kalim, Kărmā*
Handbook Vol. 2

Size: Village hen. **Field Characters:** A handsome but clumsy purplish blue rail with long red legs and toes. The bald red forehead (frontal shield) continued back from the short heavy red bill, and the white patch under the stumpy tail (conspicuous when flicked up at each step) are leading clues. Sexes alike. Pairs, or parties, in swampy reed-beds. **Distribution:** Throughout the plains of the Indian Union; Bangladesh; Pakistan; Burma; Ceylon. Two races — *seistanicus* and *poliocephalus*. **Habits:** Typical rail. Affects reedy swamps, and margins of jheels overgrown with rushes. Stalks or skulks through the vegetation with the same jerky bobbing of head and flicking of tail as the waterhen, and the flight and general behaviour of the two are also similar. Occasionally clambers awkwardly up the reed stems. **Food:** Shoots and vegetable matter; also insects and molluscs. Locally destructive to young paddy crops. **Calls:** A variety of loud hooting, cackling and hoarse notes. Particularly noisy during breeding season. Male has ludicrous courtship display, holding water weeds in his bill and bowing to female with loud chuckles. **Nesting:** *Season* — June to September (SW. monsoon). *Nest* — a large pad of interwoven reed flags etc., on a mass of floating debris or amongst matted reeds slightly above water level. *Eggs* — 3 to 7, pale yellowish stone to reddish buff, blotched and spotted with reddish brown.

(See also BANDED CRAKE, p. 144, BAILLON'S CRAKE, p. 144.)

80. Indian or Yellowlegged Button Quail. *Turnix tanki* Blyth
HINDI NAME : *Lowwā* (cf. 67)
Handbook Vol. 2

Size: Rain Quail $\pm$. **Field Characters:** The broad orange-rufous half collar on hindneck of the female (illustrated) and the bright yellow legs and bill of both sexes are diagnostic. In flight, which is feebler even than that of 64, the orange-rufous hind collar, breast and flanks, and whitish underparts are pointers. Male lacks the hind collar and is less richly coloured. Singly, in damp grassland or crops. **Distribution:** Practically the entire Indian Union up to about 4000 ft elevation; Bangladesh; Andamans; Nicobars; Burma. Absent in Pakistan and Ceylon. **Habits:** Affects scrub and grassland. Rises in feeble flight when almost trodden upon, only to plunge into cover again a dozen yards further. Female polyandrous as in 64. **Call:** A prolonged drumming *drr-r-r-r* similar to the blue-legged species but softer. Both are reminiscent of a two-stroke motorcycle engine running in the far distance. **Food:** Grass- and weed seeds, grain, green shoots and small insects. **Nesting:** *Season* — undefined, varying locally. *Nest* — a grass-lined scrape or natural hollow under shelter of a grass tussock in grassland. *Eggs* — 4, like those of the Bustard-Quail, but usually more boldly coloured.

(See also BLUELEGGED BUSTARD-QUAIL, p. 32)

81. Coot. *Fulica atra* Linnaeus
HINDI NAMES : *Aari, Thēkări, Khuskul, Kēsrār*
Handbook Vol. 2

Size: Village hen or 3/4 grown duckling. **Field Characters:** A slaty black, dumpy, practically tailless waterbird, very duck-like when swimming in the distance. The ivory white pointed (not flat) bill and frontal shield (on forehead) are diagnostic. The peculiar lobed or scalloped toes are also characteristic. Sexes alike. Gregariously, on tanks and jheels. **Distribution:** Throughout the Indian Union up to 8000 ft in the Himalayas; Bangladesh; Pakistan; Burma; northern Ceylon. Resident and also winter visitor. **Habits:** As a resident found sparingly on rush-bordered irrigation tanks etc. In winter numbers vastly augmented by immigrants from central and western Asia and then abundant on most large jheels, especially in northern India. Skitters along the water to take off, half running half flying; rises with much labour and pattering, but flies strongly when properly launched. The rapid almost hovering wing beats, the blunt barrel-shaped body and the legs trailing behind rail-like, distinguish it from a duck in flight. **Food:** Grass and paddy shoots, aquatic weeds and insects, molluscs, etc. **Call:** A clear and loud trumpet-like cry, often heard at night. **Nesting:** *Season* — principally July/August. *Nest* — a large compact mass of rushes among matted reeds slightly above water level. *Eggs* — 6 to 10 buffy stone-colour, stippled and spotted with reddish brown or purplish black.

(See also KORA or WATERCOCK, p. 143.)

82. Painted Snipe. *Rostratula benghalensis* (Linnaeus)
HINDI NAMES : *Rājchăhā, Ohādi*
Handbook Vol. 2

Size: Quail + . **Field Characters :** A typical rail with long, straight and slender snipe-like bill, slightly decurved at tip. Upper plumage chiefly metallic olive-green with buff and blackish streaks and markings; lower plumage chiefly brown and white. Whitish ' spectacles ' with a white patch behind eye and white bands over shoulders to sides of breast (like straps of a rucksac), distinctive. Male less showy than female, lacking the chestnut and black on neck and breast, Singly, or in wisps, in reedy swamps. **Distribution:** Throughout the Indian Union up to 5000 ft in the Himalayas; Bangladesh; Pakistan; Ceylon; Burma. Resident and locally migratory. **Habits:** Affects reed-covered swamps, margins of jheels and tanks, and inundated paddy fields. Largely crepuscular. Often flushed when snipe shooting, but it is a feeble and clumsy flier, indifferent as a table bird and hardly worth powder and shot. A typical rail also in its other habits and behaviour. The female, as in the bustard-quails, is polyandrous and the dominant partner in the courtship ceremonials. She also fights rival hens for the possession of an eligible cock. **Call:** A deep, hollow *oook* likened to the sound produced by blowing softly into a bottle. **Food:** Paddy grains, vegetable matter, insects, worms and molluscs. **Nesting:** *Season* — practically all year. *Nest* — a pad of rush stems on marshy ground or on *bunds* separating irrigated rice fields. *Eggs* — 3 or 4, yellowish stone colour, blotched and streaked with brown.

41

83. Pheasant-tailed Jaçana. *Hydrophasianus chirurgus* (Scopoli)
HINDI NAMES : *Piho, Pihuya*

Handbook Vol. 2

Size: Partridge ± . **Field Characters:** In breeding dress (illustrated), identified in flight by the large amount of white and chocolate-brown in plumage, and the pointed downcurved tail. Non-breeding birds chiefly pale brown and white, with a black ' necklace ' on upper breast, and minus the sickle-shaped ' pheasant ' tail. Spidery elongated toes as in 84. Sexes alike. Singly, or gregariously, on vegetation-covered jheels etc. **Distribution:** Throughout the Indian Union, normally up to 5000 ft in Kashmir; Bangladesh; Pakistan; Ceylon; Burma. **Habits:** Not appreciably different from those of the Bronzewinged species. In off season collects in flocks of 50 to a hundred. At rest the non-breeding plumage is very obliterative in the environment of dry floating water-lily stems and leaves. As the birds rise in alarm and fly away, the white wings flash into prominence in the same way as the Pond Heron's. **Call:** A peculiar nasal mewing *tewn, tewn,* etc. **Food:** Same as of 84 — vegetable matter, aquatic insects, and molluscs. This species possesses a pointed spur at the bend of the wing whose function is uncertain. **Nesting:** *Season* — June to September (SW. monsoon). *Nest* — same as in 84 ; sometimes lays directly on floating singāra leaves partially submerged in water. *Eggs* — 4, peg-top shaped, glossy greenish bronze or rufous-brown, unmarked. Female polyandrous, like Painted Snipe.

84. Bronzewinged Jaçana. *Metopidius indicus* (Latham)
HINDI NAMES : *Pipi, Kundai, Kattoi* (Bihar)

Handbook Vol. 2

Size: Partridge ± . **Field Characters:** A leggy swamp bird somewhat like a moorhen, with glossy black head, neck and breast, metallic greenish bronze back and wings, and chestnut-red stub tail. A broad white stripe behind eye to nape. Enormously elongated spider-like toes. Immature birds chiefly whitish, rufous and brown. Sexes alike. Singly, or gregariously, on tanks with floating vegetation. **Distribution:** The entire Indian Union (excepting W. Rajasthan); Bangladesh; Burma. Not Ceylon. **Habits:** Affects jheels and tanks abounding in floating vegetation such as waterlily and singāra (*Trapa*). The elongated, widely spreading toes help to distribute the bird's weight and enable it to trip along with ease over the floating tangles of leaves and stems. Becomes tame and fearless on village tanks if unmolested. A typical rail in flight and general behaviour. Swims well with the carriage of a moorhen, and also dives on occasion. **Food:** Seeds, roots, etc. of aquatic plants; insects and molluscs. **Call:** A short harsh grunt; also a wheezy piping *seek-seek-seek* etc. Becomes noisy during the breeding season. **Nesting:** *Season* — June to September (SW. monsoon). *Nest* — a skimpy pad of twisted weed-stems etc., on floating leaves often partially submerged, or amongst marginal rushes. *Eggs* — 4, glossy, handsome, bronze-brown with an irregular network of blackish scrawls. Female polyandrous, like Painted Snipe.

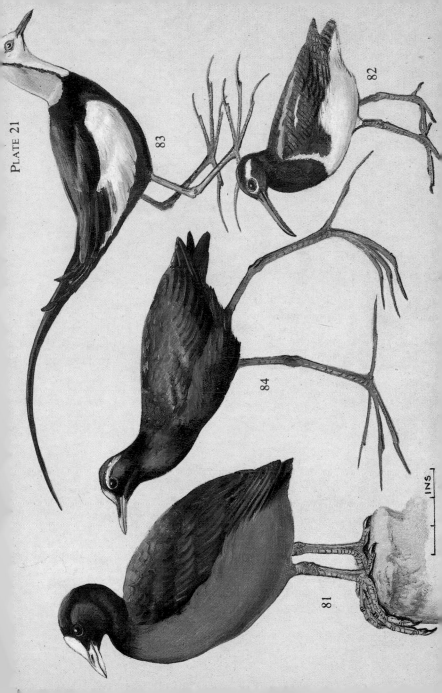

PLATE 21

PLATE 22

85

86

87

88

85. Redwattled Lapwing. *Vanellus indicus* (Boddaert)

HINDI NAMES : *Titeeri, Titūri*
Handbook Vol. 2

Size: Partridge + ; more leggy. **Field Characters:** A familiar plover, bronze-brown above, white below, with black breast, head and neck, and a crimson fleshy wattle in front of each eye. A broad white band from behind eyes running down sides of neck to meet the white underparts. Sexes alike. Producer of the well-known *Did-he-do-it?* calls. Scattered pairs at tanks, puddles, etc. **Distribution:** Throughout the Indian Union up to about 6000 ft in the Himalayas and peninsular hills; Bangladesh; Pakistan; Ceylon; Burma. The Indian race *indicus* concerns us mostly. **Habits:** Affects open country, ploughed fields, grazing land, and margins and dry beds of tanks and puddles. Also met with in forest glades around rain-filled depressions. Runs about in short spurts and dips forward obliquely to pick up food in the typical plover manner. Is uncannily and ceaselessly vigilant, day or night, and foremost to detect intrusion and raise the alarm. **Call:** A loud, penetrating, *Did-he-do-it?* or *Pity-to-do-it?* repeated placidly or frantically as the occasion demands. **Food:** Insects, grubs, molluscs, etc. **Nesting:** *Season* — chiefly March to August. *Eggs* — 4, stone colour or greyish brown, blotched with blackish; peg-top shaped. Laid on bare ground in open waste land, occasionally with the depression ringed around with a few pebbles. They match the soil to perfection and are difficult to find.

86. Yellow-wattled Lapwing. *Vanellus malabaricus* (Boddaert)

HINDI NAMES : *Zirdi, Chāfān*
Handbook Vol. 2

Size: Partridge ± ; more leggy. **Field Characters:** A sandy brown plover with white belly, black cap and bright yellow fleshy lappets above and in front of the eyes. In flight, a white wing-bar conspicuous on the black wings. Sexes alike. Pairs, or small parties, on dry waste land. **Distribution:** Throughout the Indian Union excepting Assam; Pakistan (part); Bangladesh; Ceylon. Not Burma. Resident and locally migratory. **Habits:** Inhabits dry open country and fallow land, and is less dependent upon the neighbourhood of water than 85. Also less noisy and demonstrative, but otherwise similar to it in general habits and food. **Call:** A sharp, plaintive, bisyllabic *ti-ee* uttered every couple of seconds, punctuated from time to time by a high-pitched, quick-repeated *twit-twit-twit-twit*. **Nesting:** *Season* — chiefly April to July. *Eggs* — 4; typical plovers' in shape, buff to olive stone-colour, irregularly blotched with dark brown and purplish grey. Laid on bare soil in dry waste land, with the scrape sometimes encircled by pebbles. Both eggs and newly-hatched downy chicks are remarkably obliterative in their natural environment. As in 85, the parents demonstrate noisily when the nest or young are in danger, circling overhead frantically and diving at the intruder.

87. **Little Ringed Plover.** *Charadrius dubius* Scopoli
HINDI NAMES : *Zirrea, Mērwā*
Handbook Vol. 2

Size: Quail — . **Field Characters:** A typical little plover with thick head, bare yellow legs, and short pigeon-like bill. Sandy brown above, white below. White forehead; black forecrown, ear-coverts and round the eyes. A complete black band round neck separates the white hindneck collar from back. Absence of white wing-bar distinguishes it in flight from the very similar KENTISH PLOVER (*C. alexandrinus*). Sexes alike. Pairs or small scattered flocks by rivers, tanks, etc. **Distribution:** Throughout the Indian Union up to about 4000 ft in the Himalayas; Bangladesh; Pakistan; Ceylon; Burma. Smaller race *jerdoni* resident; larger *curonicus* winter visitor. **Habits:** Essentially a bird of mudflats, shingle banks and sandspits by rivers, estuaries and tanks. Scattered parties run about in short spurts with a swift mincing gait, stopping abruptly now and again to pick up some tit-bit in the characteristic plover manner. Coloration remarkably obliterative; birds often completely invisible till betrayed by movement. Though scattered when feeding, the party flies off together on alarm uttering a short plaintive whistling *phiu*, twisting and wheeling in the air in unison. **Food:** Insects, sand-hoppers, tiny crabs, etc. **Nesting:** *Season*.— March to May. *Eggs* — 4, buffish stone to greenish grey with hieroglyphic scrawls and spots of dark brown, and phantom purple markings. Of the typical ' peg-top ' shape of all plovers' eggs, broad at one end abruptly pointed at the other. Laid on bare shingle on sandbanks where they harmonize perfectly with their surroundings.

88. **Indian Whiskered Tern.** *Chlidonias hybrida* (Pallas)
HINDI NAMES : *Tehāri, Koorri* (all terns)
Handbook Vol. 3

Size: Pigeon $\pm$; considerably slimmer. **Field Characters:** In winter plumage rather like the river tern, grey above white below. Distinguishable by its much shorter and only slightly forked (almost square cut) tail, a characteristic of this group known as ' marsh terns '; also by *red* instead of yellow bill. At rest, tips of closed wings project beyond tail. In summer dress, black cap and black belly conspicuous. Sexes alike. Numbers at jheels, inundated paddy fields, etc. **Distribution:** Our race *indica* is found throughout the Indian Union; Pakistan; Ceylon. Only as a winter visitor south of central India and in Ceylon. **Habits:** Affects jheels and marshes inland, and tidal creeks and mud flats on the seaboard. Flies gracefully back and forth over a marsh, bill and eye directed intently below for signs of life. Plunges into water after fish or stoops on insects or crabs on the ground and bears them away in its stride. Although possessing webbed feet, terns hardly ever alight on the water. When not hunting they rest on a rock or mudbank on their ridiculously short legs. **Food:** Tiny fishes, tadpoles, crabs, grasshoppers and other insects. **Nesting:** *Season* — in N. India and Kashmir, June to September. *Nest* — a rough circular pad of reeds and rushes on tangles of floating singāra and such-like aquatic vegetation in jheels and swamps, usually in colonies. *Eggs* — 2 or 3, greenish, brownish, or bluish, spotted and streaked with dark or purplish brown. Both sexes share the domestic duties.

89. Spurwinged Plover. *Vanellus spinosus* (Linnaeus)
HINDI NAME :
Handbook Vol. 2

Size: Partridge + . **Field Characters:** An obvious cousin of the Red-wattled Lapwing. Vinous grey and light brown above and on breast, white below. Forehead, crown, occipital crest, and throat black bordered with white. A black patch on abdomen. Rump and tail white with a broad black tip to latter. In flight a large white patch or bar on the wing, black wing-tips, and contrasting black and white pattern on head diagnostic. On ground, the hunched posture with head and neck almost furtively drawn in is a notable feature. Sexes alike. Pairs or small parties on sand- and shingle banks of large rivers. **Distribution:** A large portion of northern and eastern India from western U.P. south through western M.P. and Andhra. Bangladesh; Burma. Not Ceylon. Extends into the Indochinese subregion. **Habits:** Affects shoals and sandbanks in the larger rivers and hardly ever met with away from them. Flight, movements, and behaviour in general very like those of the Redwattled Lapwing. **Call:** A single-noted high-pitched, insistent *did, did, did,* etc. of the quality of the Yellow-wattled Lapwing's call. The pointed black horny spur on the bend of the wing could be an effective weapon of offence, but it has not been observed to be so used. **Nesting:** *Season* — March to June. *Nest* — a shallow scrape in sand on an exposed river bank or shoal. *Eggs* — 3 or 4, olive-stone or yellowish stone, blotched and spotted with shades of brown and black — very like those of the Redwattled Lapwing.

90. Golden Plover. *Pluvialis dominica* P. L. S. Müller
HINDI NAME : *Chhōtā bătān*
Handbook Vol. 2

Size: Partridge. **Field Characters:** Typical plover with thick head, slender bare legs, pigeon-like bill. Brown above, spangled with white and gold; whitish below mottled on breast with brown, grey, yellow. In flight narrow pointed wings *without wing-bar,* and fanned-out *brown tail* conspicuous. In summer (breeding) plumage underparts black. On arrival in India (autumn) and before departure (spring) commonly with parti-coloured black and white underparts. Sexes alike. Flocks on wet pasture land, moist grassy edges of jheels, etc.

The GREY PLOVER (*Pluvialis squatarola*), easily confused with this, has upper parts mottled only with silver-grey, no gold. On arrival (Sept./Oct.) and again before leaving (Mar./April) seen in partial breeding plumage: black above barred and spotted with silver-white; underparts black. *White tail,* brown-barred near tip; a conspicuous black oval patch (axillaries) at armpit, and *white wing-bar* diagnostic in flight. Usually on sea coast; seldom inland.

Distribution: The Golden Plover (eastern race *fulva*) is a winter visitor practically throughout India; Bangladesh; Pakistan; Ceylon; Burma. Breeds in N. Siberia, June/July. **Habits:** Typical plover. Runs about on moist grassland, stopping erect now and again and dipping forward steeply to pick up food — tiny snails, crabs, insects, berries, etc. When one bird rises on alarm the scattered flock follows almost simultaneously, wheeling and banking on rapidly beating wings in compact formation. **Call:** A clear high-pitched rather mournful double whistle *tu-ee.* Its palatability combined with its natural wariness and speed on the wing make it a coveted sporting bird.

91. Ruff and Reeve. *Philomachus pugnax* (Linnaeus)
HINDI NAMES : *Geh-wala, Băgbăd*
Handbook Vol. 2

Size: Male (Ruff) = Partridge; female (Reeve) = Quail + . **Field Characters:** A rather dumpy greyish brown wader with bold scaly patterned upper plumage and relatively short sandpiper-like bill. In flight a narrow white wing-band and whitish patches on either side at base of tail, suggestive clues. Sexes alike, but Reeve considerably smaller. In summer plumage, sometimes partially acquired before emigration (April/May), Ruff extremely variable with much black, white, purple, chestnut, and buff in it, and with a peculiar ruff and ear tufts. Reeve as in winter, but blacker above. Flocks on marshes and tidal mudflats, etc. **Distribution:** Winter visitor to practically all India; Bangladesh; Pakistan; Ceylon; Burma. Commoner in N. India. Breeds in temperate Europe and N. Asia. **Habits:** Gregarious; on first arrival in N. India sometimes seen in enormous concentrations. Behaviour, food, etc. not markedly different from other migrant waders, but takes larger quantities of weed seeds. A good sporting bird. Ruff best known for its promiscuous breeding habits and its fantastic communal sparring tournaments or courtship displays. A number of Ruffs in variegated breeding plumages gather at selected spots known as " leks " or " hills ", each occupying an adjacent " territory " of a few square inches. The neighbours posture threateningly with ruff and ear tufts erected, legs flexed, head lowered, bill pointing to ground, and tilt and leap at one another. Ready-to-breed females visit the " hills " from time to time and mate with the Ruff of their choice. He takes no part in the nesting chores.

92. Blacktailed Godwit. *Limosa limosa* (Linnaeus)
HINDI NAMES : *Gudēra, Gairiya, Jangral, Khāg, Mālgūjhā*
Handbook Vol. 2

Size: Partridge + . **Field Characters:** A variegated brown and white wader very like the Whimbrel or Curlew (95) in general effect, but with a slender, straight, slightly upcurved bill. In flight the broad black band across end of white tail, and a white band along the trailing edge of the wings are diagnostic points. In summer plumage, sometimes acquired before emigration in March/April, the head, neck, and breast become rusty red (as illustrated). Sexes alike. Small parties or large flocks on marshy jheels and tidal mudflats.

Rarer, and sometimes seen in association with the above in Pakistan and NW. India, is the slightly smaller and relatively shorter legged BARTAILED GODWIT (*Limosa lapponica*). Shorter legs, *barred* (instead of black-ended) tail, white rump, and absence of white wing-bands are its distinguishing characters.

Distribution: Winter visitor to practically all India; Bangladesh; Pakistan; Ceylon; Burma; in two races which breed from N. Europe and E. Siberia to Japan. **Habits:** Similar to those of the Curlew and Whimbrel. Keeps to marshes of both fresh and brackish water, often in large close-packed flocks and in association with other waders. **Food:** Worms, molluscs, crabs, insects. Godwits are excellent for the table, and this combined with their swift flight and ever watchful alertness makes them good sporting birds, eagerly sought by sportsmen.

PLATE 23

Plate 24

93

94

95

96

93. Avocet. *Recurvirostra avosetta* Linnaeus
HINDI NAME : *Kusya chăhā*
Handbook Vol. 2

Size: Partridge + ; more leggy. **Field Characters:** An elegant black-and-white marsh bird with long bare bluish legs. Its chief diagnostic feature is the slender black upcurved bill. Sexes alike. Pairs or parties, at marshes and on tidal mudflats etc. **Distribution:** The entire Indian Union, rare in Assam, sparse in the south; Pakistan; Ceylon. Not Bangladesh. Rare in Burma. Chiefly winter visitor, but partly also resident. **Habits:** Runs about actively on squelchy ground and wades into shallow water for food. The partially webbed toes enable it also to swim with ease. Occasionally in large flocks. In feeding the curiously upturned bill is wielded rather like a hockey stick, the curved part skimming the semi-liquid mud with a back and fore rotatory or churning motion, washing out the food particles: small crustacea, worms, aquatic insects, etc. **Call:** A clear, loud, high-pitched *kleet* repeated quickly, usually on the wing. **Nesting:** *Season* — at the only known breeding place within Indian limits, the Great Rann of Kutch — April. *Eggs* — 4, closely resembling those of both the Stilt and the Redwattled Lapwing in shape, colour and markings. Laid on bare sunbaked ground, on the surface or in a shallow depression. Colony of many nests a few yards from one another.

(See also OYSTERCATCHER, p. 30)

94. Blackwinged Stilt. *Himantopus himantopus* (Linnaeus)
HINDI NAMES : *Găz-păun, Tinghŭr, Sărgyne*
Handbook Vol. 2

Size: Partridge ± ; with bare slender legs about 10 inches long. **Field Characters:** A lanky black, greyish brown and white wading bird with a straight slender black bill and enormously long, thin reddish legs. The sexes differ in details of coloration, as also the summer and winter plumages. Pairs or flocks at jheels etc. **Distribution:** The Indian Union; Bangladesh; Pakistan; Ceylon; Burma. Resident and locally migratory; also winter visitor. **Habits:** Affects marshes, jheels, village tanks, salt pans and tidal mudflats. Its stilt legs enable it to wade into comparatively deep water where it probes into the squelchy bottom mud for worms, molluscs, aquatic insects, etc. head and neck submerged at a steep angle and hind part of body sticking out, rather like a duck ' up ending '. Also swims well. Flight weak and flapping with neck extended and long red legs trailing beyond the tail. **Call:** A squeaky, piping *chek-chek-chek-chek*, somewhat like a moorhen's, uttered when alarmed and flying off. **Nesting:** *Season* — principally April to August. *Nest* — a depression in the ground on the margin of a jheel, or a raised platform of pebbles in shallow water, lined with vegetable scum or flags of reeds. Often breeds in large colonies. *Eggs* — 3 or 4, light drab in colour, densely blotched with black; closely resembling eggs of Redwattled Lapwing.

95. Curlew. *Numenius arquata* (Linnaeus)
HINDI NAMES : *Gūinyār, Băda gūlindā*
Handbook Vol. 2

Size: Village hen. **Field Characters:** A darkish sandy brown wading bird, streaked with black and fulvous to produce the well-known ' game-bird pattern '. Lower back and rump white, conspicuous in flight. Its most characteristic feature is the downcurved slender bill five or six inches long. Sexes alike. Singly or small parties, on jheels, rivers and the seashore.

The WHIMBREL (*Numenius phaeopus*), a smaller edition of the Curlew is also found in similar habitats during winter. A whitish stripe along the centre of its dark crown (' centre parting ') and whitish eyebrows are diagnostic. **Call:** A musical *tetti-tetti-tetti-tet*. Usually keeps in larger flocks.

Distribution: Throughout the Indian Union; Bangladesh; Pakistan; Ceylon; Burma. Winter visitor; chiefly the race *orientalis* with finely streaked underparts. **Habits:** Runs or stalks along the water's edge or on the seashore at low tide, probing into soft ooze for food: molluscs, crustaceans, insect larvae, etc. Also eats berries of marsh plants, grass shoots, seaweed and other vegetable matter. **Call:** A shrill and wild, plaintive scream *coor-lee* or *cur-lew* uttered chiefly on the wing. Usually exceedingly wary and difficult to circumvent. A good sporting bird and esteemed for the table. **Nesting:** *Season* — in N. Europe east to Siberia, April to June.

96. Wood or Spotted Sandpiper. *Tringa glareola* Linnaeus
HINDI NAMES : *Chūpkā, Chobāhā, Titwāri*
Handbook Vol. 2

Size: Quail $\pm$. **Field Characters:** A snipe-like wader, sepia brown above, indistinctly spotted with white. Lower back and rump white. Breast pale brownish. Whitish stripe above eye from bill to nape. Summer (breeding) plumage brighter, with spots more defined. In flight, the white rump and barred brown-and-white tail diagnostic. No wing-bar. Sexes alike. Singly or small flocks, at jheels and marshes.

The GREEN SANDPIPER (*Tringa ochropus*), another common species in winter, is somewhat larger than above with dark bronze-green gloss on upperparts. In flight white rump and unbarred white tail conspicuous. The low whistling *titui* uttered as it flushes is also diagnostic. Usually seen singly.

Distribution: Throughout the Indian Union; Bangladesh; Pakistan; Ceylon; Burma. Winter visitor. **Habits:** One of the commonest and also most gregarious of the group of little wading birds found near inland waters and at marshes, flooded paddy fields and tidal mudflats; popularly and collectively known as ' snippets '. They run along on the squelchy mud picking up ţit-bits, or probe with their bills for food; insects, larvae, worms and molluscs, wagging the tail end of the body ridiculously up and down. The flushing notes of the different species are useful pointers to their identity. The Spotted Sandpiper utters a shrill *chiff-chiff-chiff* as it makes off. **Nesting:** *Season* — in Europe and N. Asia, May/June. *Nest* — a scantily lined-depression on a dry patch in marshy grass-covered localities.

97. Common Sandpiper. *Tringa hypoleucos* Linnaeus
HINDI NAME :
Handbook Vol. 2

Size: Quail ± . **Field Characters:** Greyish olive-brown above, white
below with pale dusky breast and a few dark streaks on foreneck. In
flight the *brown* rump and tail (excepting only the white outer feathers)
distinguish it from the Spotted Sandpiper (96). Also a prominent
wing-bar usually present. Sexes alike. Singly, at ponds, tanks, tidal
creeks and on rocky seashore. **Distribution:** Throughout the Indian
Union; Bangladesh; Pakistan; Ceylon; Burma. Winter visitor. **Habits:**
One of our earliest immigrants (August) and also one of the last to
leave (May). A few non-breeding individuals remain in their winter
quarters all the year. Never collects in flocks, but a few scattered
examples sometimes seen together as when driven up the seashore
rocks by the rising tide. Flies with characteristic stiff rapidly vibrating
wing strokes close over the water, uttering a shrill piping *tee-tee-tee*.
Besides this flushing note has a pretty, long-drawn trill *wheeit*, *wheeit*
repeated several times when the bird is perfectly undisturbed. **Food:**
As of other sandpipers, insects, worms, molluscs, etc. **Nesting:** *Season*
— in Indian limits (Kashmir, Garhwal, Kumaon, etc.) May/June.
Nest — a slight depression sparsely lined with leaves and rubbish, on a
shingle bank or islet amid stream. *Eggs* — 4, yellowish buff or stone-
colour, blotched and speckled with reddish brown, with phantom
marks of lavender or pinkish grey.

98. Redshank. *Tringa totanus* (Linnaeus)
HINDI NAMES : *Chhōtā bătān, Sūrmā*
Handbook Vol. 2

Size: Partridge — . **Field Characters:** A large sandpiper, greyish brown
above, white below finely streaked with brown on breast. In flight,
white lower back and rump prominent; also the broad white semi-
circular band along the trailing edge (hind border) of wing, and the
long slender *red* legs projecting behind. Tail white, barred with brown.
In summer (breeding plumage) upperparts somewhat streaked and
spotted with black and fulvous, and breast more heavily streaked
with brown. Sexes alike. Singly, or small flocks, at jheels, estuaries, etc.

Another large sandpiper seen singly in winter is the GREENSHANK
(*Tringa nebularia*). Slightly larger than the Redshank, dark greyish
brown above, white below. White forehead, lower back, rump and
faintly barred tail. No wing-bar, olive-green legs, and slightly upcurved
bill distinguish it.

Distribution: The entire Indian Union; Bangladesh; Pakistan;
Ceylon; Burma. Winter visitor. Two races. **Habits:** Typical sandpiper.
Often seen in mixed flocks with other species. The flushing notes of this
species and the Greenshank are rather similar, a shrill piping *tiwee-
tiwee-tiwee* or *tiu-tiu-tiu*. **Nesting:** *Season* — within Indian limits
(Kashmir, Ladakh, etc.) May to July. *Eggs* — 4, yellowish to greenish
stone-colour, handsomely blotched with reddish brown or purplish
black with underlying lavender or reddish grey spots. Laid in a
depression within a grass clump near a bog.

99. Little Stint. *Calidris minuta* (Leisler)

HINDI NAMES : *Chhōtā pānlowwā, Rūnni*

Handbook Vol. 2

Size: Quail — . Field Characters: A diminutive wader, mottled greyish brown or dusky above white below, with *blackish* legs and bill. Rump and middle tail feathers dark brown, outer tail feathers smoky brown. In flight, a faint narrow whitish bar on the pointed wings noticeable. Summer plumage richer —'more black and rufous. Sexes alike. Flocks on tidal mudflats, tank margins, etc.

The similar TEMMINCK'S STINT (*C. temminckii*) frequently found associated with it, is slightly darker above and with outer tail feathers white instead of brownish. Legs *olive-green*.

Distribution: Throughout the Indian Union; Bangladesh; Pakistan; Ceylon; Burma. Winter visitor. Habits: Sociable and gregarious. Keeps in flocks, often mixed with other small waders. Affects marshes inland, and tidal mudflats on the seaboard. The flock spreads itsel out to feed, running about actively on the mud, picking up tiny insects, crustaceans and molluscs. When disturbed, the birds fly off swiftly, all together in an orderly compact mass, their white undersides flashing in the sun from time to time as they turn and twist in unison. Call: A soft musical *wit-wit-wit* or a low *tr-rr* uttered on the wing. Nesting: *Season* — in NE. Europe and Siberia, June/July. *Nest* — a cup-shaped depression lined with willow leaves, on grassy marshland. *Eggs* — 4, pyriform, greenish to buffish stone-colour, spotted and blotched with reddish brown.

100. Common or Fantail Snipe. *Gallinago gallinago* (Linnaeus)

HINDI NAME : *Chăhā*

Handbook Vol. 2

Size: Quail + . Field Characters: An obliteratively coloured marsh bird with straight slender bill about 2½ inches long. Dark brown above, streaked with black, rufous and buff; whitish below. Sexes alike. Singly or in wisps, on marshes.

The PINTAIL SNIPE (*C. stenura*) often found alongside it, is difficult to distinguish in the field except with much practice. Its stiff narrow pin-like outer tail feathers help diagnosis in the hand.

Distribution: Practically the entire Indian Union; Bangladesh; Pakistan; Ceylon; Burma. The nominate race concerns us mainly. Resident in Kashmir and the Himalayas; winter visitor elsewhere. Habits: Arrives in the plains about September; leaves by April. Frequents squelchy paddy stubbles, and grassy margins of jheels, tidal creeks, etc. Completely invisible when crouching on mud, even in the open. Flushes abruptly on close approach of observer with a characteristic harsh note — *pench* or *scape* — and flies off at great speed in a series of lightning zigzags. This is what supplies the element of ' sport ' to snipe shooting and is usually responsible for disappointing bags. Food: Worms, insect larvae, etc. obtained by probing into soft mud with the. long, slender bill. Nesting: *Season* — in Kashmir and the Himalayas, May/June. *Nest* — a shallow grass-lined depression in grassy marshland. *Eggs* — 4, variable, yellowish stone-colour or olive-green, blotched or mottled with chocolate-brown or black.

PLATE 25

97

98

99

100

INS

PLATE 26

101

103

102

104

INS

101. **Stone Curlew.** *Burhinus oedicnemus* (Linnaeus)
HINDI NAMES : *Kǎrwǎnǎk, Bǎrsiri*
Handbook Vol. 3

Size: Partridge + ; more leggy. **Field Characters:** A brown-streaked plover-like ground bird with thick head, long bare yellow 'thick-kneed' legs, and large yellow 'goggle' eyes. In flight two narrow white bars on the dark wings conspicuous. Sexes alike. Pairs, or parties, in open stony country. **Distribution:** Practically throughout the Indian Union up to about 3000 ft in the Himalayas; Bangladesh; Pakistan; Ceylon; Burma. The race *indicus* concerns us mainly. **Habits:** Affects dry plains country with scanty scrub, ploughed and fallow land, shingly stream beds and ravines, light deciduous jungle and mango topes, etc., near villages. Largely crepuscular and nocturnal, and sluggish during daytime. When suspicious or alarmed, squats with body pressed to ground and neck extended when its coloration affords perfect camouflage. **Food:** Insects, worms, small reptiles, etc., to which a quantity of grit is added. **Call:** A series of sharp, clear whistling 'screams' *pick, pick, pick, pick. . . . pick-wick, pick-wick, pick-wick,* etc. (accent on second syllable). Mostly heard at dusk and during moonlit nights. **Nesting:** *Season* — February to August. *Eggs* — 2, pale buff to olive-green, boldly blotched with brownish or purplish; remarkably obliterative. Laid on ground in scrape in dry river bed, open country or mango grove. Both sexes share parental duties.

(See also GREAT STONE PLOVER, p. 143.)

102. **Indian Courser.** *Cursorius coromandelicus* (Gmelin)
HINDI NAME : *Nūkri*
Handbook Vol. 3

Size: Partridge ± . **Field Characters:** A sandy brown lapwing-like bird with chestnut and black underparts. Rich rufous crown; a black and a white stripe through and above eyes; long bare china white legs. Sexes alike. A good example of obliterative coloration. Scattered pairs, or parties, on fallow land and semi-desert. **Distribution:** The drier portions of the Indian Union (excepting Assam); Pakistan; northern Ceylon. Resident and locally migratory.

Largely replaced in Pakistan by the Palaearctic cream coloured species, *C. cursor*, without chestnut and black underparts.

Habits: Bare stony plains, waste and fallow land adjoining cultivation, and ploughed fields is the Courser's typical habitat. Runs about swiftly, zigzagging and dipping forward obliquely now and again in the characteristic plover manner to pick up some insect. On alarm or suspicion spurts forward a few yards with rapid mincing steps, halts abruptly and stretches itself erect to survey the intruder, makes another spurt, and so on. When pressed, rises with a peculiar note, flying fairly low over the ground and commencing to run immediately upon touching down a hundred yards or so farther. **Food:** Beetles and their larvae, crickets, grasshoppers and other insects. **Nesting:** *Season* — chiefly March to August. *Eggs* — 2 or 3, stone-coloured, thickly spotted and blotched with black. Laid in shallow scrape or on bare ground in open, arid country, where they are perfectly camouflaged.

(See also JERDON'S COURSER, p. 20)

103. Brownheaded Gull. *Larus brunnicephalus* Jerdon
HINDI NAME : *Dhomrā*
Handbook Vol. 3

Size: Jungle Crow + . **Field Characters:** A typical gull, grey above, white below with coffee-brown head in summer. In winter, while birds mostly with us, head greyish white. Distinguishable from the equally common somewhat smaller BLACKHEADED GULL (*L. ridibundus*) by the prominent white patch or ' mirror' near tip of the all-black first primary (see pl. 80). In *ridibundus* first primary all white, with black edges and tip. First year birds (both species) have a black subterminal bar to white tail. Gregariously, on the seacoast; sparingly on large rivers and jheels. **Distribution:** The western and eastern seaboards of India, and to a lesser extent also on inland waters; Bangladesh; Pakistan; Ceylon; Burma. Winter visitor. **Habits:** Arrives about September/October, departs end April. Frequents harbours and coastal fishing villages, circling in effortless gliding flight round ships lying at anchor or escorting outgoing and incoming vessels and fishing boats for scraps or garbage cast overboard. These are either scooped off the surface in flight, or by the bird alighting on the water beside them and gobbling them up. In seaports it has to compete for the food with other gull species and with Pariah and Brahminy Kites. In inland localities it also eats insects, grubs, slugs and shoots of various crops. **Call:** A variety of loud, raucous notes, one commonly heard being a querulous scream *keeah* rather like the raven's. **Nesting:** Breeds in colonies in Ladakh and Tibet, in bogs around Rhamtso, Manasarovar, Rakhas Tal and other lakes, June/July.

104. River Tern. *Sterna aurantia* J. E. Gray
HINDI NAMES : *Tehāri, Koorri*
Handbook Vol. 3

Size: Pigeon ± ; much slimmer. **Field Characters:** A slender, graceful, grey and white tern with long, deeply forked ' swallow ' tail; deep yellow bill and short red legs. In summer entire forehead, crown and nape glossy jet black; in winter greyish white flecked and streaked with black, especially on nape. Sexes alike. Gregariously, on rivers and jheels, flying up and down. **Distribution:** Throughout the Indian Union; Bangladesh; Pakistan; Burma. Not Ceylon.

Another common tern of inland waters is the BLACKBELLIED (*Sterna acuticauda*) while the GULLBILLED (*Gelochelidon nilotica*) occurs on the seacoast as well. The latter is distinguished from all our other terns by its *black* bill and legs.

Habits: Flies over the water a few feet above with deliberate beats of the long, slender, pointed wings intently scanning the surface for fish venturing within striking depth. From time to time it plunges in with closed wings, often becoming completely submerged but soon re-appearing with the quarry held across the bill. As it resumes its flight, the victim is jerked up in the air and swallowed head foremost. In addition to fish, crustaceans, tadpoles and water insects are also eaten. **Nesting:** *Season* — chiefly March to May. *Eggs* — 3, greenish grey to buffy stone blotched and streaked with brown and inky purple. Laid on bare ground on sandbanks of large rivers in colonies.

(See also WHISKERED TERN, p. 44, SKIMMER, p. 132, CASPIAN TERN, p. 146.)

105. Shikra. *Accipiter badius* (Gmelin)
HINDI NAME : *Shikră*
Handbook Vol. 1

Size: Pigeon $\pm$. **Field Characters:** A lightly built hawk, ashy blue-grey above, white below cross-barred with rusty brown. Female browner above, and larger. Immature, brown and rufous above with broad brown vertical streaks on the underside. Tail with broad, blackish cross bands. Singly, or pairs, in lightly-wooded country. **Distribution:** Throughout the Indian Union, up to about 5000 ft in the Himalayas; Bangladesh; Pakistan; Ceylon; Burma. Three races chiefly concern us, differing in size and depth of coloration. **Habits:** Affects open wooded country and avoids heavy forest. Fond of groves of large trees in the neighbourhood of villages and cultivation. From its lookout in a leafy branch it swoops down and carries off its prey before the victim is aware of danger. Flight swift; several rapid wing strokes followed by a glide. Usually flies close to ground, shooting upward to alight on a branch. **Food:** Lizards, mice, squirrels, birds, etc. When feeding its nest-young sometimes becomes an inveterate chicken-lifter from the poultry yard. **Call:** Loud, harsh, challenging; rather like Black Drongo's. **Nesting:** *Season* — principally March to June. *Nest* — an untidy loose platform of twigs, like a crow's nest, lined with grass and roots, high up in a large leafy mango or such-like tree. *Eggs* — 3 or 4, bluish white, sometimes faintly speckled and spotted with grey. Both sexes share domestic duties; apparently female alone incubates.

106. Blue Rock Pigeon. *Columba livia* Gmelin
HINDI NAME : *Kăbūtăr*
Handbook Vol. 3

Size: House Crow — ; about 13 inches. **Field Characters:** A familiar slaty grey bird with glistening metallic green, purple and magenta sheen on neck and upper breast. Two dark bars on wings, and a band across end of tail. Sexes alike. Flocks and colonies, about cliffs and human habitations. **Distribution:** Throughout the Indian Union, locally up to 13,000 ft in the Himalayas; Bangladesh; Pakistan; Ceylon; Burma. Resident, but also partial local migrant. Two races concern us, differentiated on size and coloration details. **Habits:** In its perfectly wild state affects open country with cliffs and rocky hills. Mostly seen in a semi-domesticated condition, living as a commensal of man and largely adulterated through interbreeding with fancy artificial strains. This semi-feral stock has become thoroughly inured to the din and bustle of urban life and is now well established in most Indian towns. Grain warehouses, railway stations, and old or disused buildings are their favourite haunts. Wild birds occupy cliffs, and crumbling battlements of hill forts, etc., and glean in outlying cultivation. **Food:** Cereals, pulses, groundnuts, etc. **Call:** A deep *gootr-goo, gootr-goo*. **Nesting:** *Season* — undefined; practically all year in semi-feral birds. *Nest* — a flimsy collection of a few sticks on a ledge or in a fissure of cliff, or on rafters and ceilings of dwelling houses, deserted or occupied. *Eggs* — 2, white, elliptical. Both sexes share all the domestic duties.

53

107. Common Green Pigeon. *Treron phoenicoptera* (Latham)
HINDI NAME : *Hāriăl*

Handbook Vol. 3

Size: Pigeon. **Field Characters:** A stocky yellow, olive-green and ashy grey pigeon with a lilac patch on shoulders and a conspicuous yellow bar in the blackish wings. Sexes alike. *Yellow* legs (not red) always diagnostic for this species. Flocks, in wooded country. **Distribution:** Practically throughout the Indian Union; Bangladesh; Ceylon; Burma. Three races on size and details of coloration. **Habits:** Gregarious and arboreal, only rarely descending to the ground. Affects well-wooded country; commonly found in roadside trees, particularly banyan and peepul when in fruit, and also in gardens and groves near towns and villages. Large numbers collect to feed on banyan and peepul figs. They clamber about deftly among the fruit-bearing twigs, often clinging upside down to reach out for a ripe one. Their coloration obliterates them completely in the green foliage so long as they remain still, and the birds have learnt to take the fullest advantage of this. The unsuspected numbers that will tumble out of a banyan and fly away on a shot being fired is often quite bewildering. **Food:** Fruits and berries. **Call:** A pleasant, musical, mellow whistle up and down the scale, with a peculiar human quality. Flight swift, strong and direct, accompanied by a noisy, metallic, flapping sound. **Nesting:** *Season* — mainly March to June. *Nest* — a sketchy twig platform like a dove's, concealed in foliage up in a moderate-sized tree. *Eggs* — 2, white, glossy. Both sexes share all the domestic duties.

(See also NILGIRI WOOD PIGEON, p. 133, MAROONBACKED IMPERIAL, p. 145, GREYFRONTED GREEN, p. 145.)

108. Emerald or Bronzewinged Dove. *Chalcophaps indica* (Linnaeus)
HINDI NAME :

Handbook Vol. 3

Size: Myna + . **Field Characters:** A brownish pink dove, with glistening emerald bronze-green upperparts (excluding tail) and conspicuous white forehead and eyebrows. In flight, chestnut underside of wings diagnostic. Sexes alike. Singly or pairs, in forest. **Distribution:** The entire Western Ghats country including the Nilgiris and associated hills; the sub-Himalayas from Dehra Dun to eastern Assam; Eastern Ghats; eastern Madhya Pradesh; Bangladesh; Ceylon; Burma. The Ceylonese race *robinsoni* differs from the Indian (*indica*) in details of size and coloration. **Habits:** Affects bamboo jungle, and deciduous as well as evergreen forest. Partial to tangles of castor plants growing up on the site of abandoned forest clearings. Feeds on ground along dusty forest roads etc. Flight swift, strong and direct. Often seen flying across glades at top speed. **Food:** Seeds and berries gleaned on the ground. **Call:** A soft, deep and low *hoon* with a nasal ending. **Nesting:** *Season* — January to May, varying locally. *Nest* — a flimsy twig platform, typical of the doves, perhaps slightly more compact, up in a low tree or bamboo culm. *Eggs* — 2, creamy yellow to ' white coffee ' colour.

PLATE 27

108

107

105

106

INS

PLATE 28

109

110

111

INS

109. Spotted Dove. *Streptopelia chinensis* (Scopoli)
HINDI NAMES : *Chitrokā fākhtā, Chittā fākhtā, Pǎrki*

Handbook Vol. 3

Size: Between Myna and Pigeon. **Field Characters:** White-spotted pinkish brown and grey upperparts, and white-and-black ' chessboard ' on hindneck are leading clues to its identity. Sexes alike. Pairs or parties, in open wooded country, gleaning in stubble fields, on cross-country cart tracks, etc. **Distribution:** All the Indian Union excepting the arid northwestern parts. Bangladesh; Ceylon; Burma. The Indian race differs from both the Burmese and the Ceylonese races in details of size and coloration. **Habits:** Affects open well-wooded and cultivated country; avoids arid tracts. Becomes quite tame and confiding if unmolested, freely entering gardens and verandas of bungalows. Flight as of other doves, swift and strong, attained by vigorous wing strokes. **Call:** An oft-repeated, pleasant though somewhat mournful *kroo-kruk-krukroo . . . . kroo-kroo-kroo*, the number of final *kroo*s varying from 3 to 6. **Nesting:** *Season* — undefined; practically all year. *Nest* — the customary flimsy dove structure of ' two crossed sticks ' low down in a tree or bush; also under eaves and on cornices and beams etc., in verandas of inhabited bungalows. *Eggs* — 2, white. Both sexes share in all the domestic duties.

110. Red Turtle Dove. *Streptopelia tranquebarica* (Hermann)
HINDI NAMES : *Serōti fākhtā, Girwi fākhtā, Biki, Itwā*

Handbook Vol. 3

Size: Myna + . **Field Characters:** Female differs from male (illustrated) in having the mantle pale brownish grey instead of bright pinkish brick-red. She looks a smaller edition of the Ring Dove. Loose parties, gleaning in stubble fields etc. **Distribution:** Throughout the Indian Union; Bangladesh; Pakistan; Ceylon; Burma. Locally migratory in many areas. Excepting Burma, only the nominate race *tranquebarica* concerns us. **Habits:** The least common of the doves dealt with here. Affects open cultivated country, usually single or in pairs but sometimes large flocks in association with other doves. Gleans grain and seeds on the ground. **Call:** A rather harsh rolling *groo-gurr-goo, groo-gurr-goo* repeated several times quickly. **Nesting:** *Season* — undefined; practically throughout the year. *Nest* — a sparse, flimsy platform of twigs, sometimes lined with wisps of grass, near the end of a branch 10 to 20 ft up. *Eggs* — 2, white. Both sexes share in building the nest.

111. Ring Dove. *Streptopelia decaocto* (Frivaldszky)
HINDI NAMES : *Dhŏr fākhtā, Părki, Păndŭk*
Handbook Vol. 3

Size: Pigeon — . **Field Characters:** A pale vinous grey and brown pigeon with a prominent narrow black half-collar or ring on the hindneck. Sexes alike. Pairs or loose flocks, in open scrub and culti-vated country. **Distribution:** Throughout the drier portions of the Indian Union, ascending locally and seasonally to 10,000 ft in the Himalayas. Bangladesh; Pakistan; Ceylon; Burma. Only the typical race concerns us in India. **Habits:** Affects open, cultivated though essentially dry country, abounding in groves, e.g. of babool (*Acacia*) or dhāk (*Butea*) trees in which to retire during the midday heat. Locally abundant in the neighbourhood of human habitations, and freely enters gardens and bungalow verandas etc. **Call:** A deep, trisyllabic *kūk-koo-kook*, repeated several times in succession. Has pretty court-ship display, rising vertically a few feet on noisily flapping wings and fanned-out tail, and volplaning down in a graceful spiral or arc to the accompaniment of an aggressive-sounding prolonged *koon-koon-koon*. **Nesting:** *Season* — practically all year. *Nest* — the typical scanty twig platform in a bush or small tree; rarely in a dwelling house. *Eggs* — 2, white. Both sexes share all the domestic duties.

112. Little Brown Dove. *Streptopelia senegalensis* (Linnaeus)
HINDI NAMES : *Chhŏtā fākhtā, Tŏrtrā fākhtā*
Handbook Vol. 3

Size: Myna + . **Field Characters:** A small, slim dove earthy brown and grey above, pinkish brown and white below, with a miniature ' chessboard ' in rufous and black on either side of neck. Sexes alike. Pairs or loose flocks in dry scrub or semi-desert country. **Distribution:** The drier portions of practically the entire Gangetic Plain and penin-sular India east to about Calcutta; Pakistan. Not Ceylon or Bangla-desh. Only the one race *cambayensis* concerns us. **Habits:** Affects dry stony scrub country with ' cactus ' (*Euphorbia* and *Opuntia*) brakes etc., in the neighbourhood of villages and cultivation, often side by side with 111. Tame and confiding. Freely enters bungalows and nests on rafters and cornices. **Food:** Seeds and grain gleaned on the ground. **Call:** A soft *coo-rooroo-rooroo*. The male has peculiar courtship display on the ground, bobbing and calling at the female and advancing on her in ludicrous stiff hops, the whole performance reminiscent of a *Calotes* or Bloodsucker lizard. It also has the aerial display described under 111. **Nesting:** *Season* — practically throughout the year. *Nest* — the usual ridiculously flimsy twig platform in a *Euphorbia* clump; frequently also on rafters etc. in inhabited dwellings. *Eggs* — 2, white, elliptical.

113. **Alexandrine** or **Large Indian Parakeet.** *Psittacula eupatria*
(Linnaeus)
HINDI NAMES : *Rāi-tōtā, Hirāmǎn-tōtā*
Handbook Vol. 3

Size: Pigeon $\pm$; slenderer, with long pointed tail. **Field Characters:**
A large grass-green parakeet with the typical short, massive deeply
hooked red bill, and a conspicuous maroon patch on each shoulder.
The female lacks the rose-pink and black collar of the male. Noisy
parties in cultivation, and wooded country. **Distribution:** Practically
the entire Indian Union; Bangladesh; Ceylon; Burma. In Pakistan
apparently only in the environs of Karachi, presumably the
descendants of escaped cage birds. Four races, on differences in
details of size and coloration. **Habits:** Affects wooded country,
orchards and cultivation. Occasionally collects in large flocks which do
considerable damage to ripening fruit and standing crops of maize
and jowar. Has communal roosts amongst groves of leafy trees where
enormous numbers collect each night to the accompaniment of much
noise and chatter. Voice deeper and more powerful than that of the
commoner Roseringed species. Flight graceful and swift in spite of
the seemingly leisurely wing beats. A popular cage bird, and learns to
repeat a few words rather indistinctly as compared with the Hill
Myna. **Nesting:** *Season* — chiefly December to April, varying locally.
Nest — an unlined hollow in a tree-trunk excavated or appropriated
by the birds, at moderate heights and up to 100 ft up. Occasionally
natural tree hollows or holes in walls of buildings are used. *Eggs* — 2
to 4, white, blunt ovals. Both sexes share all domestic duties.

114. **Roseringed Parakeet.** *Psittacula krameri* (Scopoli)
HINDI NAMES : *Tōtā, Lybār tōtā*
Handbook Vol. 3

Size: Myna + ; with a long pointed tail. **Field Characters:** A smaller
edition of the Alexandrine Parakeet, but lacking the maroon shoulder-
patches. Female lacks the black and rose-pink collar of male. Noisy
flocks about cultivation, in lightly-wooded country. **Distribution:**
Practically the entire Indian Union, from the Himalayan foothills south.
Plains and locally up to 5000 ft in the peninsular hills. Bangladesh;
Pakistan; Ceylon; Burma. **Habits:** One of the most familiar of Indian
birds, as much at home on the countryside as within villages and
towns. Often bands itself into large flocks and is highly destructive at
all times to crops and orchard fruit, gnawing and wasting far more
than it actually eats. **Call:** A loud, sharp screaming *keeak, keeak,
keeak,* etc. uttered both at rest and on the wing. Flight swift and
direct, with rapid wing beats. Is a popular cage bird, large numbers of
young taken from nest being on sale in all bird markets. Learns to
repeat a few words, and to perform various table-top tricks like
loading and firing off a toy cannon. **Nesting:** *Season* — chiefly February to April, varying locally. *Nest* — a natural hollow in a tree-
trunk, or one excavated by the birds themselves. Holes in rock scarps
and walls of buildings, ruined or in occupation, often within noisy
towns, are freely utilized. *Eggs* — 4 to 6, pure white, roundish ovals.
Both sexes share all domestic duties.

(See also BLOSSOMHEADED PARAKEET and LORIKEET, p. 69)

115. Koel. *Eudynamys scolopacea* (Linnaeus)

HINDI NAMES : *Koel, Kokila*

Handbook Vol. 3

Size: House Crow; slenderer, with longer tail. **Field Characters:** Male glistening black, with yellowish green bill and crimson eyes. Female brown, profusely spotted and barred with white. Familiar shrieking crescendo calls, *kuoo-kuoo-kuoo*. Singly or pairs, in groves of trees, etc. **Distribution:** The entire Indian Union; Bangladesh; Pakistan; Ceylon; Burma. Two races, the Assam-Burma race *malayana* being larger than the India-Ceylon *scolopacea*. Resident and also locally migratory. **Habits:** Brood-parasitic. Arboreal. Frequents gardens, groves and open country abounding in large leafy trees. Silent in winter, thus often overlooked and recorded as absent. Becomes increasingly noisy with the advance of the hot weather, and then one of the earliest bird voices at dawn. The call begins with a low *kuoo*, rises in scale with each successive *kuoo* until it reaches fever pitch at the seventh or eighth, and breaks off abruptly. It is soon commenced all over again. The female only utters a sharp, quick-repeated *kik-kik-kik* as she dashes from tree to tree. **Food:** Largely fruits and berries; also caterpillars and insects. Flight straight and swift with rapid wing beats. **Nesting:** *Season* — mainly April to August, coincident with that of its normal hosts, the House and Jungle crows. *Eggs* — smaller but similar to the crows': pale greyish green or stone colour, speckled and blotched with reddish brown. As many as 13 have been found in a single crow's nest.

116. Crow-Pheasant or Coucal *Centropus sinensis* (Stephens)

HINDI NAMES : *Māhokā, Kūkā*

Handbook Vol. 3

Size: Jungle Crow; with long, broad tail. **Field Characters:** A clumsy, glossy black bird with conspicuous chestnut wings and long, broad, black, graduated tail. Sexes alike. Singly or pairs, stalking along the ground in undergrowth. **Distribution:** The Indian Union (from about 6000 ft in the Himalayas); Bangladesh; Pakistan; Ceylon; Burma. Three races on size and coloration details. **Habits:** One of the non-parasitic cuckoos, and largely terrestrial. Affects open forest, scrub-and-bush country interspersed with grassland and shrubbery, and groves about human habitations. Stalks along the ground, or clambers and hops with agility amongst branches of shrubs in search of food: caterpillars, large insects, lizards, young mice, and birds' eggs and nestlings. Particularly destructive to the last two. **Call:** A deep, resonant *coop-coop-coop* etc., in series of 6 or 7 and up to 20, repeated quickly in varying tempo. Two birds frequently join in an uneven duet. Also utters a variety of harsh croaks and gurgling chuckles. **Nesting:** *Season* — February to September, varying locally. *Nest* — a large untidy globular mass of twigs, leaves, etc., with a lateral entrance. Placed in the centre of a tangled thorny shrub at moderate height. *Eggs* — 3 or 4, chalky, glossless white. Both sexes share all domestic duties.

PLATE 29

113

114

♀

♂

115

116

Plate 30

117. Common Hawk-Cuckoo or Brainfever Bird. *Cuculus varius* Vahl
HINDI NAMES : *Păpihā, Păpiyā, Kăpăk, Ūpăk*
Handbook Vol. 3

Size: Pigeon. Slenderer with longer tail. **Field Characters:** Ashy grey above; whitish below, cross-barred with brown. Broadly barred tail. Sexes alike. Superficially very like the Shikra hawk; also in flight and movements. Singly, in wooded country.

Another common cuckoo of similar appearance, identified by the broad black subterminal band to its tail, is the INDIAN CUCKOO (*Cuculus micropterus*). It is best known by its calls, *orange-pekoe, bo-kotako,* or *cross-word-puzzle,* repeated *ad nauseam,* day or night.

Distribution: The Indian Union from about 2500 ft in the Himalayas south; Bangladesh; Ceylon. Resident and locally migratory. **Habits:** Nest-parasitic. Inhabits light forest; also partial to gardens, groves and mango topes, etc., near human habitations. Mostly silent during winter, and therefore liable to be overlooked. Becomes increasingly obstreperous with the advance of the hot weather. **Call:** A loud, screaming *brain-fever, brain-fever,* repeated with monotonous persistency 5 or 6 times, rising in crescendo and ending abruptly. Heard all through the day and frequently during moonlit nights. The call is rendered in Hindi as *pee-kăhăn?* (' Where is my love?') and in Mahratti as *păos-āla* (' Rain's coming! '). **Food:** Hairy caterpillars and other insects, berries and wild figs, etc. **Nesting:** *Season* — March to June, coinciding with that of *Turdoides* babblers on whose nests it is parasitic. *Eggs* — usually a single in each nest, blue, like that of the host. Hatchling reared to maturity by foster parents.

118. Pied Crested Cuckoo. *Clamator jacobinus* (Boddaert)
HINDI NAMES : *Păpiyā, Chātăk*
Handbook Vol. 3

Size: Myna ± ; with longer tail. **Field Characters:** A handsome, crested black-and-white cuckoo. White tips of tail feathers, and a roundish patch on wings conspicuous in flight. Singly, or pairs, in wooded country. **Distribution:** Practically the entire Indian Union up to about 8000 ft in the Himalayas; Bangladesh; Pakistan; Ceylon; Burma. Two races, the larger *serratus* of N. India being a rains visitor, presumably from Africa. Resident and locally migratory. **Habits:** Nest-parasitic. Frequents open, well-wooded country. Commonly found in the neighbourhood of habitations. Its local migrations are largely controlled by the SW. monsoon. Arrival and presence in a locality advertised by the birds chasing one another, flying from tree to tree, and calling excitedly a rather plaintive, metallic, *piu-piu-pee-pee-piu . . . pee-pee-piu,* or merely ·a tinkling *piu. . .piu,* etc. Chiefly arboreal, but occasionally descends to ground and hops about in search of food : grasshoppers, hairy caterpillars, and sometimes berries. **Nesting:** *Season* — chiefly June to August, coinciding locally with the breeding of its accustomed hosts. Parasitic chiefly on babblers of the *Turdoides* group. *Eggs* — blue, similar to those of the fosterers, but when more than one cuckoo egg in a nest, uncertain whether these the product of the same or different females.

119. Crimsonbreasted Barbet or Coppersmith. *Megalaima haemacephala* (Müller). HINDI NAME : *Chhotā bāsănth*

Handbook Vol. 4

Size: Sparrow + ; more dumpy. **Field Characters:** A heavy-billed grass-green barbet with crimson breast and forehead, yellow throat and green streaked yellowish underparts. Short truncated tail, distinctly triangular in flight silhouette. Sexes alike. Singly, or loose parties, on banyan and peepul trees in fruit. **Distribution:** The greater part of the Indian Union from about 2500 ft in the Himalayas south; Bangladesh; Pakistan; Ceylon; Burma. Replaced in the humid-forest tracts of SW. India by the allied CRIMSONTHROATED species. *M. rubricapilla.* **Habits:** Arboreal. Found commonly wherever there are fruiting trees, especially the various species of wild fig, be it in outlying forest or within a noisy city. **Call:** A familiar, loud, monotonous ringing *tūk, tūk* repeated every second or two in long runs throughout the day, reminiscent of a distant coppersmith hammering on his metal. **Food:** Fruits and berries; especially fond of banyan and peepul figs. Sometimes eats winged termites captured by ungainly flycatcher-like sallies. **Nesting:** *Season* — January to June. *Nest* — a hole excavated in a snag of a dead softwood branch such as of the Coral or Drumstick trees, at moderate heights. When in a horizontal branch, the entrance hole is on the underside. *Eggs* — 3, glossless white. Both sexes share all domestic duties.

120. Bluethroated Barbet. *Megalaima asiatica* (Latham)
HINDI NAME : *Nilkănt băsănth*

Handbook Vol. 4

Size: Myna ± . **Field Characters:** A gaudily coloured dumpy green arboreal bird with a heavy conical bill. Forehead and crown crimson with transverse black band above the eyes. Sides of head, chin, throat and foreneck pale blue. A large crimson spot on each side of the neck and a crimson speck on either side at base of lower mandible. Sexes alike. Singly, or parties, in leafy fruiting trees.

Another widely distributed Indian species, oftener heard than seen on account of its concealing coloration is the LARGE GREEN BARBET 120 A (*Megalaima zeylanica*), Hindi: *Băḍā băsănth.* Its loud familiar call *kor-r-r — kutroo, kutroo, kutroo* resounds endlessly in the forest. Slightly larger than the Myna; grass green above, with the head, neck and breast brown streaked white, and rest of underparts pale green. A patch of naked orange skin round eye.

Distribution: The country along the base of the Himalayas from Chamba to E. Assam. Also Bangladesh and Burma. Plains and upto about 6000 ft. Several races, of which we are concerned chiefly with the typical one. **Habits:** Arboreal. Affects wooded country, groves and gardens even in populous cities, e.g. Calcutta. **Food:** Fruits and berries, figs of the various species of *Ficus* being special favourites. Like other barbets, frequently catches flying termites in the air. **Call:** Similar to that of the Large Green Barbet, perhaps somewhat higher pitched, reiterated at all times of the day. Flight noisy and dipping, a few rapid wing beats followed by a short pause. **Nesting:** *Season* — overall March to June. *Nest* — a hole in dead tree-trunk or branch excavated by the birds, 10 to 25 ft up. *Eggs* — 3 or 4, glossless white. Both sexes share all domestic duties.

121. Sirkeer Cuckoo. *Taccocua leschenaultii* Lesson
HINDI NAME : *Jāngli tōtā*

Handbook Vol. 3

Size: House Crow ± ; with longer, broader tail. **Field Characters:** An obvious relation of the Crow-Pheasant. A heavy-tailed earthy brown and rufous bird, with fine black shaft-streaks to the feathers. White tips to the graduated cross-rayed tail feathers prominent. Also the bright cherry-red and yellow stout hooked bill. Sexes alike Singly or pairs, on ground in broken scrub country and deciduous secondary jungle. **Distribution:** All India south and east of a line from Kutch to Simla; Bangladesh; Ceylon. Three races, differentiated on size and details of coloration. **Habits:** Largely terrestrial. Stalks about amongst thickets like Crow-Pheasant, searching for food: insects, lizards, fallen fruits and berries, etc. Runs swiftly through undergrowth looking like mongoose, but is a feeble flier. Ascends trees rapidly, hopping from branch to branch with great agility. **Call:** Occasional. A sharp loud *kek-kek-kek-kerek-kerek-kerek* of quality of Roseringed Parakeet's shrieks; also reminiscent in a way of call of Barred Jungle Owlet (*Glaucidium radiatum*, 131). **Nesting:** Non-parasitic. *Season* — March to August, varying with locality. *Nest* — a shallow saucer of twigs lined with green leaves, in a thorn bush or sapling 5 to 20 ft up. *Eggs* — 2 or 3, white, with a chalky texture.

(See also GREENBILLED MALKOHA, p. 147.)

122. Plaintive Cuckoo. *Cacomantis passerinus* (Vahl)
HINDI NAME :

Handbook Vol. 3

Size: Between Bulbul and Myna. **Field Characters:** A slim arboreal bird, dark grey above, whitish below with grey chin and throat. White-tipped black tail, and a white patch on underside of black wings prominent in flight. *Female* similar but sometimes ' hepatic ', i.e. bright chestnut above and on throat, barred with black on back and on white underparts. Singly, in scrub and openly wooded country. In normal plumage confusable with DARK GREY CUCKOO-SHRIKE (*Coracina melaschistos*); in hepatic phase with BAYBANDED CUCKOO (*Cacomantis sonneratii*). The latter has a very different call *wēē-ti-tēē-ti* reminiscent of *cross-word-puzzle* of Indian Cuckoo (117) but in much higher key. **Distribution:** Indian race *passerinus* practically throughout India south of the Himalayas (except the arid NW. portions), east to W. Bengal; Ceylon (winter). Replaced by the Burmese *querulus* (paler above; rufous below) in Assam and Bangladesh. **Habits:** Solitary, arboreal, insectivorous, with hawk-like flight. **Food:** Plant bugs, caterpillars, and other insects. **Calls:** Normally a high-pitched *p'teer, p'teer, p'teer*, or *peter-peter*. Also a pleasant, plaintive whistling song *pi-pi-pipeepeepi-pipeepee* etc. delivered from exposed tree-top, with tail depressed and wings drooping. **Nesting:** *Season* — July to September (SW. monsoon). Parasitic chiefly on Tailor Birds and Ashy Wren-Warblers (216, 215), its eggs matching their in coloration and markings in varying degree.

61

123. Crested Tree Swift. *Hemiprocne longipennis* (Tickell)
HINDI NAME: *Tājdār ăbābeel*

Handbook Vol. 4

Size: Bulbul — . **Field Characters:** A slender swift, blue-grey above, paler and whitish below, with a prominent erectile crest on forehead, long pointed wings, and deeply forked tail. Chin and throat chestnut in male, grey in female. In overhead flight very like Palm Swift (133), but larger and with more deeply forked tail. Pairs or small parties hawking midges and tiny winged insects over deciduous forest. **Distribution:** Ceylon; practically all India (except the arid NW. portions) up to and along the base of the Outer Himalayas into Assam; Bangladesh; Burma; Thailand, etc. Local and patchy. **Habits:** Perches bolt upright on bare topmost twigs with wing-tips crossed on either side of the spiky tail feathers. **Calls:** A variety of loud and harsh but not unpleasant notes uttered from perch and also on the wing, the commonest being *whit-uck, whit-uck, whit-uck,* etc. Others are reminiscent of the ' scolding ' of a shikra hawk (*Accipiter badius*). **Nesting:** *Season* — December to July and possibly later, varying with locality. *Nest* — a ridiculously tiny, shallow and flimsy half saucer of scraps of bark and feathers gummed together with the bird's saliva. Attached to upper surface of a slender leafless branch 12 to 40 ft up, difficult to detect from the ground. *Egg* — a singleton, pale grey, elliptical, almost completely filling the nest.

124. Malabar Pied Hornbill. *Anthracoceros coronatus* (Boddaert)
HINDI NAMES: *Dhăn chiri, Suleimani mūrghi*

Handbook Vol. 4

Size: Kite. **Field Characters:** A heavy-billed arboreal bird with black neck, back, and wings, white tips to the flight feathers, and white underparts. Tail longish, with outer feathers *all* white. A ponderous wax-yellow and black horn-shaped bill surmounted by a casque sharply ridged along top, flat on sides, ending in a point. *Female* differs only in colour details of bare parts. Noisy flocks in fruit-laden trees in well-wooded deciduous country. **Distribution:** Ceylon; south and central India; north to southeastern U.P.; Bihar; and Orissa.

The very similar LARGE PIED HORNBILL (*A. malabaricus*) with outer tail feathers white-tipped black, and sides of casque convex, has a more northerly range, Kumaon into Assam. The GREAT INDIAN HORN-BILL (*Buceros bicornis*) of the W. Ghats and tropical E. Himalayas is much larger: black with white neck, black-and-white wings and tail, and concave-topped casque.

Habits: Sociable, mainly frugivorous. Also eats lizards, mice, and baby birds. Flight: a few noisy flaps followed by a glide, with wing-tips upturned. **Calls:** A variety of loud raucous cackling and inane screams reminiscent of the protestations of a dak bungalow *mūrghi* seized by the cook, and also the yelps of a smacked puppy! **Nesting:** *Season* — March to June. Little recorded, but presumably of the same general pattern as other hornbills (cf. p. 137). *Eggs* — 2 to 4, white, usually wood-stained brownish.

(See also COMMON GREY HORNBILL, p. 74)

124

121

123

122

N

PLATE 32

125. Barn or Screech Owl. *Tyto alba* (Scopoli)
HINDI NAMES : *Kurāyā, Karail*
Handbook Vol. 3

Size: Jungle Crow $\pm$. **Field Characters:** A typical owl, golden buff and grey above finely stippled with black and white; silky white below tinged with buff and normally spotted dark brown. Large round head with a conspicuous ruff of stiff feathers surrounding a comically pinched white monkey-like facial disc. Sexes alike. Singly or pairs, about deserted buildings and ruins. **Distribution:** The entire Indian Union; Bangladesh; Pakistan; Ceylon; Burma. Two races chiefly concern us. In numerous other races, the Barn Owl has an almost world-wide range. **Habits:** Inseparable from the haunts of man. Deserted buildings and cities, and ancient forts and ruins invariably hold their quota. Purely nocturnal. Spends the daytime standing upright and dozing in some dark niche. Emerges after dusk with a wheezy screech, flying about silently and ghost-like, hunting for rats and mice. **Calls:** A mixture of harsh discordant screams and weird snoring and hissing notes. **Food:** Almost exclusively rats and mice, hence of great economic usefulness. **Nesting:** *Season* — undefined. Practically all year. *Nest* — a collection of straw, twigs, rags and rubbish padded into tree-hollows, holes in ruined walls, or in the space between ceiling and roof of a dwelling house. The same site is used year after year. *Eggs* — 4 to 7, white, smooth, roundish.

126. Brown Fish Owl. *Bubo zeylonensis* (Gmelin)
HINDI NAMES : *Amrāi-ka-ghughu, Ūlloo*
Handbook Vol. 3

Size: Pariah Kite $\pm$. **Field Characters:** A large heavy brown owl, the underparts paler with dark vertical streaks, especially about the breast. Feather tufts projecting above the head like long ears. Large round yellow forwardly directed eyes. *Unfeathered* legs diagnostic. Sexes alike. Singly or pairs, in ancient trees near water. **Distribution:** Throughout the Indian Union; Bangladesh; Pakistan; Ceylon; Burma. Two races concern us, the Ceylonese *zeylonensis* being smaller and darker than the Indian *leschenault*. **Habits:** Nocturnal. Affects well-wooded, well-watered tracts. Fond of overgrown ravines etc., in the neighbourhood of jheels and streams, and groves of ancient densely foliaged trees about village tanks. **Calls:** A deep hollow, moaning, *boom-o-boom* with a peculiar ·eerie and ventriloquistic quality, uttered at sundown on leaving the daytime retreat, and during night and early morning. **Food:** Fish, frogs, crabs, small mammals, birds, reptiles; occasionally carrion. **Nesting:** *Season* — December to March, but varying with locality. *Nest* — a natural tree-hollow or cleft of rock near water, occasionally lined with a few twigs. Sometimes an old eagle's nest is used. *Eggs* — 1 or 2, white, roundish with a slightly glossed though pitted texture. Vicinity of nest invariably bestrewn with cast-up pellets and remains of birds and small animals.

63

127. Indian Great Horned Owl. *Bubo bubo* (Linnaeus)
HINDI NAME : *Ghūghū*
Handbook Vol. 3

Size: Pariah Kite ± . Field Characters: Similar to the Fish Owl (126) in general effect, but fully *feathered* legs diagnostic. Sexes alike. Singly or pairs, in wooded rocky ravines or shady groves. Distribution: The entire Indian Union; Bangladesh; Pakistan; Burma. Not Ceylon. The only race that concerns us is *bengalensis*. This genus of Horned Owls has a practically world-wide distribution. Habits: Mainly nocturnal. Inhabits well-wooded but open and cultivated country, and avoids heavy forest. Favourite haunts are bush-covered rocky hillocks and ravines, and steep outscoured banks of rivers and streams. Spends the day under shelter of a bush or rocky projection, or in ancient mango and similar thickly foliaged trees near villages. Call: A deep,. solemn, resounding *bu-bo* (2nd syllable much prolonged), not loud but with a curious penetrating quality. Food: Small mammals, birds, reptiles; occasionally large insects, fish and crabs. A beneficial species on account of the heavy toll it takes of field rats and mice in agricultural areas. Nesting: *Season* — principally November to April. *Eggs* — 3 or 4, creamy white, broad roundish ovals with a smooth texture. Laid without nest on bare soil in a natural recess in earth bank, on ledge of cliff, or under shelter of bush on level ground.

(See also MOTTLED WOOD OWL, p. 141.)

128. Common Indian Nightjar. *Caprimulgus asiaticus* Latham
HINDI NAMES : *Chhipäk, Däb-chiri, Chäpkä*
Handbook Vol. 4

Size: Myna ± . Field Characters: A soft-plumaged crepuscular and nocturnal bird, mottled grey-brown, buff and fulvous, black-streaked above, of a complicated camouflaging pattern. White patches on wings conspicuous in flight. Sexes alike. Singly, in scrub country, crouching on ground by day, hawking insects at dusk.

Several other species of nightjars are locally common. They resemble one another superficially and are hard to tell in the field except by their calls which are always diagnostic.

Distribution: Throughout the Indian Union; Bangladesh; Pakistan; Ceylon; Burma. Resident and partly local migrant. The Ceylon race *eidos* is smaller than the Indian *asiaticus*. Habits: Frequents scrub and stony country, dry overgrown nullahs, compounds and groves in the neighbourhood of cultivation and human habitations. Spends the day squatting under shelter of a bush or along a low bough. Active after sunset, and all through night, hawking insects. Flight peculiarly moth-like, silent and wandering — long sailing glides alternated with somewhat leisurely flapping of the wings. Call: Familiar and diagnostic, *chuk-chuk-chuk-chuk-r-r-r*, well likened to a stone gliding over a frozen pond. Food: Beetles, moths and other insects. Nesting: *Season* — not well-defined, chiefly February to September. No nest. *Eggs* — 2, pale pink to deep salmon colour, spotted and blotched with reddish brown and inky purple; laid on bare ground in bamboo or bush jungle.

129. Collared Scops Owl. *Otus bakkamoena* Pennant
HINDI NAME : *Tharkavi choghād*
Handbook Vol. 3

Size: Myna ± ; = Spotted Owlet. **Field Characters:** A pretty little
' horned ' owlet, grey-brown or rufous-brown above, vermiculated and
mottled with whitish. A pale half-collar on upper back. Chin and
throat buffy white, the latter barred and stippled with black. Underparts buff streaked with black and with fine wavy reddish brown bars.
Sexes alike. Singly or pairs, in open wooded country. **Distribution:**
Throughout the Indian Union; Bangladesh; Pakistan; Ceylon; Burma.
Several races, differing chiefly in details of coloration. **Habits:** Nocturnal. Affects open deciduous forest, and groves of trees in or near
towns and villages. Oftener heard than seen. **Call:** a soft interrogative *wut?* repeated monotonously every 2 or 3 seconds over long
stretches of time, between dusk and dawn. Also an occasional bubbling, chattering note in ascending scale. **Food:** Beetles and other
insects; occasionally mice and lizards. **Nesting:** *Season* — principally
January to April. *Nest* — a natural hollow in a tree-trunk or bough,
or a disused woodpecker or barbet nest-hole, without any lining.
Eggs — 3 to 5, white, spherical.

130. The Spotted Owlet. *Athene brama* (Temminck)
HINDI NAMES : *Khăkūsăt, Khūsăttia, Choghăd*
Handbook Vol. 3

Size: Myna ± . **Field Characters:** A squat, white-spotted greyish
brown little owl, with the typical large round head and forwardly
directed staring yellow eyes. Sexes alike. Pairs or family parties,
about villages, in ruins, and groves of ancient trees, etc. **Distribution:**
Throughout the Indian Union; Bangladesh; Pakistan; Burma. Not
Ceylon. Three races, on size and depth of coloration. **Habits:** Chiefly
crepuscular and nocturnal. Our commonest and most familiar owl.
Affects all types of country excepting heavy forest. Particularly abundant about human habitations. Pairs spend the daytime in some hollow
in an ancient tree-trunk or sitting huddled together on a secluded
branch. They fly out fussily when suspicious of being observed, and
bob and stare at the intruder from a distance in clownish fashion.
Calls: A large variety of harsh chattering, squabbling and chuckling
notes, two individuals frequently combining in a discordant duet.
Food: Chiefly beetles and other insects; also young birds and mice,
and lizards, etc. **Nesting:** *Season* — principally November to April.
Eggs — 3 or 4, white, roundish ovals. Laid on an untidy pad of tow
or fibres in tree-hollows, holes in crumbling walls, or between ceiling
and roof of deserted as well as occupied dwellings. Both sexes share
all the domestic duties.

131. Barred Jungle Owlet. *Glaucidium radiatum* (Tickell)
HINDI NAME : *Jāngli choghād*

Handbook Vol. 3

Size: Same as 130. **Field Characters:** General effect as of 130, but dark brown above and conspicuously barred (not spotted) with pale rufous. Underparts rufous and white, closely barred with blackish brown. Sexes alike. Singly, in open deciduous forest. **Distribution:** Patchily over a great part of the Indian Union, excepting Rajasthan and the adjoining arid portions, and perhaps also the E. Ghats; Bangladesh (?); Ceylon. Not Burma or Pakistan. **Habits:** Crepuscular and nocturnal, but apparently little inconvenienced by sunlight and frequently on the move in daytime. Its preferential habitat, shared with the Racket-tailed Drongo, is open forest such as of mixed teak and bamboo. **Call:** A loud, not unpleasant *kāo-kāo-kāo*, followed by *kāo-kūk*, *kāo-kūk*, *kāo-kūk*, and so on, in increasing tempo. It is somewhat reminiscent of the Grey Junglecock's crow heard in the distance. **Food:** Mainly beetles and other insects. **Nesting:** *Season* — overall March to May. *Nest* — a natural tree hollow, usually unlined. *Eggs* — 2 to 4, white, roundish ovals.

(See also BROWN HAWK-OWL, p. 141.)

132. Osprey. *Pandion haliaetus* (Linnaeus)
HINDI NAMES : *Māchhlimār*, *Māchhārāng*

Handbook Vol. 1

Size: Pariah Kite $\pm$. **Field Characters:** A dark brown hawk with a brown-and-white head, and white underparts. Across the upper breast is a broad brown band, or ' necklace ', which is diagnostic both when the bird is at rest and on the wing. Sexes alike. Singly, at irrigation tanks, jheels, and on the sea coast. **Distribution:** In winter the entire Indian Union; Bangladesh; Pakistan; Ceylon; Burma. **Habits:** A fish-eating hawk, commonly found in winter on many of our larger rivers, irrigation tanks and jheels. Flies up and down over the water scanning the surface for any fish coming up within striking depth. Occasionally hovers like a kestrel to investigate more closely, with legs dangling below in readiness. At a suitable opportunity the bird closes its wings and hurls itself upon the quarry, striking the water with a great splash and often becoming completely submerged. The fish is grasped in the talons and carried off to some convenient rock nearby, where it is torn to pieces and devoured. **Call:** Seldom heard in its winter quarters; described as a clear *kai, kai, kai*. **Nesting:** In Europe the season is April to June. Its alleged breeding in the Himalayas, and elsewhere within Indian limits has not been proven.

PLATE 33

132

130

129

131

INS

PLATE 34

133

135

134

136

133. Palm Swift. *Cypsiurus parvus* (Lichtenstein)
HINDI NAMES : *Tādi bătāsi, Tāl chăttā, Pătta deuli*
Handbook Vol. 4

Size: Sparrow — . **Field Characters:** A slim, plain sooty-grey bird with narrow deeply forked tail, and long slender bow-like wings. Sexes alike. Flying about gregariously over open country dotted with palmyra palms. **Distribution:** Practically throughout the Indian Union, coincident with the range of the *tād* or palmyra palm (*Borassus flabellifer*). Also Bangladesh; Ceylon; Burma. Two races based on size and coloration details. **Habits:** Inseparable from the *tād* palm, the rigid folds and furrows of whose leaves provide it with eminently suitable roosting and nesting sites. The birds spend the day hawking tiny winged insects in the vicinity of the palms, turning and twisting in the air adroitly to the accompaniment of a shrill joyous triple note *ti-ti-tee*. The deep fork in the tail is particularly noticeable when the bird wheels or banks in its flight. **Nesting:** *Season* — undefined; varying locally. *Nest* — a tiny half-saucer of feathers and vegetable down agglutinated with the bird's saliva, attached in a fold on the underside of a *tād* leaf. In the Garo and Naga Hills of Assam, nests are sometimes built in the palm leaf thatching of inhabited huts. *Eggs* — 2 or 3, pure white, long pointed ovals.

134. House Swift. *Apus affinis* (J. E. Gray)
HINDI NAMES : *Băbĭla, Bătāsi*
Handbook Vol. 4

Size: Sparrow — . **Field Characters:** A small smoky-black bird with white throat, white rump, short square tail, and long narrow wings. Sexes alike. Flying about gregariously near human habitations. **Distribution:** Patchily throughout the Indian Union from about 6000 ft in the Himalayas; Bangladesh; Pakistan; Ceylon; Burma. Five races, on details of size and coloration. **Habits:** Fond of ancient forts, ruined mosques and buildings, and dwelling houses — deserted or occupied — often in the midst of noisy cities. Flies about at great speed almost incessantly throughout the day, hawking flies and midges. The inordinately widened gape facilitates capture of tiny prey in the air. **Food:** Chiefly dipterous insects. Owing to peculiar structure of foot — all four toes directed forward — swifts cannot perch in the ordinary way, but only cling to rough surfaces. In the evenings disorderly rabbles ' ball ' high up in the air in play, uttering shrill joyous twittering screams. **Nesting:** *Season* — February to September. *Nest* — a round untidy cup of feathers and straw cemented with the birds' saliva, with a slit between wall and nest for entrance. Usually in colonies, plastered in angle of walls and ceiling in verandas, porches and arched gateways of buildings. *Eggs* — 2 to 4, pure white, longish ovals. Both sexes share in building, incubation (?), and feeding young.

(See also SOUTHERN TROGON, p. 147.)

135. Alpine Swift. *Apus melba* (Linnaeus)
HINDI NAME : *Bǎdi bǎtāsi*
Handbook Vol. 4

Size: Bulbul + . **Field Characters:** A large swift, dark brown above, white below with a diagnostic dark brown band across the breast. Tail short and square-cut. Wings, very long, pointed and bow-like. Sexes alike, Loose parties, dashing at terrific speed around hilltops etc. **Distribution:** Practically throughout the Indian Union, plains and hills; Bangladesh; Pakistan; Ceylon; Burma. Resident, sporadic, and locally migratory. Three races, on size and shade of coloration. **Habits:** An extremely fast and sustained flier, with a speed estimated at between 130 and 250 km p.h. They cover enormous distances during the day's foraging and make sudden and momentary appearances in localities a hundred (or perhaps many hundred) kilometres from likely roosting sites, passing on as suddenly as they appeared. The birds spend the daylight hours hawking insects high up in the air, but descend to lower levels in cloudy overcast weather. In the evenings they ' ball ' up in the heavens with noisy twittering in the manner of the House Swift. **Food:** Hemipterous bugs and other tiny winged insects. **Nesting:** *Season* — May/June in the north; December/January in the south. *Nest* — a rough pad of straw, feathers and rubbish agglutinated with the bird's saliva placed on ledges in fissures of cliffs and natural caves, in colonies. The cliffs flanking Jog Falls in Mysore are a well-known nest locality in S. India. *Eggs* — 2 to 4, glossless white, pointed ovals.

Swifts do not normally cling on wires. The illustration is of one in captivity, purposely to show the underparts.

(See also CRESTED TREE SWIFT, p. 62.)

136. Hoopoe. *Upupa epops* Linnaeus
HINDI NAME : *Hūdhūd*
Handbook Vol. 4

Size: Myna ± . **Field Characters:** A fawn coloured bird with black and white zebra markings on back, wings and tail. A conspicuous fan-shaped crest, and long, slender, gently curved bill. Sexes alike. Singly or pairs, usually on the ground in lightly-wooded country. **Distribution:** Practically throughout the Indian Union; Bangladesh; Pakistan; Ceylon; Burma. Resident and also locally migratory. Three races chiefly concern us, differentiated on details of size and coloration. **Habits:** Affects open country, plains and hills up to about 5000 ft elevation. Fond of lawns, gardens and groves in and around villages and towns. Walks and runs with a quail-like but waddling gait, probing into the soil for food with bill partly open like forceps. When digging, the crest is folded back and projects in a point behind the head. It is flicked open and erected fanwise from time to time. **Call:** A soft, musical, penetrating, *hoo-po* or *hoo-po-po* repeated in runs, often intermittently for 10 minutes at a stretch. **Food:** Insects, grubs and pupae; hence is beneficial to agriculture. **Nesting:** *Season* — principally February to May. *Nest* — a natural tree-hollow or hole in wall or ceiling of a building, untidily lined with straw, rags and rubbish. *Eggs* — 5 or 6, white. The nest is notorious for its filthiness and stench. Both sexes share in feeding the young.

137. Blossomheaded Parakeet. *Psittacula cyanocephala* (Linnaeus)

HINDI NAME: *Tuïyā tōtā*

Handbook Vol. 3

Size: Myna; slenderer and with long, pointed tail. **Field Characters:** Distinguished from 114 by smaller size, bluish red head and maroon shoulder-patches. In female, head greyer with a bright yellow collar round neck, and no maroon shoulder-patches. White tips to the two long central tail feathers diagnostic in flight, as also the sharp, interrogative *tooi?* uttered on the wing. Flocks in wooded country, about forest cultivation. **Distribution:** Throughout the Indian Union from about 6000 ft in the Himalayas; Bangladesh; Ceylon; Burma. In Pakistan only in the Himalayan foothills about Murree. Resident and locally migratory. Three races on details of coloration. **Habits:** Typical of the parakeets. Prefers better-wooded country than 114. Flight very swift. Flocks on the wing turn and twist their way through stems of forest trees with astonishing celerity and orderliness, uttering their distinctive shrill *tooi* or *tooi-tooi?* as they dash along. **Nesting:** *Season* — chiefly between January and May. *Nest* — a hole in a tree-trunk often excavated by the birds themselves. Sometimes several pairs nest in neighbouring trees in a loose colony. *Eggs* — 4 to 6, pure white, smooth, roundish ovals. Both sexes share all the domestic duties.

138. Lorikeet. *Loriculus vernalis* (Sparrman)

HINDI NAMES: *Bhora, Bhoara, Lătkăn*

Handbook Vol. 3

Size: House Sparrow ± . **Field Characters:** A dainty little bright grass-green parrot with short square tail and rich crimson rump. A small blue throat-patch in male; lacking in female. Singly, or small parties, in orchards and well-wooded country. **Distribution:** Eastern Himalayas from Sikkim through Assam. Western India from about Bombay to Kanyakumari, including the Nilgiri and associated hills. The Visakhapatnam area of the E. Ghats. Bangladesh; Andamans; Burma. Resident and locally migratory.

An allied species, *L. beryllinus*, with crimson crown and orange nape occurs in Ceylon.

Habits: Arboreal. Affects leafy fruiting or flowering trees where its small size and green coloration obliterates it completely among the foliage. Seldom seen except when dashing across from one tree to another. Flight swift, several rapid wing strokes followed by a short pause with closed wings and a consequent slight dip. **Call:** A pleasant, sharp, trisyllabic *chee-chee-chee* repeated every couple of seconds, uttered in flight as well as while clambering amongst the foliage and blossoms. **Food:** Pulp of wild figs and other fruits, and flower nectar. Coral flowers (*Erythrina*) are specially favoured. The Lorikeet is unique among Indian birds for its habit of roosting at night like a bat, hanging head downwards. **Nesting:** *Season* — January to April. *Nest* — a hole excavated by the birds (?) in a rotten branch or tree-stump; usually a natural hollow. *Eggs* — 3, small white roundish ovals.

(See also BLUEWINGED PARAKEET, p. 140.)

139. Roller or Blue Jay. *Coracias benghalensis* (Linnaeus)
HINDI NAMES : *Nīlkānt, Sābzāk*
Handbook Vol. 4

Size: Pigeon. **Field Characters:** A striking Oxford-and-Cambridge-blue bird, with biggish head, heavy black bill, rufous brown breast, and pale blue abdomen and under tail. The dark and pale blue portions of the wings show up as brilliant bands in flight. Sexes alike. Singly perched on telegraph wires etc., in open cultivated country.

The KASHMIR ROLLER, 139 A (*C. garrulus semenowi*) is a common passage migrant over Sind, Kutch, Kathiawar and Gujarat in autumn. Its uniformly blue-black flight feathers, and wholly light blue underparts are diagnostic.

Distribution: Practically throughout the Indian Union from the Himalayan foothills south; Bangladesh; Pakistan; Ceylon; Burma. Resident and partial local migrant. Three races on details of size and coloration. **Habits:** Affects open cultivated country and light deciduous forest. From a lookout on a telegraph wire or other point of vantage it pounces upon some large insect, frog or lizard on the ground, returning with it either to the same perch or flying leisurely across to another nearby. Here the quarry is battered to death and swallowed. Highly beneficial to agriculture since it destroys vast quantities of injurious insects. Has a variety of loud, raucous croaks and chuckles. Indulges in a spectacular courtship display, somersaulting and nosediving in the air to the accompaniment of harsh, grating screams. **Nesting:** *Season* — chiefly March to July. *Nest* — a collection of straw, rags and rubbish in a natural tree-hollow at moderate heights; sometimes in a hole in wall of building. *Eggs* — 4 or 5, glossy white roundish ovals.

140. Small Green Bee-eater. *Merops orientalis* Latham
HINDI NAME : *Pătringā*
Handbook Vol. 4

Size: Sparrow. **Field Characters:** A dainty grass-green bird tinged with reddish brown on head and neck. Central pair of tail feathers prolonged into blunt pins. Slender, long, slightly curved bill. Conspicuous black ' necklace '. Sexes alike. Pairs, or parties, in open country on telegraph wires, fence-posts, etc. **Distribution:** Throughout the Indian Union from about 5000 ft in the Himalayas; Bangladesh; Pakistan; Ceylon; Burma. Resident and locally migratory. Four races, mainly on depth of coloration. **Habits:** Inhabits open country — the neighbourhood of cultivation, forest clearings, fallow land, gardens, golf links, etc. Also partial to the zone above sandy beach along the seacoast. Launches aerial sallies after bees etc., snapping them up in its bill and circling back gracefully on outstretched motionless wings to the perch, where the quarry is battered to death and swallowed. **Food:** Insects, chiefly diptera and hymenoptera. **Call:** A pleasant jingling *tit, tit* or trilly *tree-tree-tree* constantly uttered on the wing or at rest. Large numbers collect to roost in favourite leafy trees, and much noise and flying around in rabbles precedes retirement for the night. **Nesting:** *Season* — principally February to May. *Nest* — a horizontal or oblique tunnel ending in a widened egg chamber, dug in the side of an earth-cutting, borrow-pit or in uneven sandy ground. *Eggs* — 4 to 7, pure white, roundish ovals. Both sexes share in excavating nest-tunnel and feeding young.

PLATE 35

137

140

139

138

NS

PLATE 36

141

142

143

144

INS

141. Bluetailed Bee-eater. *Merops philippinus* Linnaeus
HINDI NAME : *Bădā pătringā*
Handbook Vol. 4

Size: Bulbul. **Field Characters:** Distinguished from 140 by larger size, black stripe through the eyes, deep chestnut throat and breast, blue rump and tail. Sexes alike. Small flocks in open country, especially about tanks and jheels. **Distribution:** Patchily throughout the Indian Union from about 3000 ft in the Himalayas; Bangladesh ; Pakistan ; Ceylon; Burma. Resident and locally migratory.

The somewhat larger BLUECHEEKED BEE-EATER (*M. superciliosus*) has a partly overlapping range in India. No blue on rump; tail bronze-green; chestnut patch on breast paler and smaller. Both species subject to seasonal local movements imperfectly understood.

Habits: Inhabits more or less the same type of country as 140 but on the whole definitely prefers better-wooded tracts and the neighbourhood of jheels and streams. **Call:** *te-tew?, te-tew?* deeper and readily distinguishable from that of the Small Bee-eater. In the distance these calls sound rather like the *pettigrew* notes of the Redvented Bulbul. In food and general habits there is little difference between the several bee-eaters. **Nesting:** *Season* — overall March to June. *Nest* — a tunnel in a river-bank or sandy mound as of 140, usually in colonies, occasionally in association with Bank Mynas. *Eggs* — 5 to 7, pure white roundish ovals. Both sexes share in excavating nest-tunnel, incubation (?) and feeding young.

142. Chestnut-headed Bee-eater. *Merops leschenaulti* Vieillot
HINDI NAME : *Lālsir pătringā*
Handbook Vol. 4

Size: Bulbul — . **Field Characters:** Similar in general effect to 141, but central pin feathers projecting only slightly beyond tail. Head and upper back bright chestnut; chin and throat yellow. Sexes alike. Small flocks on exposed branches of trees in wooded country. **Distribution:** The W. Ghats country south of about Belgaum; the Himalayan terai from Dehra Dun to E. Assam; Orissa. Bangladesh; Ceylon; Burma. Rare or absent in central and eastern peninsular India. **Habits:** Occurs patchily and locally in fairly well-wooded country intermediate between the moist evergreen and the dry deciduous types. Prefers foothills up to 4000 ft elevation. Large gatherings collect at nightly roosts in favourite leafy trees. Food and general habits similar to 140 and 141. Voice and notes closely resemble those of the Bluetailed Bee-eater. **Nesting:** *Season* — overall February to May, varying locally. *Nests* — tunnels in earth-cuttings and sandy soil similar to those of the other bee-eaters, commonly in banks of streams in forested country. Singly or in small colonies. *Eggs* — 5 to 6, glossy, pure white, roundish ovals.

143. Pied Kingfisher. *Ceryle rudis* (Linnaeus)
HINDI NAMES : *Koryālā, Kilkilā, Kārōnā*
Handbook Vol. 4

Size: Between Myna and Pigeon. **Field Characters:** A speckled and barred black-and-white kingfisher with the typical, stout, dagger-shaped bill. Female similar to male but with a single black gorget broken in the middle, as against two more or less complete ones in the male. Singly or pairs, by streams and tanks, perched on rock or hovering above water.

The HIMALAYAN PIED KINGFISHER (*Ceryle lugubris*), much larger and with a prominent crest, replaces this species above 2500 ft in the Himalayas.

Distribution: Throughout the plains of India, Bangladesh; Pakistan, Ceylon, Burma the race *leucomelanura* occurs, excepting Kerala to which is confined the much darker *travancorensis*. **Habits:** Frequents rivers, jheels, irrigation tanks and tidal creeks. Usually seen perched on a favourite rock or stake near water, flicking up its tail and bobbing its head now and again. Its chief characteristic is its spectacular method of fishing. It hovers stationary for considerable periods, 30 ft or so above the water, ' standing on its tail ', and hurls itself, wings pulled in at the sides, at fish coming up within striking depth. On emergence with the quarry, the bird flies off to a convenient rock where the victim is battered before being swallowed. **Call:** A sharp, cheery *chirruk, chirruk* uttered on the wing. **Food:** Fish, tadpoles, frogs and aquatic insects. **Nesting:** *Season* — between October and May. *Nest* — a horizontal tunnel dug in a precipitous mud-bank of a stream. *Eggs* — 5 or 6, glossy white roundish ovals. Both sexes share excavation, incubation (?) and feeding the young.

144. Small Blue Kingfisher. *Alcedo atthis* (Linnaeus)
HINDI NAMES : *Chhōtā kilkilā, Shăreefăn*
Handbook Vol. 4

Size: Sparrow + . **Field Characters:** A dapper blue-and-green little kingfisher, with deep rust coloured underparts, short stumpy tail and long, straight, pointed bill. Sexes alike. Singly by stream, tank or puddle; perched on an overhanging branch or flying swiftly over the water. **Distribution:** Throughout the Indian Union; Bangladesh; Pakistan; Ceylon; Burma. Three races, on size and details of coloration. **Habits:** From time to time as the bird sits scanning the water from an over-hanging branch, it bobs its head, turning it this side and that, and jerks its stub tail to the accompaniment of a subdued *click*. A sharp *chichee, chichee* is uttered as it dashes off at top speed, low over the surface, from one corner of its beat to another. Its normal method of hunting is to drop bill foremost upon its quarry from an overhanging perch. Occasionally it also hovers like 143. **Food:** Small fish, tadpoles and aquatic insects. **Nesting:** *Season* — principally March to June. *Nest* — a horizontal tunnel dug into the earth-bank of a stream or ditch, a foot to 4 ft in length, ending in a widened egg chamber. *Eggs* — 5 to 7, pure white, glossy, roundish ovals. Both sexes share all the domestic duties.

145. Whitebreasted Kingfisher. *Halcyon smyrnensis* (Linnaeus)
HINDI NAMES : *Kilkilā, Kourillā*

Handbook Vol. 4

Size: Between Myna and Pigeon. **Field Characters:** A brilliant turquoise-blue kingfisher with deep chocolate-brown head, neck and underparts, a conspicuous white ' shirt front ', and long, heavy, pointed red bill. A white wing-patch prominent in flight. Sexes alike. Singly, in cultivated and wooded country, both near and away from water. **Distribution:** Plains and lower hills throughout the Indian Union; Bangladesh; Pakistan; Ceylon; Burma. Four races based on size and coloration differences. **Habits:** The most familiar of our kingfishers and also the least dependent upon water. Seen at ponds, puddles, rain-filled ditches, inundated paddy fields and near the seashore, but also in light forest at considerable distances from water. From a favourite lookout on telegraph wire or post, it pounces down on creeping prey and flies off with it to another perch nearby where the victim is battered to death and swallowed. **Food:** Fish, tadpoles, lizards, grasshoppers and other insects. Occasionally also young birds and mice. **Call:** a loud cackling chiefly uttered in flight. Also has a loud, not unmusical, frequently-repeated chattering song, delivered from a tree-top or some exposed elevated perch. **Nesting:** *Season* — principally March to July. *Nest* — typical of the kingfishers; in a horizontal tunnel dug into the side of a dry nullah or earth-cutting. *Eggs* — 4 to 7, white, spherical. Both sexes excavate, incubate (?), and feed the young.

146. Blackcapped Kingfisher. *Halcyon pileata* (Boddaert)
HINDI NAME : *Kourillā*

Handbook Vol. 4

Size: Between Myna and Pigeon. Same as 145. **Field Characters:** Deep cobalt blue above; pale rusty below. A velvety black cap on head separated from back by a prominent white collar on hindneck. Bright coral red bill. In flight, a large white patch in wing (primaries) conspicuous and diagnostic. Sexes alike. Singly, near the seacoast. **Distribution:** Practically the entire coastline of India south of about Bombay; Bangladesh; Ceylon; Burma. **Habits:** Affects the seacoast and tidal rivers, frequently ascending along these for considerable distances inland in forested country. Mangrove swamps bordering tidal creeks are favourite haunts. Except that it is largely dependent on the presence of water, chiefly salt or brackish, for its food — fish, crabs, etc. — its habits are quite similar to those of the more familiar whitebreasted species. **Call:** like the Whitebreasted Kingfisher's, but somewhat shriller. **Nesting:** *Season* — May to July. *Nest* — a tunnel excavated in the earth-bank of a river or creek ending in a widened egg chamber. *Eggs* — 4 or 5, white, spherical, also very like those of 145.

147. Brownheaded Storkbilled Kingfisher. *Pelargopsis capensis* (Linnaeus)

HINDI NAMES : *Gūriāl, Bādāmi kourillā, Tānāk*
Handbook Vol. 4

Size: Pigeon — . **Field Characters:** Head brown, upper parts pale greenish blue, underparts pale yellowish brown or ochraceous. Easily distinguished from all other brightly coloured kingfishers by its large size and enormous, compressed blood-red bill. Sexes alike. Singly, or separated pairs, at forest streams. **Distribution:** Practically the entire Indian Union excepting Rajasthan and the adjoining arid portions; Bangladesh; Ceylon; Burma. In India only the nominate race concerns us. **Habits:** Affects well-watered country, and except in Bengal and Assam where it is commonly seen on telegraph wires along the railway, keeps to shady forest streams, jungle pools, and swampy glades. Also mangrove- and *Pandanus*-lined tidal creeks. Sits on branches overhanging water, hidden by foliage. Seen chiefly when coursing up and down forest streams. Its method of hunting resembles that of the Small Blue Kingfisher, but it does not hover and plunge from the air. **Call:** A raucous, explosive, chattering ' laugh ' *ké-ke-ke-ke-ke-ke* (accent on first *ké*). Also utters a pleasant soliloquy *peer-peer-pūr* when resting contentedly on some shady branch. **Food:** Fish, crabs, reptiles, frogs, and occasionally also young birds and eggs from nests. **Nesting:** *Season* — January to July. *Nest* — the typical horizontal tunnel of kingfishers, excavated in a steep outscoured bank of a forest stream, *Eggs* — 4 or 5, white, glossy, roundish ovals.

148. Common Grey Hornbill. *Tockus birostris* (Scopoli)

HINDI NAMES : *Chălōtrā, Dhănēsh*
Handbook Vol. 4

Size: Pariah Kite. **Field Characters:** A clumsy brownish grey bird with an enormous black-and-white curved bill surmounted by a peculiar protuberance or casque, and long graduated tail. In female the casque is smaller. Small parties, in lightly-wooded country with groves of ancient trees.

Replaced in the heavy rainfall W. Ghats country north to Bombay, and Ceylon, by the MALABAR GREY HORNBILL (*T. griseus*) which lacks the casque above the bill.

Distribution: Throughout the Indian Union excepting Malabar, parts of Rajasthan, and Assam. Absent in Bangladesh; Ceylon; Burma. **Habits:** Arboreal. Commonly met with among fig-laden banyan and peepul trees along roadsides or near villages, feeding in company with green pigeons and other frugivorous birds, or flying across from one tree to another in follow-my-leader fashion. Flight typical of the hornbills, laboured, undulating and noisy — a few rapid wing strokes followed by a dipping glide with the primaries upturned. **Calls:** A loud, cackling *k-k-k-kaē* and a variety of squealing and chattering conversational notes. **Food:** Mainly fruit, but also large insects, lizards, young mice, etc. **Nesting:** *Season* — principally March to June. *Nest* — a natural tree-hollow, walled up with the bird's droppings after the female has settled herself within, leaving only a narrow slit through which the male feeds her during the self-imposed confinement. The wall is broken down after the young hatch out, and both parents forage for the young thereafter. *Eggs* — 2 or 3, dull glossless white.

(See also MALABAR PIED HORNBILL, p. 62.)

PLATE 37

146

145

147

148

INS

PLATE 38

149

150

151

152

INS

149. **Rufous Woodpecker.** *Micropternus brachyurus* (Vieillot)
HINDI NAME : *Kātphorā*
Handbook Vol. 4

Size: Myna ± . **Field Characters:** A chestnut-rufous woodpecker, cross-barred with black on wings and tail. The pale-edged feathers of the throat produce a scaly effect. A crescent-shaped crimson patch of feathers under eye in male; absent in female. Otherwise sexes alike. Pairs in thin deciduous forest. **Distribution:** Practically the entire Indian Union; Bangladesh; Ceylon; Burma. Plains and hills up to about 5000 ft locally. Five races, chiefly on details of coloration. **Habits:** A typical woodpecker. Affects open secondary jungle. **Food:** Largely the eggs, pupae and adults of tree ants (*Cremastogaster*) obtained by digging with its bill into the arboreal carton-like nests of these insects. Occasionally eats the pulp of ripe banyan and other wild figs, and nectar of Silk Cotton and Coral flowers. **Call:** A high-pitched, quick-repeated nasal *keenk-keenk-keenk* very like one of the more familiar calls of the Indian Myna. **Nesting:** *Season* — chiefly February to April. *Nest* — a hole excavated in the ball-shaped carton-like nests of *Cremastogaster* tree ants, strangely enough while they are alive and swarming with the ferocious insects! *Eggs* — 2 or 3, pure white, unglossed. The eggs and chicks, as well as the incubating parent, seem to suffer no harm from the ants amongst whom the brood is raised.

(See also WRYNECK, p. 77, HEARTSPOTTED WOODPECKER, p. 148.)

150. **Goldenbacked Woodpecker.** *Dinopium benghalense* (Linnaeus)
HINDI NAME : *Kātphorā* (for all woodpeckers)
Handbook Vol. 4

Size: Myna + . **Field Characters:** Upper plumage golden yellow and black; lower buffy white streaked with black, more boldly on breast. Crown and occipital crest crimson. Female similar, but with fore-crown black stippled with white, and only occipital crest crimson. Singly or pairs, on tree-trunks in open wooded country, orchards, etc. **Distribution:** Practically the entire Indian Union; Bangladesh; Pakistan; Ceylon. Four races in India, two in Ceylon, based chiefly on details of coloration. Burma has three superficially similar but distinct species of golden-backed woodpeckers. **Habits:** Affects open tree and scrub jungle and is partial to mango topes, groves of ancient trees and coconut plantations. Works up stems and boughs of trees, in jerky spurts, directly or in spirals, occasionally sliding a few feet down in ' reverse gear ', tapping on the bark and chiselling away rotten wood for beetles and insects hiding in the crannies. Black ants, sometimes taken on ground, form a considerable proportion of its diet, and pulp of ripe fruit as well as flower nectar are also eaten. **Call:** A loud, harsh, chattering ' laugh ' uttered mostly on the wing. Flight dipping, as typical of woodpeckers. **Nesting:** *Season* — March to August. *Nest* — an unlined hollow in a tree-stem or branch, excavated by the birds, 8 to 30 ft up. *Eggs* — 3, glossy china white. Both sexes share all domestic duties.

151. Yellowfronted Pied or Mahratta Woodpecker.
Picoides mahrattensis (Latham)
HINDI NAME : *Kătphorā*

Handbook Vol. 4

Size: Bulbul ± . **Field Characters:** A small typical woodpecker with long, stout, pointed bill and stiff, wedge-shaped tail. Irregularly spotted black and white above. Whitish, brown-streaked breast and flanks; scarlet-crimson on abdomen and vent. Female lacks scarlet in crest. Singly or pairs, in groves and thin jungle. **Distribution:** Practically throughout the Indian Union from about 2500 ft in the Himalayas southward. Also Ceylon; Bangladesh; Pakistan; Burma. **Habits:** Affects open scrub country, light deciduous forest, mango orchards and groves around villages. Scuttles up tree-trunks in jerky spurts, tapping on the bark and digging into rotten wood for insects and grubs. The tail, pressed against the stem, serves as the third leg of a tripod to support the clinging bird. The long, extensile barb-tipped tongue helps to skewer out grubs from borings. Ants also eaten. Flight typical of woodpeckers', swift and undulating — a series of rapid wing beats followed by a short pause with wings closed. **Call:** A sharp *click*, *click* or *click-r-r-r*. **Nesting:** *Season* — principally January to May. *Nest* — a hole excavated in decaying branch at moderate height, with entrance on underside. *Eggs* — 3, glossy, white. Both sexes share domestic duties.

(See also PIGMY WOODPECKER, p. 77, SMALL YELLOWNAPED, p. 148.)

152. Indian Pitta. *Pitta braçhyura* (Linnaeus)
HINDI NAME : *Naorăng*

Handbook Vol. 4

Size: Myna ± . **Field Characters:** A gaudy stub-tailed thrush-like bird, green, blue, fulvous, black and white, with crimson abdomen and under tail. In flight a round white spot near tip of wing conspicuous. Sexes alike. Singly, on ground in undergrowth in scrub jungle. **Distribution:** Well-wooded portions of the Indian Union, from about 2500 ft in the Himalayas southward; Ceylon; Bangladesh. Resident and locally migratory. **Habits:** Mainly terrestrial; roosts in trees. Affects wooded country and is fond of dry nullahs and ravines with tangled undergrowth. Hops along like thrush turning over dead leaves and digging into damp earth for insects and grubs which comprise its food. Stumpy tail wagged slowly and deliberately up and down. **Call:** A loud, clear double whistle, *wheet-tew*, uttered chiefly morning and evening, and oftener on cloudy overcast days. Three or four birds sometimes answer one another from different directions. Its local migrations appear to be controlled by the SW. monsoon. **Nesting:** *Season* — May to August. *Nest* — large, globular, of twigs, grass, roots, etc., on ground under a bush or more commonly up in the fork of a low tree. *Eggs* — 4 to 6, glossy china white with spots, specks and fine hair lines of dull or dark purple.

153. Pigmy Woodpecker. *Picoides nanus* (Vigors)
HINDI NAME :
Handbook Vol. 4

Size: Sparrow — . **Field Characters:** A diminutive pied woodpecker, barred dark brown and white above; dusky white below with faint brown longitudinal streaks. A conspicuous broad white stripe from above eye down sides of neck. Female lacks the narrow scarlet streak on either side of hindcrown. Singly or pairs in openly wooded deciduous country. **Distribution:** Practically the entire Indian Union and Bangladesh; Pakistan. Himalayan foothills and terai (including Nepal and Sikkim), and peninsular plains and hills. Also Ceylon. Four slightly differing races of which one peculiar to Ceylon. **Habits:** Like the Mahratta and other woodpeckers, but more commonly associating with the mixed itinerant hunting parties of small birds. Feeds on stems of saplings close to ground as well as high up among the slender branches and end-twigs of tall trees, running jerkily up and down and around them with the agility of a nuthatch and flying on to the next tree-top. **Food:** Insects, flower-nectar, and soft pulp of berries and banyan and peepul figs. **Call:** A feeble, mousy *click-r-r-r* as contact note between a pair. **Nesting:** *Season* — February to April, varying locally in the different parts of its range. *Nest* — a natural hollow in a rotten branch, or hole excavated by the birds themselves. *Eggs* — 2 or 3, glossy white, short blunt ovals.

154. Wryneck. *Jynx torqui'la* Linnaeus
HINDI NAME : *Viri mōt* (Kashmir)
Handbook Vol. 4

Size: Sparrow + . **Field Characters:** Silvery grey-brown above, streaked and vermiculated with black and fulvous; whitish below, with black arrowhead markings producing a finely cross-barred pattern. Deceptively sparrow-like, particularly in flight. On a flashing glimpse, also easily mistaken for Great Reed Warbler in the appropriate habitat. Sexes alike. Singly in stunted thorn jungle and open deciduous country; not abundant but fairly common though often escaping notice by its unobtrusive behaviour. **Distribution:** Breeds in Kashmir; winter visitor to Bangladesh; Pakistan and practically the entire Indian Union excepting the heavy rainfall evergreen forest tracts. Three slightly differing races. **Habits:** Although closely related to woodpeckers, appearance and behaviour rather sparrow-like. Clings to stems and branches of trees tapping on the bark like woodpecker, as well as perches crosswise in the typical passerine manner. Hops about on ground with tail raised like Indian Robin, picking up ants and other insects which comprise its diet. Has a comical way of stretching neck and bill upwards and twisting its head slowly from side to side, especially when surprised within its nest-hole or handled — evidently a threatening gesture. **Call:** A shrill, quick-repeated nasal *chewn, chewn, chewn* (4 or 5 times at about 3 per second) which betrays the bird's presence in a locality oftener than it is seen. **Nesting:** *Season* — in Kashmir chiefly May and June. *Nest* — a hollow in a rotten branch or tree stem, natural or a disused woodpecker boring, at varying heights. *Eggs* — 6 to 8, white, unglossed oval, often somewhat pointed at the smaller end.

77

155. Blackheaded Yellow Bulbul. *Pycnonotus melanicterus*
(Gmelin). HINDI NAME : *Zắrd būlbūl*
Handbook Vol. 6

Size: Myna — ; same as Redvented Bulbul. **Field Characters:** Head, face and throat glossy black (as is also the pointed erect crest in the northern race *flaviventris*, illustrated). Upperparts olive-yellow; lower bright oil-yellow. Pale yellow eyes conspicuous at short range and through glasses. Sexes alike. Singly or in pairs or small parties in secondary scrub jungle, shrubbery around cultivation and on the outskirts of forest. **Distribution** (*flaviventris*): lower Himalayas from Mussooree to Assam (including Nepal, Sikkim, and Bhutan) up to about 5000 ft, south to northern Madhya Pradesh, Orissa, and northern Andhra. The Rubythroated crestless race (*gularis*) occurs in Kerala and Mysore; Ceylon has the nominate *melanicterus*, smaller and crestless with a yellow throat. **Habits:** Similar to the Redvented and other bulbuls described on pages 97 and 98. Mainly frugivorous, but also eats insects. **Call** very pleasant; something between the cheery notes of the Redwhiskered Bulbul and the tinkling song of the Whitespotted Fantail Flycatcher. **Nesting:** *Season* — principally January to June, but also breeds in other months. *Nest* — like other bulbuls', a cup of fine twigs, rootlets, grass, etc. often bound with cobwebs, placed fairly low down in a bush or small tree. *Eggs* — 2 or 3, reddish white stippled and blotched with various shades of red. Both sexes share in nest building, incubation, and care of the young.

156. Yellow Wagtail. *Motacilla flava* Linnaeus
HINDI NAMES : *Pillắkh, Pẵn pillắkh*
Handbook Vol. 9

Size: Sparrow $\pm$. **Field Characters:** A slim, lively, long-tailed bird chiefly yellowish- or olive-green above, yellow below, seen running about in marshy fields and pastureland, constantly wagging its tail up and down. The three commonest races wintering in India are the Blackheaded (*melanogrisea*) and Blueheaded (*beema*) — A and B — and the Greyheaded (*thunbergi*). They are easily identified in adult summer plumage, but difficult to tell apart in juvenile and winter dress. **Distribution:** Common winter visitor to the entire Indian Union, Bangladesh and Pakistan. Also Nepal, Sikkim, Bhutan, Ceylon, Andaman and Nicobar islands. **Habits:** Similar to the other wagtails described on pages 117 and 118. Runs about in short spurts with brisk mincing steps, picking up tiny insects, occasionally springing into the air to capture a fleeing midge. Flies in undulating curves — a few quick wing flaps followed by a pause — accompanied by the distinctive call-note *weesp*. Roosts in reedbeds and standing sugarcane crops in enormous swarms often commuting long distances — up to 20 miles or more — at sunrise and sunset between the feeding ground and roost, milling around in dense ' clouds ' above the roosting fields before dropping into them like a rain of falling leaves! Some indication of the vast abundance of these winter visitors over the country as a whole can only be obtained after witnessing this astounding spectacle.

PLATE 39

153

154

155

156 B

156 A

JPIrani

IN ___ 2

MM

PLATE 40

157

158

159

160

INS

157. Crested Lark. *Galerida cristata* (Linnaeus)
HINDI NAME : *Chāndūl*

Handbook Vol. 5

Size: Sparrow + . **Field Characters:** The larger size and prominent pointed crest distinguish it from most other larks. Sexes alike. Singly or pairs in dry open country. Occasionally flocks in winter. **Distribution:** Rajasthan and continental India south to Madhya Pradesh, east to Bengal. Also Pakistan. We are mainly concerned with the resident race *chendoola*.

Two allied crested larks, smaller and more rufous, between them occupy most of peninsular India, viz. Sykes's (*G. deva*) with few and narrow streaks on breast, and MALABAR (*G. malabarica*) with pectoral streaks numerous and broader.

Habits: Affects open, sandy or stony semi-desert with scanty grass ground cover. Runs about in search of food: grass seeds, small beetles and other insects, etc. Normal call note a pleasant *tee-ur*. A short, pleasant song uttered during the display flight which consists of soaring a few feet up on leisurely fluttering wings. It is also delivered from a clod or bush-top. **Nesting:** *Season* — March to June. *Nest* — a shallow cup of grass, lined with hair, etc., in open country at the base of a grass tuft or clod. *Eggs* — 3 or 4, dull yellowish white, blotched with brown and purple. Both sexes share in building the nest and tending the young. Female alone believed to incubate.

158. Indian Small Skylark. *Alauda gulgula* Franklin
HINDI NAME : *Bhārāt*

Handbook Vol. 5

Size: Sparrow. **Field Characters:** Like the pipit, but squatter in build and with shorter tail. Sexes alike. Pairs or scattered parties in open country and cultivation. Occasionally large flocks in winter. **Distribution:** Throughout the Indian Union; Bangladesh; Pakistan; Ceylon; Burma. Resident, but also locally migratory. Three races mainly concern us, differing in details of size and coloration. **Habits:** Essentially a bird of grassy meadows and open cultivation, both plains and hills. Particularly fond of damp grassland bordering jheels. Feeds on ground on seeds and insects. Has a peculiar fluttering flight. The song, delivered on the wing, is the skylark's chief claim to distinction. From the ground the bird springs almost vertically upwards on fluttering wings, rising higher and higher till it becomes a speck in the sky. There it remains more or less stationary on rapidly vibrating wings and pours forth a deluge of spirited, melodious warbling, often for over 10 minutes at a stretch. The singer descends to the ground thereafter, but the performance is soon repeated. **Nesting:** *Season* — variable; mainly February to July. *Nest* — a cup-like depression in the ground, or a hoof-print, lined with grass under shelter of a clod or grass tussock. *Eggs* — 2 to 4, pale brownish grey or whitish, spotted and streaked with brown.

159. Redwinged Bush Lark. *Mirafra erythroptera* Blyth
HINDI NAME : *Jăngli aggiyā*
Handbook Vol. 5

Size: Sparrow. **Field Characters:** Distinguished from other larks of same size by the large chestnut patch on the wings, particularly conspicuous in flight. Sexes alike. Loose parties, in dry stony scrub-and-bush country. More commonly perched singly on leafless bush. **Distribution:** Patchily throughout the greater part of the Indian Union excepting the humid heavy rainfall tracts. Pakistan. Represented in Burma and Ceylon by closely allied species.

The SINGING BUSH LARK (*Mirafra cantillans*), with less chestnut in wings and outer tail feathers largely white, is also widely distributed. Its song and song-flight are easily mistaken for the Skylark's.

Habits: The most characteristic and diagnostic habit of the Red-winged Bush Lark is its spectacular song-flight. From a bush-top the male flutters straight up in the air, 30 ft or so, trilling a quick-repeated mousy *si-si-si-si*. This is succeeded immediately by a squeaky *wisee, wisee, wisee, wisee*, etc., getting slower in tempo and fading out as the performer parachutes back to his perch, wings stiffly outstretched in a wide V above the back, and legs dangling. This performance lasts about 20 seconds, and during the breeding season is repeated again and again. **Nesting:** *Season* — April to October, varying locally. *Nest* — a shallow cup of grass, lined with hair, etc., and sometimes domed. Usually well concealed at the base of a bush. *Eggs* — 2 to 4, pale greyish white, yellowish or stone colour, speckled and blotched with various shades of brown.

(See also BLACKBELLIED and RUFOUSTAILED FINCH-LARKS, p. 122)

160. Indian Pipit. *Anthus novaeseelandiae* Gmelin
HINDI NAMES : *Rūgēl, Chărchări*
Handbook Vol. 9

Size: Sparrow $\pm$. **Field Characters:** Rather like female House Sparrow in coloration, dark brown above marked with fulvous; pale fulvous below, streaked with brown on breast. Slimmer, with slenderer bill and longer tail in which outermost feathers white. Sexes alike. Pairs or loose parties, on fallow land etc.

Several other pipits visit our area in winter. They resemble one another closely in appearance and habits, and considerable practice is needed to differentiate them in the field.

Distribution: Throughout the Indian Union; Bangladesh; Pakistan; Ceylon; Burma. Three resident races, separated mainly on depth of coloration; a fourth and larger race, winter visitor. **Habits:** Mainly terrestrial. Affects open country, plains and hills up to about 6000 ft. Ploughed and stubble fields, grazing land and grass-covered stony hillsides are favourite haunts. **Food:** Weevils and other small insects. Runs about briskly in spurts and wags tail up and down like a wagtail, but much more slowly. Has the same undulating flight accompanied by a distinctive *pipit, pipit* or *tseep, tseep*, etc. During the breeding season the male soars and flutters a few feet up in the air uttering a feeble cheeping ' song ', and presently returns to earth. It is a tawdry un-impressive version of the skylark's song-flight. **Nesting:** *Season* — February to October, principally March to June. *Nest* — a shallow cup of grass, rootlets and hair placed under shelter of a clod or in an old hoof-print. *Eggs* — 3 or 4, yellowish- or greyish white, blotched and spotted with brown, more densely at broad end. Both sexes share in nest building and tending the young.

161. Redrumped or **Striated Swallow.** *Hirundo daurica* Linnaeus
HINDI NAME : *Măsjid-ăbābeel*
Handbook Vol. 5

Size: Sparrow ± . **Field Characters:** Glossy deep blue above, fulvous white below finely streaked with dark brown. The chestnut half-collar on hindneck, the deeply forked ' swallow ' tail, and the chestnut rump (conspicuous when banking in flight) are diagnostic points. Sometimes the red rump looks very pale — almost whitish. Sexes alike. Pairs or parties hawking insects on the wing about cliffs, ancient hill forts, ruined buildings, etc. Also in open country. **Distribution:** All India up to 4000 ft in the Himalayas; Bangladesh; Pakistan; Ceylon; Burma. Several races, of which the most widespread resident race is *erythropygia* — Sykes's Striated Swallow — distinguished by very narrow brown streaks on the underparts. In winter, when migratory races are present, differentiation in field difficult, but the commonest of these — seen perched in thousands on telegraph wires — is *nipalensis*, conspicuously broad-streaked below. **Habits:** Similar to those of the Common Swallow and often seen hawking in association with it, and with crag martins and swifts. **Nesting:** *Season* — April to August, varying locally. *Nest* — a retort-shaped structure of plastered mud with a narrow tubular entrance, stuck flat against the ceiling of a rock overhang, cave, or veranda of occupied dwelling. The bulbous egg chamber is lined with feathers. *Eggs* — 3 or 4, pure white. Both sexes share in building the nest and feeding the young.

162. Wiretailed Swallow. *Hirundo smithii* Leach
HINDI NAME : *Leishrā*
Handbook Vol. 5

Size: Sparrow ± . **Field Characters:** Glossy steel blue above, with a chestnut cap. Readily distinguished from other swallows by its glistening white underparts and two long, fine ' wires ' in the tail. Sexes alike, but tail wires of female shorter. Pairs or parties, in open cultivation, near water. **Distribution:** All India from about 9000 ft in the Himalayas south to the Nilgiris; Bangladesh; Pakistan; Burma. Not Ceylon. Mainly resident, but also locally migratory. Only the once race *filifera* concerns us.

Habits: Typical of the swallows, but is more confined to the neighbourhood of water. Seldom encountered away from streams, tanks, reservoirs, etc., or in large flocks. Utters a lively *chit-chit* while hawking midges over a jheel or ploughed field. Male has a pretty twittering song in breeding season. **Nesting:** *Season* — practically all year; principally March to September. *Nest* — a mud-saucer bracket, very similar to Crag Martin's, attached under a culvert or rock overhang near water. *Eggs* — 3 to 5, like those of the Common Swallow. Both sexes share in building the nest and feeding the young.

(See also INDIAN CLIFF SWALLOW, p. 131)

163. Common Swallow. *Hirundo rustica* Linnaeus
HINDI NAME : *Ābābeel*

Handbook Vol. 5

Size: Sparrow $\pm$. **Field Characters:** Glossy steel blue or purplish blue above, pale pinkish white below. Chestnut forehead and throat, the latter bordered by a broad glossy black pectoral band. Deeply forked ' swallow ' tail, especially prominent in flight. Sexes alike. Gregarious. Usually seen huddled on telegraph wires or hawking midges over open country or marshland. **Distribution:** In winter throughout the Indian Union; Bangladesh; Pakistan; Ceylon; Burma. Chiefly two races differing slightly in size and coloration. The NE. Siberian race *tytleri*, with chestnut underparts, visits E. Bengal, Assam and Burma. **Habits:** Winter visitor. Commences arriving September/October; departs April/May. Hawks winged insects high up in air or close to ground. Roosts in large congregations amongst reed-beds and tamarisk thickets standing in water. Flight swift and graceful — a few rapid wing strokes followed by a long glide. Deeply forked tail adds to agility in turning, twisting and wheeling movements. **Food:** Chiefly flies and midges. **Call:** A pleasant, low twittering. **Nesting:** Within our limits, only the Himalayas from Kashmir to NE. Assam, 4000-7000 ft elevation. *Season* — April to July. Often 2 successive broods raised. *Nest* — similar to that of Crag Martin, but with the mud reinforced with grass. Commonly built against beams and rafters within dwelling houses and stables. *Eggs* — 4 or 5, similar in colour and markings to those of the Crag Martin. Both sexes share all domestic duties.

164. Dusky Crag Martin. *Hirundo concolor* Sykes
HINDI NAME : *Chătăn ăbābeel*

Handbook Vol. 5

Size: Sparrow —. . **Field Characters:** Sooty brown, with short square tail and swallow-like wings and flight. A roundish white spot on all tail feathers except the middle and outermost pairs, conspicuous when the bird banks or wheels in the air. Sexes alike. Small numbers about cliffs, ruined forts, etc. in company with swallows and swifts.

In winter the migratory CRAG MARTIN (*Hirundo rupestris*) is also found in association with our resident birds. It is slightly larger and paler, and readily distinguishable by its whitish underparts.

Distribution: All India excepting Assam. Local and patchy. Absent in Bangladesh; Pakistan; Ceylon; and Burma. **Habits:** A close relation of the swallows. Inseparable from crags, rock caves, ancient forts and buildings, irrigation dams, etc. Insectivorous. Hawks midges and other tiny winged insects in the air. Utters a soft *chit-chit* as it flies. **Nesting:** *Season* — principally between June and October when wet mud for nest building is easily obtainable. *Nest* — a deepish oval saucer of mud lined with tow, feathers, etc. Attached like a bracket to vertical rock face or wall, under natural overhang or archway in building. *Eggs* — 2 or 3, white, minutely speckled and spotted with reddish brown. Both sexes share all domestic duties.

PLATE 41

161

162

164

163

INS

PLATE 42

165

168

166

167

INS

165. Grey Shrike. *Lanius excubitor* Linnaeus
HINDI NAME : *Săfēd lătorā*
Handbook Vol. 5

Size: Myna ± . **Field Characters:** A silver-grey bird with longish black-and-white tail. A broad black stripe from bill backward through eye. Black wing quills with a white patch or ' mirror ' conspicuous in flight. Heavy, hooked hawk-like bill. Sexes alike. Singly, on bush-tops in dry open country. **Distribution:** The dry and semi-desert portions of India and Pakistan, from the foot of the Himalayas south to Belgaum, east to Calcutta. Not Eastern Ghats, Assam, Bangladesh, Ceylon or Burma. The race chiefly concerned is the Indian *lahtora*. **Habits:** Inhabits semi-desert and dry cultivation interspersed with patches of thorny scrub and waste land. From exposed perch on bush-top, swoops to ground to carry off locusts, lizards, mice, etc. Prey held under foot and torn to pieces with hooked bill before devouring. When disturbed, drops from perch and flies flat along ground shooting up at end to another bush-top 50 yards away. **Call:** Harsh grating notes; breeding males have a pleasing tinkling song. A good mimic of other birds' calls. Shrikes are known as Butcher Birds from their habit of killing more than needed immediately for food, and storing the surplus impaled on thorns. **Nesting:** *Season* — January to October, chiefly March/April. *Nest* — a deep cup of thorny twigs, with grass, rags, wool or feathers as lining, in thorny trees between 4 and 12 ft up. *Eggs* — 3 to 6, variable, mostly pale greenish white blotched and spotted with purplish brown, especially at broad end.

166. Baybacked Shrike. *Lanius vittatus* Valenciennes
HINDI NAMES : *Chhotā lătorā, Păchănāk*
Handbook Vol. 5

Size: Bulbul ± . **Field Characters:** The smallest Indian shrike. Hook-tipped bill, grey and white head with broad black band across forehead and backward through the eyes; chestnut-maroon back; white underparts. Black-and-white graduated tail; whitish rump; white ' mirrors ' on black wing quills. Sexes alike. Singly, in dry, thinly-wooded country, babool jungle, and cultivation. **Distribution:** Pakistan and practically the entire Indian Union (excepting Assam) from the Himalayan foothills to Kanyakumari; east to West Bengal. Not Bangladesh, Ceylon or Burma. No races. **Habits:** Very similar to those of the Grey Shrike. Avoids pure desert areas as well as humid forest. Normally utters harsh churring notes, but in breeding season male has pleasant warbling song in which imitations of other birds' calls are freely intermingled. **Food:** Locusts and other large insects, lizards, etc. **Nesting:** *Season* — April to September, chiefly June/July. *Nest* — a neat compact cup of grass, rags, wool and feathers bound outside with cobwebs. In fork of small tree or in hedge at moderate height. *Eggs* — smaller replicas of the Grey Shrike's with the same range of variations.

167. **Rufousbacked Shrike.** *Lanius schach* Linnaeus
HINDI NAMES : *Māttiyā lătorā, Kājăla lătorā*
Handbook Vol. 5

Size: Bulbul ± ; Myna — . **Field Characters:** Forehead and a band through the eyes black. Head grey. Lower back and rump bright rufous. Underparts washed with rufous. Typical stout hooked bill. Sexes alike. Singly, in open lightly-wooded and scrub country. **Distribution:** Practically through the Indian Union; Bangladesh; Pakistan; Ceylon; Burma. Up to about 8000 ft in the Himalayas. Seasonal visitor in some parts. Four races, on details of size and coloration. **Habits:** General habits and behaviour typical, but affects less arid country than the two foregoing species. **Call:** Harsh, scolding notes. In breeding season a pretty rambling song of considerable duration uttered in nature of soliloquy. A very accomplished mimic of calls and noises heard in its habitat, quick at learning them and with a retentive memory. Harsh squeals of a frog caught by snake, yelps of newly born puppy, tame grey partridge's call prefaced by its human owner's whistles, and calls of numerous birds even long after many have migrated, are imitated to perfection. **Food:** Grasshoppers and large insects, lizards, young mice, etc. **Nesting:** *Season* — February to July, locally variable. *Nest* — deep compact cup of twigs, grass, wool, rags, etc., in fork of branch of small tree usually under 15 ft. *Eggs* — 3 to 6, somewhat smaller than Grey Shrike's, but more or less identical with them in colour and markings.

168. **Common Wood Shrike.** *Tephrodornis pondicerianus* (Gmelin)
HINDI NAME : *Tārti tuiyā*
Handbook Vol. 6

Size: Bulbul ± . **Field Characters:** A plain greyish brown bird with a dark stripe below the eye and a distinct whitish supercilium. Hook-tipped shrike bill; short square tail. Sexes alike. Pairs or parties, in light jungle. **Distribution:** Practically the entire Indian Union south of the Himalayan foothills; Bangladesh; Pakistan; Ceylon; Burma. Three races, chiefly on depth of coloration. **Habits:** Affects scrub-and-bush country and light deciduous forest. Commonly seen in gardens, among roadside trees and in groves of babool, neem, etc., around cultivation and villages. Parties hunt amongst foliage often in mixed company of other small birds, and follow one another gliding from tree to tree, calling in rich liquid whistling notes — *weet-weet* followed by a quick interrogative *whi-whi-whi-whi?*. **Food:** Moths, beetles, cater-pillars, etc., captured in trees; occasionally in the air like a flycatcher; seldom on ground as in true shrikes. **Nesting:** *Season* — between February and September, mainly March/April. *Nest* — a neat cup of soft bark and fibres cemented together and draped exteriorly with cobwebs and spiders' egg cases, in fork of leafless saplings normally under 20 ft. *Eggs* — 3, pale greenish grey, speckled with purple-brown more densely at broad end to form a ring. Both sexes share parental duties.

(See also PIED FLYCATCHER-SHRIKE, p. 131)

169. **Black Drongo** or **King Crow.** *Dicrurus adsimilis* (Bechstein)
HINDI NAMES : *Būjăngă, Kŏtwāl, Kālkălăchi*
Handbook Vol. 5

Size: Bulbul ± . **Field Characters:** A slim and agile glossy black bird with long, deeply forked tail. Sexes alike. Singly, on the open countryside and about cultivation. **Distribution:** Throughout the Indian Union; Bangladesh; Pakistan; Ceylon; Burma. Four races, on size differences in wing, tail, and bill. **Habits:** A familiar bird of open country, usually perched on telegraph wires, or attending on grazing cattle. From exposed look-outs it keeps vigilant watch for grasshoppers and other insects. These are pounced upon and carried off, held under foot, torn to pieces and swallowed. It rides on the backs of grazing cattle and takes toll of the insects disturbed by the animals' movements through the grass. Forest fires or fired grass patches invariably attract numbers of drongos for the same reason. Highly beneficial to agriculture by the vast quantities of injurious insects it destroys. A variety of harsh scolding or challenging calls are uttered, some closely resembling those of the Shikra hawk. **Food:** Insects; flower nectar also regularly eaten. **Nesting:** *Season* — principally April to August. *Nest* — a flimsy-bottomed cup of fine twigs and fibres cemented with cobweb; in fork at extremity of branch 12 to 30 ft up in large trees preferably standing alone in the open. *Eggs* — 3 to 5 variable; mostly whitish with brownish red spots. Both sexes share all domestic duties and are bold in defence of their nest.

170. **Whitebellied Drongo.** *Dicrurus caerulescens* (Linnaeus)
HINDI NAMES : *Păhări būjăngă, Dhāpri*
Handbook Vol. 5

Size: Bulbul ± . **Field Characters:** Glossy indigo above, with white belly and under tail-coverts. Long, deeply forked tail. Sexes alike. Singly, in lightly-wooded country. **Distribution:** Practically all India south of a line roughly from Kutch to Garhwal, and as far east as Western Bengal and Bihar; Ceylon. Plains and hills; to about 6000 ft in the Himalayas. Three races, on size and details of coloration. **Habits:** Affects well-wooded deciduous tracts; avoids treeless country as well as humid forest. Partial to bamboo and thin tree jungle, and here to shady paths and glades. Makes graceful, agile swoops after winged insects, turning and twisting dextrously in the air and snapping up the quarry in its stride. Often seen as a member of the mixed hunting parties of birds that rove the forest. **Food:** Chiefly insects; also nectar of *Butea, Salmalia* and *Erythrina* flowers. **Call:** Of 3 or 4 pretty whistling notes. An excellent mimic. **Nesting:** *Season* — March to June. *Nest* and *eggs* not appreciably different from those of Black Drongo. The nest site, however, is usually in open deciduous forest.

171. **Racket-tailed Drongo.**   *Dicrurus paradiseus* (Linnaeus)
HINDI NAMES : *Bhimrāj, Bhăngrāj*
Handbook Vol. 5

Size: Myna. **Field Characters:** A glossy black drongo with prominently tufted forehead and two long wirelike spatula-tipped feathers or ' streamers ' in the tail. In flight the broadened tips sometimes give the illusion of the bird being pursued by a pair of large bumble bees. Sexes alike. Singly or loose parties, in forest. **Distribution:** Patchy, more or less throughout India south of the Himalayas east of about Mussooree; Bangladesh; Ceylon; Burma; Andamans & Nicobars. Eight geographical races within this area, on comparative sizes of wing, tail, crest and bill. **Habits:** Inhabits forest, preferably moist-deciduous, plains and hills. In the Himalayas to 6000 ft. Teak and bamboo jungle in broken foothills country is its typical habitat. Commonly seen in hunting parties associated with tree pies and jungle babblers. Very noisy; has a large repertoire of loud metallic calls and is a convincing mimic besides. Its mimicry often confounds the observer into imagining birds which are not there! Makes an amusing pet and is much sought after by fanciers. **Food:** Moths and large insects; also flower nectar. **Nesting:** *Season* — chiefly March to June, with considerable local variations. *Nest* — a deep flimsy cup of fine twigs, rootlets and fibres bound together and secured to the site with cobweb. Built in the end fork of a branch, 15-50 ft up, in forest. *Eggs* — 3 or 4, mostly creamy white blotched and speckled with reddish brown.

(See also HAIRCRESTED DRONGO, p. 146.)

172. **Ashy Swallow-Shrike.**   *Artamus fuscus* Vieillot
HINDI NAME : *Tādi ăbābeel*
Handbook Vol. 5

Size: Bulbul + . **Field Characters:** A rather dumpy but sleek slaty grey bird with paler underparts and a pale rump. When perched, the closed wings reach the end of the tail. Heavy, bluish, sparrow-like bill. Sexes alike. In flight very like swallow or crag martin, but heavier in build. Parties, huddled together on bare branches or telegraph wires in open country, or hawking winged insects in graceful sailing flight. **Distribution:** India east and south of a line from Simla to Godhra (Gujarat); Bangladesh; Ceylon; Burma. Plains and hills to *c.* 6000 ft. Patchy, and locally migratory. **Habits:** Affects open country particularly where dotted with palmyra palms or tall dead trees to serve as look-out posts and foraging bases. While perched, tail constantly moved up and down slowly and twisted sideways. **Food:** Moths, butterflies and winged insects, hawked in the manner of bee-eaters, the birds sailing gracefully back to their perch after each capture, accelerated by intermittent series of rapid beats of the pointed wings. **Call:** A harsh, shrike-like *chek-chek-chek.* **Nesting:** *Season* — April to June. *Nest* — a loosely built cup of grass, roots and fibres up on a horizontal bough or at the base of leaf stalks in a palm tree. *Eggs* — 2 or 3, greenish white, spotted with light brown, chiefly at the broad end.

PLATE 43.

171

170

169

172

NS

PLATE 44

175

176

173

174

INS

173. Golden Oriole. *Oriolus oriolus* (Linnaeus)
HINDI NAME : Peelăk
Handbook Vol. 5

Size: Myna. **Field Characters:** Bright golden yellow with black in wings and tail, and a conspicuous black streak through the eye. Female duller and greener. Singly or pairs, among leafy trees in wooded country. **Distribution:** Practically all the Indian Union excepting Assam, up to about 5000 ft in the Himalayas. Bangladesh; Pakistan. Occasionally Ceylon. Not Burma. Resident in some areas, local migrant in others. Our only Indian race *kundoo* differs from the European chiefly in that its black eye-streak extends behind the eye. **Habits:** Arboreal. A dweller of open but well-wooded country, partial to groves of large trees around villages and cultivation, and in gardens and along roadsides even in noisy towns. Has strong dipping flight. **Call:** A harsh *cheeah* and clear fluty whistles something like *peelolo*. **Food:** Insects, banyan and peepul figs and other fruits and berries; also flower nectar. **Nesting:** *Season* — April to July. *Nest* — a beautifully woven deep cup of grass and bast fibres bound with cobweb, suspended hammockwise in fork of leafy twig 12 to 30 ft up. *Eggs* — 2 or 3, white, spotted with black or reddish brown. Both sexes share all domestic duties.

174. Blackheaded Oriole. *Oriolus xanthornus* (Linnaeus)
HINDI NAME : Peelăk
Handbook Vol. 5

Size: Myna. **Field Characters:** Brilliant golden yellow, with jet black head, throat and upper breast. Black in wings and tail. Bright pink bill; crimson eyes. Sexes alike, but black of head duller in female. Young birds have yellow forehead and the black head streaked with yellowish. Singly or pairs, among leafy trees in wooded country. **Distribution:** All India east of a line from Kathiawar through Mount Abu to the Sutlej river, up to 4000 ft in the Himalayas; Bangladesh; Ceylon; Burma. Partial local migrant. Three races, differing in size and details of coloration. **Habits:** Arboreal. Not appreciably different from the Golden Oriole's. Liquid flute-like calls also very similar. A harsh nasal *kwaak*, commonly heard, and other harsh notes mistakable for a tree pie's. **Food:** Insects, fruits and berries, and flower nectar. **Nesting:** *Season* — April to July; in Ceylon October to May. *Nest* — like the Golden Oriole's. *Eggs* — somewhat smaller; more pinkish, less glossy. Orioles of both species, and such other mild-mannered birds as doves and babblers often build in the same tree as holds a nest of the Black Drongo, presumably on account of the protection afforded against marauders by that bold and pugnacious species.

175. Hill Myna. *Gracula religiosa* Linnaeus
HINDI NAME : *Păhări mynā*
Handbook Vol. 5

Size: Myna +. **Field Characters:** A glossy jet black myna with a conspicuous white patch on the wings, yellow bill and legs, and bright orange-yellow patches of naked skin and wattles on the head. Sexes alike. Pairs or noisy flocks, in hill forest. **Distribution:** Restricted and patchy. In India proper in three distinct areas: (1) Himalayan foot-hills to about 2500 ft elevation from Almora to Assam, (2) Chota Nagpur, Orissa and SE. Madhya Pradesh, (3) the Western Ghats north to about Bombay. Also the Andamans, Ceylon, and Tenasserim (South Burma). Four races, mainly on overall size and differences in arrangement of head wattles. **Habits:** Arboreal. Pairs or noisy flocks in well-wooded country feeding on the various wild figs in company with green pigeons, hornbills and other fruit-eating birds. Has habit of settling on bare tops of dead trees in forest clearings at sunset and uttering its loud, sharp, creaky shrieks. In flight the wings produce a metallic whirring noise, as in green pigeons. An accomplished mimic and talker, and much prized as a cage bird. **Nesting:** *Season —* March to October. *Nest —* a collection of grass, leaves, feathers, etc., stuffed into natural hollows in lofty tree-trunks in forest, usually 30 to 70 ft up. *Eggs —* 2 or 3, deep blue sparsely spotted and blotched with reddish brown or chocolate.

176. Rosy Pastor or Rosecoloured Starling. *Sturnus roseus* (Linnaeus)
HINDI NAME : *Tilyăr*
Handbook Vol. 5

Size: Myna. **Field Characters:** A rose-pink myna-like bird with glis-tening black head, neck and upper breast, wings, and tail. A long, recumbent, pointed crest on crown and nape, sometimes erected. Sexes alike. Young birds and adults in winter plumage (non-breeding) duller and browner. Flocks, about cultivation. **Distribution:** In winter all India; abundant in the northwestern portions and Deccan, dimi-nishing markedly towards its eastern limit in Bengal, and in South India; Pakistan. Visits Ceylon irregularly and sparingly. **Habits:** One of our earliest winter visitors. Begins arriving July-August, departs by mid April. Small flocks or ' clouds ' of up to 500 or more individuals, keep in the vicinity of cultivation, particularly *jowari*, and do considerable damage to ripening grain crops. They destroy locusts on a large scale and to that extent are beneficial to agriculture. Banyan and peepul figs, lantana, peeloo (*Salvadora*) and other berries are eaten, as also nectar of simal flowers (*Salmalia*). The birds do useful service in cross-pollinating these. Males have a chattering, warbling song of harsh as well as pleasant notes uttered chiefly when satiated and resting in a shady tree during the mid day heat. **Nesting:** Breeds in eastern Europe, western and central Asia on stony hillsides and amongst ruins, in May and June. The breeding grounds overlap those of the migratory locust whose hoppers and other stages provide the staple food of hordes of Rosy Pastors and their young from the time the latter hatch out.

177. Greyheaded Myna. *Sturnus malabaricus* (Gmelin)
HINDI NAME : *Păwei*
Handbook Vol. 5

Size: Myna — . **Field Characters:** A small, trim myna, brownish silvery grey above, rusty brown below, with blackish wing quills. Sexes alike. Flocks in thinly-wooded country. **Distribution:** Throughout India east and south of a line from Mount Abu to Dehra Dun. Assam; Bangladesh; Burma. Not Ceylon. Subject to considerable seasonal local migration. The three races that concern us mostly are: (1) the greyheaded *malabaricus* (all India-Assam), (2) the whiteheaded *blythii* (Kerala), (3) the whitewinged *nemoricola* (Burma). **Habits:** Largely arboreal. Inhabits open, thinly-forested country and the neighbourhood of teak plantations and forest cultivation, both near and away from human habitations. Flight swift, direct, typically starling. **Food:** Bēr, lantana, and other berries, banyan and peepul figs, nectar of *Salmalia* and other flowers, and insects. While feeding, keeps up incessant squabbling and chatter varied by some pleasant musical notes. **Nesting:** *Season* — March to June, varying locally. *Nest* — a collection of twigs, rootlets and grass in an old barbet or woodpecker hole in tree-trunks, 10 to 40 ft up. *Eggs* — 3 to 5, pale blue, unmarked. Both sexes share domestic duties, but female alone believed to incubate.

178. Bank Myna. *Acridotheres ginginianus* (Latham)
HINDI NAMES : *Găngā mynā, Bărăd mynā*
Handbook Vol. 5

Size: Myna — . **Field Characters:** Similar to the Indian Myna, but pale bluish grey instead of brown. Naked skin round eyes brick-red instead of yellow. Sexes alike. Flocks, in open country and human habitations. **Distribution:** Sind in Pakistan, and the greater part of northern India, east to Bangladesh, south to about the latitude of Bombay. Partial local migrant. **Habits:** Similar to those of the Indian Myna. Railway stations are particularly favoured. Saunters along confidingly on platforms, in and out of the passengers' feet and baggage, picking up bits of food. Haunts municipal refuse dumps for scraps and titbits, and attends on grazing cattle for insects. Voice somewhat softer than Indian Myna's. **Nesting:** *Season* — May to August. *Nest* — a pad of grass and rubbish stuffed in weepholes of revetments of bridges or in self-excavated tunnels in earth-cuttings; often in colonies. *Eggs* — 3 to 5, glossy pale blue.

179. Indian Myna. *Acridotheres tristis* (Linnaeus)

HINDI NAME : *Dēsi mynā*

Handbook Vol. 5

Size: Bulbul +. Pigeon — (= 9 inches). **Field Characters:** A familiar perky, well-groomed dark brown bird with bright yellow bill, legs, and bare skin round eyes. A large white patch in wing conspicuous in flight. Sexes alike. Pairs or parties, about human habitations and on country-side. **Distribution:** Throughout the Indian Union up to 9000 ft in the Himalayas in summer; Bangladesh; Pakistan; Ceylon; Burma. Ceylon birds (*melanosternus*) are darker than the Indian *tristis*. **Habits:** A confirmed associate of man, following wherever he opens up new habitations. Omnivorous. Eats fruits, insects, kitchen scraps. Follows the plough for earthworms etc., and attends on grazing cattle for the grasshoppers disturbed, side-hopping jauntily, and springing up in the air to capture them. Has a variety of sharp calls and chatter: a loud, scolding *rādio-rādio-rādio*, and *keek-keek-keek*, *kok-kok-kok*, *chur-chur*, etc., uttered with the plumage frowzled and a ludicrous bobbing of the head. **Nesting:** *Season* — April to August. *Nest* — a collection of twigs, roots, paper and rubbish in a hole in a tree, wall or ceiling. *Eggs* — 4 or 5, glossy blue. Two broods often raised in succession. Both sexes share domestic duties.

180. Brahminy or Blackheaded Myna. *Sturnus pagodarum* (Gmelin)

HINDI NAME : *Bāmăni mynā*

Handbook Vol. 5

Size: Myna —. **Field Characters:** A typical myna, grey above reddish fawn below, with glossy black crown and long recumbent crest, and black wing quills. Tail brown with white ending at tip conspicuous when spread out in alighting. Sexes alike. Young birds have crestless sooty brown head, and dull general coloration. Small flocks, in thinly-wooded country. **Distribution:** Practically all India east to Bengal, excepting the most arid and also humid evergreen parts. Commonly up to 4000 ft in the Himalayas in summer. Mainly resident, but also partial local migrant. Pakistan (Karachi environs); Ceylon (coastal Dry zone). **Habits:** Less arboreal than the Greyheaded Myna. Freely enters gardens, and towns and villages. Partial to moist grass-land, and frequently in attendance on grazing cattle, capturing the insects disturbed. **Food:** Chiefly berries, wild figs and insects, but is largely omnivorous. Has several merry creaking or chattering notes. A pleasing little song, in the nature of a soliloquy, is uttered in the breeding season. **Nesting:** *Season* — May to July. *Nest* — a pad of grass, rags, etc., in a hollow in a tree or ruined wall, often even in that of an inhabited house. *Eggs* — 3 or 4, pale blue, unmarked. Both sexes share domestic duties.

(See also JUNGLE MYNA, p. 104, and PIED MYNA, p. 126)

PLATE 45

177

178

180

179

PLATE 46

181

182

183

184

181. Jungle Crow. *Corvus macrorhynchos* Wagler
HINDI NAMES: *Jăngli kowwā, Dhāl kowwā*
Handbook Vol. 5

Size: House Crow + ; Kite — . **Field Characters:** A glossy jet black crow with a heavy bill and deep and hoarse 'caw'. Sexes alike. Singly, pairs or loose parties. **Distribution:** The Indian Union; Bangladesh; Pakistan; Ceylon; Burma. Four geographical races, mainly on size differences of wing and bill. **Habits:** Chiefly a bird of the countryside, but small numbers also in towns and villages. Associates with vultures to feed on carrion. Its movements often lead to discovery of tiger or panther kills hidden in the jungle which the bird is quick to locate. Like House Crow is omnivorous, and highly destructive to eggs and chicks of other birds including domestic poultry, and to young of small mammals. **Nesting:** *Season* — normally December to April in peninsular India; March to May in northern India, Assam and Burma. *Nest* and *eggs* like the House Crow's; the latter slightly larger. Both sexes share parental duties. Nests frequently parasitized by Koel.

182. House Crow. *Corvus splendens* Vieillot
HINDI NAMES: *Kowwā, Dēsi kowwā*
Handbook Vol. 5

Size: Pigeon ± ; (17 inches). **Field Characters:** Grey neck and smaller size distinguish it from the all-black Jungle Crow. Sexes alike. **Distribution:** Throughout the Indian Union; Bangladesh; Pakistan; Ceylon; Burma. Chiefly plains, but also many hill stations. Four geographical races, based largely on paleness or darkness of the grey collar: palest in Sind and Kashmir; darkest (blackish) in Burma. **Habits:** Perhaps the most familiar bird of Indian towns and villages. Lives in close association with man and obtains its livelihood from his works. Audacious, cunning and uncannily wary. Has no particular food preferences. Will eat almost anything: dead sewer rat, offal, carrion, kitchen scraps and refuse, locusts, termites, fruit, grain, and eggs or fledgling birds pilfered from nests. A useful scavenger but also a great bully and therefore a serious menace to defenceless ornamental bird species in urban areas. Has community roosts in selected trees or groves where large numbers collect every night. **Nesting:** *Season* — principally April to June. *Nest* — a platform of twigs frequently intermixed with iron wire, with a cup-like depression lined with tow, coir fibre, etc., 10 ft or more up in a tree; sometimes several nests in the same tree. *Eggs* — 4 or 5 pale blue-green, speckled and streaked with brown. Both sexes share incubation and nest-feeding. The Koel commonly lays its eggs in crows' nests.

183. Tree Pie. *Dendrocitta vagabunda* (Latham)
HINDI NAMES : *Măhālăt, Mătā*
Handbook Vol. 5

Size: Myna $\pm$; tail 12 inches long. **Field Characters:** A long-tailed chestnut-brown bird with sooty head and neck. Black-tipped grey tail and greyish white wing patches conspicuous in flight. Flight undulating — a swift noisy flapping followed by a short glide on outspread wings and tail. Sexes alike. **Distribution:** The Indian Union; Bangladesh; Pakistan; Burma. Not Ceylon. Four races, on size and coloration details. **Habits:** Frequents wooded country and scrub jungle. Freely enters residential compounds and gardens. Usually noisy pairs or family parties. Has a large variety of calls, some loud, harsh and guttural, others pleasing and melodious: one of the commonest of the latter being a clear *bob-o-link* or *kokila*. Omnivorous like the crows and will take fruits, insects, lizards, frogs, centipedes and even carrion, in addition to the eggs and helpless young of birds and rodents. Tree Pies are regular members of the mixed hunting associations of birds that move about in forest. **Nesting:** *Season* — February to July, chiefly March to May. *Nest* — like the crows' but deeper and often of thorny twigs, well lined with rootlets. Concealed in foliage of moderate-sized tree. *Eggs* — 4 or 5, variable in shape and colour; most commonly pale salmon-white splashed and streaked with bright reddish brown. Both sexes share parental duties.

(See also WHITEBELLIED TREE PIE, p. 140.)

184. Grey Tit. *Parus major* Linnaeus
HINDI NAME : *Rāmgăngrā*
Handbook Vol. 9

Size: Sparrow. **Field Characters:** Glossy uncrested black head, glistening white cheek-patches, grey back and whitish underparts with a broad black band down the centre. Sexes alike. **Distribution:** Practically throughout the Indian Union; Bangladesh; Pakistan; Ceylon; Burma. Plains, and hills to about 6000 ft. Five races, on size and coloration details. **Habits:** Frequents well-wooded localities, but not dense humid forest. Singly, pairs or parties, often hunting in association with other small insectivorous birds. Very active. Clings to sprigs, flowering stems and tree-trunks, etc. upside down and in other acrobatic positions in search of food — insects, their eggs and larvae, flower buds, fruit, kernels of small nuts and seeds. The latter are held down underfoot and hacked open with the strong conical bill. Joyous sweeching notes uttered while moving about. In the breeding season the male has a loud, clear, whistling song: *whee-chichi, whee-chichi, whee-chichi,* etc. **Nesting:** *Season* — varies with locality; February to November. Often two successive broods raised. *Nest* — a pad of hair, moss, feathers, etc. in a hole in a tree, wall or earth-cutting, 5 to 15 ft up. *Eggs* — 4 to 6, white or pinkish white, spotted and speckled with reddish brown. Both sexes share parental duties.

(See also YELLOWCHEEKED TIT, p. 115.)

185. Blackheaded Cuckoo-Shrike. *Coracina melanoptera* (Rüppell)
HINDI NAME : *Jăngli kăsyā*
Handbook Vol. 6

Size: Bulbul $\pm$. **Field Characters:** Male: ashy grey with black head, wings and tail, and whitish underparts. Female: head grey; underparts barred black and white. Pairs, in open, lightly-wooded country. **Distribution:** India south and east of a line from Mount Abu through Sambhar (in Rajasthan) to Kangra in Himachal Pradesh. Also parts of Assam, Bangladesh, and Ceylon. Plains and up to about 6000 ft. elevation. Two races. **Habits:** Usually seen in pairs; commonly in association with the itinerant mixed hunting parties of insectivorous birds. Partial to mango, neem, tamarind and other leafy trees growing near villages. **Food:** Chiefly insects, but also berries such as lantana. Method of capturing insects similar to the minivets'. Normally silent. In breeding season male delivers a pretty, clear, whistling song of several notes ending in a quick-repeated *pit-pit-pit*. **Nesting:** *Season* — overall March to August; earlier in Ceylon than in the Deccan. *Nest* — a shallow cup of twigs and rootlets bound together with cobweb; secured on upper surface of bough, usually under 15 ft. *Eggs* — 2 or 3, greenish white with longitudinal blotches of brown.

186. Large Cuckoo-Shrike. *Coracina novaehollandiae* (Gmelin)
HINDI NAME : *Kăsyā*
Handbook Vol. 6

Size: Pigeon — ; slimmer. **Field Characters:** A rather thick-set grey bird, whitish from breast down and with a broad dark eye-streak. Wings and tail black. Eye-streak less prominent in female and her underparts barred grey and white. Pairs, in foliage canopy, in wooded country. **Distribution:** The entire Indian Union (excepting East Punjab and Rajasthan) from about 4000 ft in the Himalayas; Bangladesh; Ceylon; Burma. Not Pakistan. Four races. **Habits:** Arboreal. Affects deciduous forest as well as secondary evergreen jungle, plains and hills alike. Partial to groves of trees about villages and cultivation, and to orchards and forest plantations. Pairs or family parties fly from tree-top to tree-top in irregular follow-my-leader fashion uttering their distinctive shrill but pleasant double-noted call *ti-eee* from time to time. **Food:** Large insects captured in the foliage, as well as berries and banyan, peepul and other wild figs. **Nesting:** *Season* — mainly May to October. *Nest* — a shallow cup of fine twigs bound together with cobweb and sparsely draped exteriorly with lichen and pieces of bark. Placed in fork of outhanging branch up in tall trees. *Eggs* — 3, pale green with scanty blotches of dark brown and purple.

187. Small Minivet. *Pericrocotus cinnamomeus* (Linnaeus)
HINDI NAMES : *Būlālchăshm, Săhēli*

Handbook Vol. 6

Size: Sparrow — . **Field Characters:** Adult male chiefly black, grey
and orange-crimson. Female and young male with no black in head
and with yellow largely replacing the red. Flocks, in foliage canopy
of trees. **Distribution:** Throughout the Indian Union; Bangladesh;
Pakistan; Ceylon; Burma. Plains and lower hills. Six races, on shades
of coloration.

The WHITEBELLIED MINIVET (*P. erythropygius*) of about the same
size, has a wide distribution in Kutch, Rajasthan and the drier portions of the Peninsula. Largely black above, white below, with only
the rump orange-red. In male breast also orange-red.

Habits: Exclusively arboreal. Affects gardens, groves and light
deciduous jungle in flocks, particularly large in winter when also
the sexes tend to keep segregated. **Food** and feeding habits similar to
those of the Scarlet Minivet. **Call:** A feeble, musical *swee-swee* uttered
both whilst hunting and on the wing. **Nesting:** *Season* — between
February and September, varying locally. *Nest* — a pretty little
shallow cup of fibres etc., coated exteriorly with cobweb and lichens.
Attached to upper surface of branch, often high up. *Eggs* — 3, pale
greenish white or creamy buff stippled with reddish brown, more
densely and in a ring round the broad end. Both sexes share parental
duties.

188. Scarlet Minivet. *Pericrocotus flammeus* (Forster)
HINDI NAME : *Păhări būlālchăshm*

Handbook Vol. 6

Size: Bulbul — . **Field Characters:** Adult male glistening black and
orange-red to deep scarlet. Female and young male grey and olive-
yellow above, yellow below with two yellow bars in the black wings.
Flocks, in foliage canopy of trees. **Distribution:** Practically the entire
Indian Union up to about 6000 ft in the Himalayas; Bangladesh;
Ceylon; Burma. Not Pakistan. Five races within these limits.

The slightly smaller, LONGTAILED MINIVET (*P. ethologus*), with
more black in the tail and red extending down along outer webs of
secondaries, breeds in the Himalayas and spreads out over the north
Indian plains during winter.

Habits: Exclusively arboreal. In winter flocks of 30 or more. Affects
well-wooded country and evergreen forest. Flits restlessly amongst
foliage, hovering and fluttering in front of sprigs to stampede lurking
insects, and following one another from tree-top to tree-top. **Food:**
Insects and their larvae; sometimes captured in air like flycatcher.
Call: A pleasant whistling *whee-tweet* or *whiriri, whiriri*, etc., uttered
in flight as well as from perch. **Nesting:** *Season* — principally April
to July. *Nest* — a neat cup of rootlets and bast fibres bound with
cobwebs and bedecked with bark, moss and lichens. Secured on upper
surface of a horizontal branch, 10 to 40 ft up. *Eggs* — 2 to 4 pale
sea-green, spotted and blotched with dark brown and lavender. Both
sexes share parental duties.

94

PLATE 47

185

186

187

188

PLATE 48

189

191

♂

190

♀

192

189. **Goldfronted Chloropsis** or ' **Green Bulbul** '. *Chloropsis aurifrons* (Temminck)
HINDI NAME : *Hărēwā*
Handbook Vol. 6

Size: Bulbul. **Field Characters:** A spruce grass-green bird with bright golden forehead, purple and black chin and throat, and slender curved bill. Female paler and duller. Pairs or parties, in leafy or flower-laden trees. **Distribution:** Locally throughout the Indian Union; Bangladesh; Ceylon; Burma. Up to about 6000 ft. Three races. **Habits:** Affects well-wooded areas, forest as well as neighbourhood of habitation. Hunts for insects and spiders in the foliage where its plumage blends perfectly; therefore, far oftener heard than seen. But is a particularly accomplished mimic of the calls of other birds — Bulbul, Drongo, Shrike, Magpie-Robin, etc. — and often passed over on this account. Sometimes mimics migratory birds during a season when they should be absent, thereby intriguing and confounding the observer. Besides insects, spiders and fruit, feeds largely on flower nectar. **Nesting:** *Season* — mainly May to August, with local variations. *Nest* — a loose shallow cup of tendrils, rootlets, etc., lined with soft grass or bast fibres, near tip of outhanging branch in fairly high tree, well concealed by foliage. *Eggs* — normally 2, cream or reddish cream, speckled with claret.

(See also GOLDMANTLED CHLOROPSIS, p. 97)

190. **Iora.** *Aegithina tiphia* (Linnaeus)
HINDI NAME : *Shaubeegi*
Handbook Vol. 6

Size: Sparrow. **Field Characters:** A black and yellow tit-like bird with two white wing bars. Female, and male in non-breeding plumage, largely greenish yellow with whitish wing bars, the latter differentiated by black tail. Pairs, in gardens, groves and light forest. **Distribution:** All India east of a line from Gulf of Cambay through Mount Abu to Gurdaspur (Punjab); Bangladesh; Ceylon; Burma. Plains and up to about 3000 ft. Five races, on differences in details of coloration. **Habits:** Arboreal. Affects gardens in towns, groves of trees (mango, tamarind, neem, etc.) on village outskirts, and secondary jungle. Hops from twig to twig, frequently clinging on sideways or upside down in search of insects among the foliage. The birds keep in touch by sweet long-drawn musical whistles and short chirrups. Its Hindi name *Shaubeegi* is onomatopaeic. During courtship display the male springs up into the air with plumage fluffed out and with a variety of sibilant whistles parachutes down in a spiral back to his perch, showing off his colours to best advantage. **Food:** Insects, their eggs and larvae. **Nesting:** *Season* — chiefly May to September with local variations. *Nest* — a compact cup of grasses, neatly and copiously plastered with cobwebs, in a crotch or fork of twig 6 to 12 ft up. *Eggs* — 2 to 4, pale pinky white, blotched with purplish brown. Both sexes share parental duties.

191. Quaker Babbler. *Alcippe poioicephala* (Jerdon)

HINDI NAME :

Handbook Vol. 7

Size: Sparrow + ; Bulbul — . **Field Characters:** A small olive-brown babbler with ashy grey head and neck, pale greyish underparts, and rusty brown wings and tail. Sexes alike. Flocks, in foliage canopy of forest trees or shrubs. **Distribution:** Peninsular India and Assam; Bangladesh; Burma. Not Ceylon. **Habits:** Largely arboreal. Frequents moist-deciduous forest preferably hilly country. Flocks of 5 to 10 or more, commonly mixed with parties of other small birds hunting insects in the foliage. Flits from sprig to sprig and clings to leaf stalks in acrobatic positions to investigate. **Call:** A clear whistling quavering song of 4 notes, constantly uttered, which proclaims the bird's presence a long way off. Also utters a harsh *chir-r, chir-r*. **Food:** Insects, spiders, flower nectar, etc. **Nesting:** *Season* — principally during SW. monsoon, June to September; in south India January to May. *Nest* — a flimsy cup of rootlets, moss, lichens, etc., in a crotch of a sapling 4 to 8 ft up, or slung hammockwise between upright weed-stems. *Eggs* — 2 or 3 pale salmon with blotches of purplish brown and pale grey. Both sexes share parental duties.

192. Spotted Babbler. *Pellorneum ruficeps* Swainson

HINDI NAME :

Handbook Vol. 6

Size: Bulbul ± . **Field Characters:** A small olive-brown babbler with a reddish brown cap. Underparts whitish, with breast heavily streaked or spotted with brown. Sexes alike. Pairs and family parties, skulking in undergrowth and on the ground. **Distribution:** Widely distributed in India to about 5000 ft elevation, from the Himalayas to Kerala; Bangladesh; Burma. With many races. An allied species in Ceylon. **Habits:** Affects well-wooded areas. Partial to dry ravines and hillsides overgrown with scrub and bamboo thickets. Rummages on the ground amongst the humus for insects, running about silently like a quail. Usually shy and difficult to observe. **Call:** Of 3 or 4 rich plaintive whistling notes, *pret-ty sweet* or *he'll beat you*, repeated monotonously for many minutes. Also has a loud percussive song of several clear whistling notes heard chiefly morning and evening, particularly during breeding season. **Nesting:** *Season* — March to May; locally up to August. *Nest* — a ball of bamboo leaves etc., with lateral entrance hole, on ground in bank of nullah in forest. *Eggs* — 2 or 3, white or creamy white speckled and blotched with brown.

193. Goldmantled Chloropsis. *Chloropsis cochinchinensis* (Gmelin)
HINDI NAME : *Hărēwā*
Handbook Vol. 6

Size: Bulbul. **Field Characters*:** Differs from 189 in absence of golden orange on forehead and presence of bright purplish blue moustachial streaks. The female has pale bluish green chin and throat, and bright greenish blue moustachial streaks. Pairs or parties, in leafy trees. Entirely arboreal. **Distribution:** The Gangetic Plain; all peninsular India; Ceylon. Plains and foothills. The nominate race *cochinchinensis* in Bangladesh, Assam, Burma. **Habits:** Same as of the Goldfronted Chloropsis (189) except that on the whole it prefers less thickly-wooded country. Partial to groves of trees around villages and scattered amongst cultivation. Invariably present at flowers of Silk Cotton, Coral, palās (*Butea*) and other trees, feeding greedily on the nectar and often acting dog-in-the-manger to other bird visitors. Also a very good mimic. Both the chloropses are popular cage birds, but bullying and pugnacious and unsuitable for mixed aviaries. **Nesting:** *Season* — chiefly April to August, varying locally. *Nest* — similar to that of Goldfronted Chloropsis, both being plastered on the outside with cobwebs. *Eggs* — 2 or 3, pale creamy or pinkish white with sparse specks, blotches and hair-lines of blackish, purplish, and reddish brown. They are very different from eggs of the other species.

(See also FAIRY BLUEBIRD, p. 138.)

194. Redvented Bulbul. *Pycnonotus cafer* (Linnaeus)
HINDI NAMES : *Būlbūl, Gūldūm*
Handbook Vol. 6

Size: Myna — ; (8″). **Field Characters:** A perky smoke-brown bird with partially crested black head, scale-like markings on breast and back, a conspicuous crimson patch below root of tail, and a white rump, the last particularly noticeable in flight. Sexes alike. Pairs or small gatherings, in gardens and lightly wooded country. **Distribution:** Throughout the Indian Union; Bangladesh; Ceylon; Burma. Up to about 4000 ft. Rare or absent in Pakistan. Seven races, on minor differences in size and coloration. **Habits:** Common in gardens and light scrub jungle, both near and away from human habitations. Large numbers collect to feed on banyan and peepul figs and winged termite swarms. Has no song as such, but its joyous notes and vivacious disposition make it a welcome visitor to every garden. Its pugnacity makes it a favourite with fanciers as a fighting bird, and large stakes are wagered on bulbul fights. **Food:** Insects, fruits and berries, peas and suchlike vegetables, and flower nectar. **Nesting:** *Season* — chiefly between February and May, varying with local conditions. *Nest* — a cup of rootlets, sometimes plastered outside with cobwebs, in a bush or tree, 3 to 30 ft up. *Eggs* — 2 or 3, pinkish white, profusely blotched with purplish brown or claret. Both sexes share parental duties.

---

* These refer chiefly to the subspecies *jerdoni*—Jerdon's Chloropsis.

97

195. Whitecheeked Bulbul. *Pycnonotus leucogenys* (Gray)

HINDI NAME : *Būlbūl*

Handbook Vol. 6

Size: As the last. **Field Characters:** An earth-brown bulbul with black head, glistening white cheeks, and sulphur yellow under root of tail. The crest varies from the rudimentary rounded black tuft of the race from Gujarat etc. (illustrated) to the long forwardly curving pointed crest of northern birds, e.g. from Kashmir. Sexes alike. Pairs or scattered parties, in gardens and open scrub country. **Distribution:** The Himalayas, west to east, up to about 9000 ft and the country along their base. Pakistan; western and central India south to Bombay, east to Jhansi. Three races, mainly on length and colour of crest. **Habits:** Jaunty and vivacious as the last. Tame and confiding. Often enters houses to be fed, and for kitchen scraps etc. Familiar visitor to house boats in Kashmir. Has a variety of cheery notes. On the countryside has a preference for semi-desert where berries of peeloo (*Salvadora persica*) and wild caper (*Capparis aphylla*) are its favourite food. Insects and flower nectar are also eaten. **Nesting:** *Season* — March to September, varying with local conditions. *Nest* — typical of bulbuls', a loosely built cup of grass and rootlets in a thorn bush or small tree, usually under 5 ft. *Eggs* — 3 or 4, very like those of Redvented Bulbul.

196. Redwhiskered Bulbul. *Pycnonotus jocosus* (Linnaeus)

HINDI NAME : *Pāhāri būlbūl*

Handbook Vol. 6

Size: Redvented Bulbul. **Field Characters:** Brown above, white below with a broken blackish necklace on breast. Black, upstanding, pointed crest, crimson ' whiskers ' and crimson patch under root of tail are distinguishing features. Sexes alike. Pairs or loose gatherings. **Distribution:** The Indian Union, excepting the arid portions of the northwest (Rajasthan etc.) ; Bangladesh ; Burma. Patchily up to about 6000 ft. Not Ceylon or Pakistan. Five races mainly on details of coloration. **Habits:** Typical of the bulbuls as described. Prefers better-wooded localities than the Redvented species and commonly found in hills up to 7500 ft. often to the exclusion of the latter. Sometimes the two species are found side by side, but normally the habitat preferences are marked. Enters gardens, and is usually tame and confiding. Its joyous querulous notes are rather similar to those of the Redvented Bulbul, but more musical and readily distinguishable. **Nesting:** *Season* — February to August; locally variable. *Nest* — like the other bulbuls', a cup of fine twigs, rootlets, grass, etc. Frequently built in thatch walls or roofs of inhabited huts. *Eggs* — 2 to 4, very similar to the last. Both sexes share parental duties.

(See also YELLOWBROWED– and BLACK BULBULS, p. 139.)

PLATE 49

195

196

♂

♀

193

194

INS

PLATE 50

198

200

199

197

197. Slatyheaded Scimitar Babbler. *Pomatorhinus schisticeps* Hodgson

HINDI NAME :

Handbook Vol. 6

Size: Bulbul + ; Myna — . **Field Characters:** A slaty-headed dark brown babbler with white throat and breast, prominent white eye-brows, and curved pointed yellow bill. Sexes alike. Pairs, or parties, in dense bush cover. **Distri'ation:** The Indian Union; Ceylon. Bangladesh and eastward. Ten races, of which *horsfieldii* of Deccan and peninsular India best known . **Habits:** Confined to forested country, chiefly broken and hilly, with tangled undergrowth and bamboo and cane brakes etc., up to about 6000 ft elevation. As a rule shy and a great skulker. Rummages on the ground under dense undergrowth, flicking the leaves aside or digging in the moist earth with its scimitar bill for insects and grubs. Also ascends into moss-covered branches of trees and bamboo culms in quest of food. Mellow bubbling or gurgling calls enable individuals of a pair or party to keep contact with one another. The male's musical flute-like call of 4 notes is promptly acknowledged by his mate nearby, so that both calls sound as parts of one and as if uttered by the same bird. Flight feeble and ill-sustained. **Food:** Chiefly insects and berries. **Nesting:** *Season* — mainly December to May. *Nest* — a loosely put-together ball of grass, moss, rootlets and leaves on the ground under a bush in a dry forest ravine. *Eggs* — 3 to 5 pure white. Both sexes share parental duties.

198. Rufousbellied Babbler. *Dumetia hyperythra* (Franklin)

HINDI NAME :

Handbook Vol. 6

Size: Sparrow. **Field Characters:** Olive-brown above, rusty fulvous below. Sexes alike. Active, cheeping flocks, in scrub and grass jungle. **Distribution:** All India from the Himalayan foothills southward; Bangladesh; Ceylon. Not Pakistan, Assam or Burma. Five races based on coloration details, the southern populatiᵒns distinguished by a white throat. **Habits:** Inhabits lightly wooded thorny scrub and tall grass country, in skulking flocks of 5 to 10. The individuals keep in touch by means of feeble but sharp cheeping calls *sweech, sweech*, etc., somewhat like a sunbird's, and utter harsh tittering notes when alarmed. The birds scatter and dive into the thickets, but soon reassemble by the more agitated cheeping and tittering that ensues. **Food:** Insects and larvae; also flower nectar. **Nesting:** *Season* — chiefly between May and September; November to March in Ceylon. *Nest* — a neat ball of coarse grass and bamboo leaves lined with softer grass and rootlets, with entrance hole at side. Placed in a bush under 3 ft and well concealed. *Eggs* — 3 or 4, glossy pinkish white, profusely speckled and blotched with reddish or dark brown.

199. Yelloweyed Babbler. *Chrysomma sinense* (Gmelin)
HINDI NAME : *Būlālchāshm*
Handbook Vol. 6

Size: Bulbul — . **Field Characters:** Cinnamon and chestnut-brown above, white below, with conspicuous orange-yellow ring round eye. Sexes alike. Small parties, in scrub and grass undergrowth. **Distribution:** The Indian Union; Pakistan; Bangladesh; Ceylon; Burma. Plains and up to about 5000 ft. Four races, mainly on coloration. **Habits:** A dweller of thorn scrub and grass jungle, commonly met with in patches of such separating cultivated fields. Hunts in small loose flocks, clinging to reed stems sideways or upside down like a tit. A great skulker, and when alarmed will hop away through the undergrowth and vanish uttering harsh tittering notes. **Call:** A clear, loud rather plaintive *cheep-cheep-cheep*. In the breeding season males clamber up to the tops of bushes etc., and deliver a loud and pretty song. Flight feeble and jerky. **Food:** Chiefly spiders and insects; also berries and flower nectar. **Nesting:** *Season* — June to September (SW. monsoon). *Nest* — a deep neat cup of grasses cemented and plastered over with cobwebs. In bushes, seldom above 5 ft high. *Eggs* — 4 or 5, yellowish white finely speckled with purplish brown. Both sexes share parental duties.

200. Common Babbler. *Turdoides caudatus* (Dumont)
HINDI NAMES : *Dūmri, Chilchil*
Handbook Vol. 6

Size: Bulbul; tail relatively longer. **Field Characters:** A slim earthy brown babbler, with upper plumage streaked darker, and long, graduated, loosely attached tail which is finely cross-rayed. Sexes alike. Flocks of a half dozen or more on the ground or in low bushes. **Distribution:** The Indian Union, excepting Assam; Bangladesh; Pakistan; dry plains and hills to about 4000 ft. Not Ceylon or Burma. **Habits:** Has a preference for dry open country and semi-desert with thorn scrub and shrubby vegetation, but is by no means restricted to such. Avoids humid forest. The birds feed on the ground and scuttle along like rats through thorn scrub and thickets, and are loth to fly. Flight feeble — a few rapid flaps followed by a glide on outspread wings and tail. **Call:** A series of short pleasant trilling whistles. When agitated, the birds utter a musical whistling *which-which-whichi-ri-ri-ri-ri-ri-ri* etc., as they nervously twitch their wings and tail and hop from bush to bush, the whole sisterhood combining to hurl invectives at the intruder in a disorderly chorus. **Food:** Insects, berries, grain and flower nectar. **Nesting:** *Season* — generally between March and July, but irregularly over the entire year. *Nest* — a neat compact cup of grass and rootlets in a low thorny bush, seldom over 5 ft up. *Eggs* — 3 or 4, turquoise coloured, glossy. Both sexes share domestic duties. Nests commonly parasitized by Pied Crested and Hawk-Cuckoos.

(See also LARGE GREY BABBLER p. 105, JUNGLE BABBLER, p. 116 and RUFOUS BABBLER, p. 136.)

201. Tickell's Blue Flycatcher. *Muscicapa tickelliae* (Blyth)

HINDI NAME :

Handbook Vol. 7

Size: Sparrow ± . **Field Characters:** A blue bird with bright azure forehead, eyebrows and shoulder-patches. Throat and breast pale rusty, fading to white on abdomen. Female paler and duller. Singly, in secondary bush jungle. **Distribution:** Practically throughout the Indian Union; Bangladesh; Ceylon. Two races differing mainly in details of coloration: Indian (*tickelliae*), and Ceylonese (*jerdoni*). **Habits:** Affects lightly-wooded deciduous country. Partial to foothills, haunting shady glades and bamboo-clad ravines. Sits bolt upright on some low twig or liana stem, flicking its tail, uttering a sharp *click-click*, and launching short agile sallies after flies and midges. Song: a pleasing little metallic trill, constantly uttered, which usually proclaims its presence in a thicket long before the bird is seen. **Food:** Flies, gnats and other dipterous insects. **Nesting:** *Season* — March to August, varying with local conditions. *Nest* — an untidy cup of twigs, rootlets, moss and leaves in hollows in tree-stumps or earth-banks, or up in a bamboo clump at moderate heights. Usually inconspicuous in its surroundings. *Eggs* — 3 to 5, pale clay-brown or olive-brown, sprayed all over with minute reddish brown specks.

(See also Redbreasted Flycatcher, p. 105; Greyheaded Fly-catcher, p. 106; Blacknaped Blue Flycatcher, p. 103)

202. Verditer Flycatcher. *Muscicapa thalassina* Swainson

HINDI NAME:

Handbook Vol. 7

Size: Sparrow +. **Field Characters:** Female differs from blue-green male (illustrated) in being duller and greyer. Singly, in wooded country, hawking flies from exposed tree-tops. **Distribution:** *Winter:* more or less over the entire Indian Union (excepting the drier portions of Rajasthan); Pakistan (excepting Punjab plains and Sind); Bangladesh; Burma. Not Ceylon. *Summer* (breeding): the Himalayas west, to east, between 4 and 10,000 ft. elevation. Ceylon has an allied species *M. sordida*, dusky grey-blue with white under tail-coverts only; no white in tail. **Habits:** Affects well-wooded country. Makes agile aerial sallies after dipterous insects and captures them in mid-air in the typical flycatcher manner. Silent in winter. Breeding males have a sweet, pleasing jingling song, rather like the White-eye's but louder. **Nesting:** *Season* — in the Himalayas, April to July. *Nest* — a thick-sided cup of moss, root hairs, etc., under eaves of a bungalow or in a hole in walls, embankments or amongst exposed roots of trees. *Eggs* — 4, pale pink with darker cap-like ring at broad end. Both sexes share domestic duties.

(See also Black-and-Orange, Whitebellied Blue, and Nilgiri Verditer flycatchers, pp. 137, 138.)

203. Whitespotted Fantail Flycatcher. *Rhipidura albicollis* (Vieillot)
HINDI NAMES : *Nāchǎn, Chǎkdil*

Handbook Vol. 7

Size: Sparrow ± . **Field Characters:** A cheery, restless smoke-brown bird with conspicuous white eyebrows, white-spotted breast and flanks, and whitish abdomen. Its most striking feature is the perky, cocked and fanned-out tail with wings drooping on either side. Pairs, in wooded country, shrubbery, gardens, etc. An allied species, the WHITEBROWED FANTAIL FLYCATCHER (*Rhipidura aureola*) — with broad white forehead and white underparts — is common more or less throughout India, Burma and Ceylon. **Distribution:** The subspecies *albogularis* (illustrated) inhabits southern Gujarat and Maharashtra, and peninsular India in and south of Madhya Pradesh, up to about 6000 ft elevation. Five other subspecies, on minor colour differences. **Habits:** Affects secondary jungle, gardens, groves and shrubbery even amidst noisy towns. Flits tirelessly in foliage and on ground, waltzing and pirouetting. Launches graceful aerial looping-the-loop sallies after flies and gnats. **Call:** A harsh *chuck-chuck*. Also a delightful clear whistling song of several tinkling notes constantly warbled as the bird prances about. **Nesting:** *Season* — March to August. *Nest* — a beautiful neat cup of fine grasses and fibres, copiously plastered outside with cobweb, in a crotch or fork of twig usually under 8 ft up. *Eggs* — 3, pinkish cream with a ring of minute brown specks round broad end. Both sexes share domestic duties.

204. Paradise Flycatcher. *Terpsiphone paradisi* (Linnaeus)
HINDI NAMES : *Shāh būlbūl, Doodhrāj*

Handbook Vol. 7

Size: Bulbul. **Field Characters:** Adult male silvery white with metallic black crested head and two long, narrow ribbonlike feathers in tail. Young male, and female, chestnut above, greyish white below, very like a bulbul in overall appearance. Young male has chestnut streamers in tail; female is without. Singly or pairs, in wooded country. **Distribution:** Practically throughout the Indian Union; Pakistan; Bangladesh; Ceylon; Burma. Plains and up to about 5000 ft in the Himalayas and peninsular hills. Resident in some localities, migratory in others. The two Indian races, *paradisi* and *leucogaster* differ in details of size and coloration. In the Ceylonese race, *ceylonensis*, the adult male never acquires the white plumage. **Habits:** Frequents shady groves and gardens, often about human habitations, and light deciduous jungle with bamboo-clad ravines. The agile fairy-like movements of the male as he twists and turns in the air after flies, with his tail-ribbons looping or trailing behind, is a spectacle of exquisite charm. **Call:** Normally a harsh grating *che* or *che-chwe*, supplemented during breeding season by some pleasanter notes, but no song. **Food:** Flies, gnats and other dipterous insects. **Nesting:** *Season* — February to July, varying locally. *Nest* — a compactly woven cup of fine grasses and fibres, plastered outside with cobwebs, built in the crotch or elbow of a twig 6 to 12 ft up. *Eggs* — 3 to 5, pale creamy pink, speckled and blotched with reddish brown. Both sexes share parental duties, but female does the major part.

PLATE 51

♂

204

♀

202

203

201

INS

PLATE 52

205

206

207

208

205. Blacknaped Blue Flycatcher. *Monarcha azurea* (Boddaert)

HINDI NAME :
Handbook Vol. 7

Size: Sparrow. **Field Characters:** A partially fantailed bright blue flycatcher with whitish abdomen, velvety black patch on nape (tuft), and black gorget across foreneck. Female browner, less blue, with grey and white underparts, and lacking the black marks. Singly or separated pairs, in wooded country; partial to mixed bamboo jungle. **Distribution:** The Indian race *styani* occurs south and east of a line from Khandesh to Lucknow; Bangladesh; Burma; Thailand, etc. Ceylon has an endemic race (*ceylonensis*). **Habits:** Typical flycatcher. Keeps chiefly to middle and lower storey of vegetation, often in the mixed foraging parties of other insectivorous birds. Hunts in trees, undergrowth, and on ground, making agile aerial pursuits, or flitting and prancing about with tail spread and partly erected, wings drooping on either side like the Whitespotted Fantail (203). **Food:** Flies and midges; also larger insects like cicadas. **Call:** A distinctive, harsh but lively *sweech-which?*. No song. **Nesting:** *Season* — April to August. *Nest* — a deep cup of fine grasses and moss, draped outside with spiders' egg-cases, lichens, etc., in fork of slender branch 5 to 25 ft up. *Eggs* — 3 or 4, pale creamy pink with reddish brown blotches. Very similar to those of Paradise Flycatcher (204) but smaller.

206. Lesser Whitethroat. *Sylvia curruca* (Linnaeus)

HINDI NAME :
Handbook Vol. 8

Size: Sparrow — . **Field Characters:** Earthy brown above, whitish below, purer white on the throat. The darker, greyer cap on the head contrasting with brown back and sharply cut off from the throat serves to accentuate the latter's whiteness. White edges and tip of tail, conspicuous in flight, are further pointers. Sexes alike. Singly, in thorn scrub and babool trees in and about fallow cultivation and waste land, and semi-desert country. **Distribution:** The Indian race *blythi* is a winter visitor practically throughout the plains of Pakistan, and northern and peninsular India; east to Bengal, south to Ceylon. Breeds in Siberia east to Manchuria, south to Tien Shan and Altai, and possibly Baluchistan. **Habits:** Similar, in general, to those of the Orphean Warbler (207). Creeps or flits restlessly amongst tangles of twigs and foliage in search of caterpillars and insects. In common with leaf and tree warblers (*Phylloscopus* and *Hippolais*) has an amusing trick, while hunting, of lunging out at an insect just out of reach of the bill and nearly toppling over in the attempt. It also feeds regularly on the nectar of *Capparis* flowers. **Call:** A subdued *tek . . . tek*, like the low clicking of one's tongue against the palate, uttered every few seconds. Usually no song in its winter quarters.

207. Orphean Warbler. *Sylvia hortensis* (Gmelin)
HINDI NAME :
Handbook Vol. 8

Size: Between Sparrow and Bulbul. **Field Characters:** A slender, bush-haunting, arboreal bird, slaty grey above buffy white below, with a black skull cap covering eyes and ear-coverts. Tail black, partly white-tipped and with outer feathers largely white; conspicuous in flight. In female cap dark grey. Singly, in babool scrub on waste land about cultivation, or amongst thorn bushes in semi-desert country. **Distribution:** Eastern race *jerdoni* breeds in NW. Pakistan, Afghanistan to Iraq; winters in Pakistan and India east to Bihar-Orissa, south to Tamil Nadu (Tiruchirapali). **Habits:** Insectivorous, shy, skulking. Hops singly amongst thorny bushes hunting insects and caterpillars, occasionally descending to ground. Fond of flower nectar; feeds regularly from blossoms of wild caper (*Capparis aphylla*) and probably effects cross-pollination. **Calls:** A harsh *chuck, chuck*, varied sometimes by a longer *chichirichich*. In breeding season male has a magnificent warbling song delivered from bush-tops etc. **Nesting:** *Season* — May/June, *Nest* — a deep cup of grass and leaves, lined with finer grass, often plastered outside with vegetable down; 2 to 5 ft up in a bush. *Eggs* — 3 to 5, greenish white, speckled and blotched with blackish and grey chiefly at the broad end.

208. Jungle Myna. *Acridotheres fuscus* (Wagler)
HINDI NAME : *Jāngli mynā*
Handbook Vol. 5

Size: Same as Indian Myna (179). **Field Characters:** Very like Indian Myna but more *greyish* brown overall; with similar white wing patches, conspicuous in flight. Absence of bare bright yellow skin round eyes, and the bushy upstanding tuft of feathers on forehead are diagnostic points. Pairs or parties on well-wooded countryside; seldom about human habitations. **Distribution:** Practically the entire Indian Union, Bangladesh and Pakistan up to 7500 ft. Burma; northern Ceylon. Resident but curiously local and patchy. Two races: northern *fuscus* more slaty grey on upperparts, with bright yellow iris; southern *mahrattensis* less grey on upperparts with bluish white iris. Other races extend the species to China and Malaysia. **Habits:** Less sophisticated than Indian Myna and usually keeps away from habitations. Attends grazing cattle, hunting the grasshoppers and other insects flushed by their movements. Largely omnivorous. Also eats wild figs and berries, and flower nectar (pl. 85). **Calls:** Indistinguishable from Indian Myna's, but the characteristic *keek-keek-kok-kok* etc. (nuptial ' song ') of the latter has not been recorded. **Nesting:** *Season* — mainly February to July. *Nest* — a collection of twigs, roots, grass and rubbish stuffed in a tree-hole (woodpecker's) 8-20 ft up, or in the weep-holes of a roadside revetment. *Eggs* — 3 or 4, glossy turquoise blue.

209. **Large Grey Babbler.** *Turdoides malcolmi* (Sykes)

HINDI NAMES : *Ghogoi, Găugai, Bhainā*

Handbook Vol. 6

Size: Myna. **Field Characters:** Similar to the Jungle Babbler (232), but pale greyish- (against earthy-) brown, with grey forehead. Tail longer and more graduated, with white outer feathers conspicuous in flight and when tail spread. Sexes alike. ' Sisterhoods' of a dozen or so, or larger flocks, rummaging on the ground in open cultivated plains country. **Distribution:** East of a line from Kutch to Punjab (Ferozepur); west of one from eastern U.P. (Ghaziabad) to eastern Maharashtra State (Chanda). Common on the Deccan Plateau; local and patchy in some areas. An endemic species, absent in Ceylon, Bangladesh and Pakistan. **Habits:** Sociable, with the same flight, food and general behaviour as the Jungle and Common Babblers (232, 200). Differs from them chiefly in its habitat — cultivated plains country dotted with babool, mango, and neem trees. Avoids the better-wooded jungly tracts preferred by the former, as well as the drier semi-desert facies of the latter, but sometimes overlaps with either species in marginal localities. **Call:** A loud discordant, almost inane, *kay, kay, kay, kay,* etc. monotonously repeated by several individuals at the same time, with plumage frowzled, wings partly drooping, and tails loosely jerked from time to time. **Nesting:** *Season* — irregular; more or less throughout the year. *Nest* — a loosely built cup of twigs, roots, and grass, usually under 15 ft up in a mango or other leafy tree. *Eggs* — 3 or 4, blue, slightly larger but very similar to those of the Common Babbler. Nests commonly parasitized by Pied Crested and Hawk-Cuckoos.

210. **Redbreasted Flycatcher.** *Muscicapa parva* Bechstein

HINDI NAME : *Tūrrā*

Handbook Vol. 7

Size: Sparrow — . **Field Characters:** A plain brown flycatcher with partly cocked black-and-white tail and wings drooping on either side of it. In adult male chin, throat, and breast bright orange-chestnut; in female and young male breast ashy fulvous, underparts white. The white patches at base of black tail feathers diagnostic in flight, and when tail switched up. Singly in leafy trees on village outskirts, roadsides, bungalow compounds, and forest plantations, etc. **Distribution:** Winter visitor practically throughout India; Bangladesh; Pakistan; Ceylon. Three races, of which only one (*subrubra*)* breeds within our limits, in Kashmir and Garhwal, at 6500 to 7500 ft altitude. **Habits:** Typical flycatcher. Flits among branches of trees, launching short twisting sallies to capture winged insects. Descends to the ground momentarily to pick up crawling prey and flits back into an overhanging branch. From time to time the cocked tail is twitched upright to the accompaniment of a sharp *click-click.* Has a pretty song of leaf warbler quality, but not heard in its winter quarters. **Nesting:** (*subrubra*) *Season* — June/July. *Nest* — of leaves, moss, and hair in a tree-hole 10-20 ft up. *Eggs* — 4 or 5, pale green marked with pinkish-brown chiefly at the broad end.

* Currently recognized as a full species.

211. Greyheaded Flycatcher. *Culicicapa ceylonensis* (Swainson)

HINDI NAME :
Handbook Vol. 7

Size: Sparrow — . **Field Characters:** A tiny, restless greenish yellow flycatcher with ashy grey head, neck, and breast, and bright yellow underparts. Sexes alike. Singly, flitting and flycatching from branches in well-wooded country. **Distribution:** Practically the entire Indian Union, Bangladesh, Pakistan (except the arid northwest portions), and Ceylon. Two races. Resident and local migrant. The species extends east to China, south to Malaysia. **Habits:** Very active. Makes lively aerial swoops after flies, turning, twisting, looping-the-loop dextrously and returning to its perch. **Calls:** A sharp, rather prolonged twittering note. Also a pretty, surprisingly loud whistling song of five notes *chik-whichee-whichee?* ending interrogatively. **Nesting:** *Season* — April to June. *Nest* — a tiny half cup of moss and lichens attached like a bracket against a mossy tree-trunk, or in the angle of outflaking bark, 10-20 ft up, usually in hilly, forested areas up to 8000 ft altitude. *Eggs* — 3 or 4, greyish or cream coloured with sparse blotches of yellowish grey often forming a ring at the broad end.

212. Bluethroat. *Erithacus svecicus* (Linnaeus)

HINDI NAMES : *Hūseni pidda, Nilkănthi*
·Handbook Vol. 8

Size: Sparrow. **Field Characters:** A sprightly, robin-like olive-brown bird with whitish eyebrow and moustachial streaks. Adult male has brilliant blue throat with a white or chestnut patch in the middle (as illustrated); female and young male merely a gorget of brown spots across the whitish breast. In both sexes the black-tipped orange-chestnut tail is conspicuous in flight, and when spread. Singly on damp ground, in tamarisk beds, reedy tank margins, sugar cane fields, etc. **Distribution:** Winter visitor from N. Europe and N. Asia practically throughout India; Bangladesh; Pakistan; Ceylon. Only one race (*abbotti*) breeds within Indian limits (Ladakh). This form is dimorphic usually having a white spot on the blue, but sometimes red. **Habits:** Hops about quietly with tail cocked and wings drooping, at the water's edge or in and out of marshy reeds and bushes, stopping every now and again to pick up an insect. When alarmed or suspicious the head and tail are lowered and the bird scuttles away with a rapid mincing gait, erecting itself every few feet to scan the intruder. **Food:** Mostly caterpillars, tiny beetles and other insects. **Call:** In winter only a harsh subdued *chur-r* or *chuck, chuck*. In summer (breeding) a sweet, loud, and rich song delivered by the male from a bush or other perch, or in his pipit-like display flight. **Nesting:** *Season* — in Ladakh, June/July. *Nest* — a deep cup of dry grass on wet ground, hidden amongst grass and scrub. *Eggs* — 4, sometimes 3, olive-green to olive-brown, minutely freckled all over with pale dull light reddish.

PLATE 53

209

210

211

212

IN

PLATE 54

214

213

215

216

INS

213. Streaked Fantail Warbler. *Cisticola juncidis* (Rafinesque)
HINDI NAME : *Ghās ki phūtki*
Handbook Vol. 8

Size: Sparrow — . **Field Characters:** A tiny bird, dark-streaked ful-vous brown above, whitish below, with a short white-tipped tail constantly flicked open like a fan. Singly, or several loosely together, among tall grass and reeds. **Distribution:** Throughout the Indian Union; Bangladesh; Pakistan; Ceylon; Burma. Plains and up to about 5000 ft. Three races, on size and details of coloration. **Habits:** Affects open grassland, reedbeds bordering a marsh, and standing cereal crops. Moves about locally with seasonal conditions. When flushed, flies a short distance and dives into the grass again. The curious mounting zigzag flight in which the fan-shaped tail is conspicuous, and the sharp *chip . . chip . . chip* accompanying it, announce its presence in any locality. These irregular wavy aerial zigzags of the male, 50 or 100 feet above the nest-site, are a common feature in the breeding season. At each successive dip in the undulating flight, every second or so, the bird utters a single *chip* remarkably like the distant snip of a barber's scissors. **Food:** Small insects and cater-pillars. **Nesting:** *Season* — coincident with the monsoon, varying in different parts of its range, but chiefly June to September. *Nest* — a deep oblong pouch of grasses with its mouth at the top, lined with vegetable down and secured to blades of grass with cobweb. Usually under 2 ft from ground. *Eggs* — 3 to 5, pale bluish white, speckled with red and purple.

214. Indian Wren-Warbler. *Prinia subflava* (Gmelin)
HINDI NAME : *Phūtki*
Handbook Vol. 8

Size: Sparrow — . Same as 215. **Field Characters:** Like 215 but rufous earthy brown above without terminal spots to tail. Winter plumage more fulvous and longer-tailed. Sexes alike. Pairs in open scrub-and-grass country. **Distribution:** The Indian Union south of the Himalayas; Bangladesh; Pakistan; Ceylon; Burma. Five races, mainly on details of coloration.

Two other commonly seen wren-warblers are: (1) FRANKLIN's — *Prinia hodgsonii*, and (2) RUFOUSFRONTED — *P. buchanani*. In winter (1) can be confused with Ashy Wren-Warbler, but is more gregarious. Summer plumage dusky grey with rust-brown wings. Underparts whitish with a broad diffuse ashy band across breast. Habitat: Deci-duous grass and secondary scrub jungle, (2) distinguishable from Indian Wren-Warbler by its rusty crown and white tips to tail feathers. Habitat: Arid semi-desert.

Habits: Affects somewhat drier habitats than Ashy Wren-Warbler; otherwise not appreciably different. **Nesting:** *Season* — March to September, chiefly SW. monsoon. *Nest* — a longish pear-shaped pouch of woven grass strips, open or with lateral entrance hole near top. Slung between upright weed stems usually under 2 ft. *Eggs* — 3 to 5, glossy greenish blue, speckled, blotched and pencilled with reddish brown. Both sexes share parental duties.

215. Ashy Wren-Warbler. *Prinia socialis* Sykes
HINDI NAME : *Phūtki*
Handbook Vol. 8

Size: Sparrow — . **Field Characters:** Ashy slate above, fulvous white below. The loose, longish, graduated, black-and-white-tipped tail is carried partially erect and constantly shaken up and down. Sexes alike. Winter plumage less slaty, more brown, than summer. Pairs, in gardens and well-watered scrub country. **Distribution:** The Indian Union; Bangladesh; Ceylon. Up to 4000 ft in the Himalayas and 7000 in south India. Four races, on details of size and coloration. **Habits:** Frequents shrubbery in gardens, reeds bordering streams, and moist grassland and scrub. Hops about quietly amongst bushes, shaking its tail loosely up and down and uttering a sharp *tee-tee-tee* from time to time. During the breeding season males warble excitedly from exposed perches. When suddenly disturbed off its nest, this warbler and several others of its near cousins, emit a peculiar *kit-kit-kit* as of electric sparks. Whether this is produced by snapping the bill or in some other way is controversial. **Food:** Insects. **Nesting:** *Season* — March to September, mainly after onset of monsoon. *Nest* — of two. types (1) like Tailor Bird's, in a funnel of stitched leaves, (2) an oblong purse of woven fibres tacked and bound with cobweb to the supporting leaves of a low bush. *Eggs* — 3 or 4, glossy brick-red with a dark ring round broad end. Incubation takes 12 days. Both sexes share all domestic duties.

216. Tailor Bird. *Orthotomus sutorius* (Pennant)
HINDI NAMES : *Dărzi, Phūtki*
Handbook Vol. 8

Size: Sparrow — . **Field Characters:** A small restless olive-green bird with whitish underparts, a rust coloured crown and two elongated pin-pointed feathers in the tail (more developed in breeding male) which is carried jauntily cocked. Sexes alike. Singly or pairs, in shrubbery. **Distribution:** The entire Indian Union up to about 5000 ft in the Himalayas; Bangladesh; Pakistan; Ceylon; Burma. Five races cover this area. **Habits:** Familiar and confiding. Equally at home in outlying scrub jungle or in gardens and shrubbery within a bustling town. Fearlessly enters verandas of occupied bungalows, hopping, amongst the trellised creepers and potted plants within a few feet of the inmates. **Call:** A loud cheerful *towit-towit-towit* or *pretty-pretty-pretty* etc. **Food:** Tiny insects, their eggs and grubs; flower nectar of *Salmalia, Erythrina* and other trees. **Nesting:** *Season* — April to September, varying locally. *Nest* — a rough cup of soft fibres, cotton wool and vegetable down placed in a funnel fashioned by cleverly folding over and stitching along edges one or more large pliant leaves. Usually under 3 ft up. *Eggs* — 3 or 4, reddish or bluish white, spotted with brownish red. Both sexes share domestic duties, but evidently female alone incubates.

(See also LESSER WHITETHROAT, p. 103; ORPHEAN WARBLER, p. 104.)

217. Magpie-Robin. *Copsychus saularis* (Linnaeus)
HINDI NAMES : *Daiyăr, Daiyā*
Handbook Vol. 9

Size: Bulbul. **Field Characters:** A trim black-and-white bird with cocked tail as in Indian Robin. Black portions of male replaced by brown and slaty grey in female. Singly or pairs, about human habitations. **Distribution:** The Indian Union; Bangladesh; Pakistan; Ceylon; Burma. Up to about 7500 ft. elevation. Absent in arid areas, e.g. W. Rajasthan and parts of Pakistán. Four races, on minor size and colour differences. **Habits:** One of the more familiar birds about towns and villages. Shy, silent and unobtrusive during non-breeding season, then skulking in shrubbery and only uttering plaintive *swee-ee* and harsh *chur-r*. Conspicuous during breeding season when male sings lustily from favourite tree-top or post, chiefly early mornings and late afternoons. Song punctuated by upward jerks of white-fringed tail. Also very good mimic of other birds' calls. Breeding territories jealously guarded, and intruding males defied with puffing-out, strutting and much show of pugnacity. **Food:** Insects, chiefly picked off the ground, and flower nectar as of *Salmalia* and *Erythrina*. **Nesting:** *Season* — India: April to July; earlier in the south. Ceylon: November to August. *Nest* — a pad of grass, rootlets, hair, etc., in hole in old wall, tree-trunk or bough, 5-20 ft up. *Eggs* — 3-5, pale blue-green, blotched and mottled with reddish brown. Female incubates; male shares other domestic chores.

218. Shama. *Copsychus malabaricus* (Scopoli)
HINDI NAME : *Shāma*
Handbook Vol. 9

Size: Bulbul; relatively longer tailed. **Field Characters:** An unmistakable cousin of the Magpie-Robin with chestnut underparts instead of white. A conspicuous white patch above root of black-and-white graduated tail diagnostic in flight. Black portions of male replaced by slaty brown in female. Singly, in deep forest. **Distribution:** Patchy but general in the forested tracts of the Indian Union (including Andamans); Bangladesh; Ceylon; Burma. Up to about 3500 ft elevation. Four races, on comparative tail lengths and coloration details. **Habits:** Affects forest-clad foothills, where shady ravines are its favourite haunts. In all respects a forest representative of the Magpie-Robin with closely similar habits; but shy and retiring and normally avoids human habitations. Therefore more familiar as a cage bird than in its wild state, and much prized as a songster. Has a loud, clear and melodious thrush-like song, rich in notes and quality. **Food:** Chiefly insects, picked off the ground or among bushes. **Nesting:** *Season* — principally April to June. *Nest* — a shallow cup of rootlets, grass, bamboo leaves, etc., in natural hollows in tree-trunks or in the tangled base of a bamboo clump. *Eggs* — 3 or 4, very like the Magpie-Robin's.

219. Indian Robin. *Saxicoloides fulicata* (Linnaeus)
HINDI NAME : *Kālchūri*

Handbook Vol. 9

Size: Sparrow + . **Field Characters:** A sprightly black bird with a white patch on wing (more conspicuous in flight) and rusty red under root of cocked tail. Hen ashy brown without the wing-patch. Pairs, in dry open lightly wooded country. **Distribution:** The Indian Union; Bangladesh; Pakistan; Ceylon. Plains and hills up to about 5000 ft. Five races, on minor differences of size and coloration: brownbacked in north, blackbacked in Ceylon. **Habits:** Familiar and confiding. Frequents stony scrub country around towns and villages, commonly perching on thatched roofs of huts and entering verandas to pick up insects. Hops along the ground, mounting a rock, termite mound or fencepost and tossing upward the jaunty cocked tail. The male utters some cheery notes — but no song as such — chiefly during courtship display. **Food:** Insects and their eggs, spiders, etc. **Nesting:** *Season* — April to June; earlier in the south. *Nest* — a pad of grass, rootlets and rubbish, lined with feathers or hair, often with bits of snake slough as adornment. Placed under stone, in hole in earthbank or tree-stump. or within a derelict tin can or earthen pot. *Eggs* — 2 or 3, creamy white, sometimes tinged greenish, speckled and blotched with ruddy brown. Female alone incubates; male shares other domestic duties.

220. Blackbird. *Turdus merula* (Linnaeus)
HINDI NAME : *Kāstūri*

Handbook Vol. 9

Size: Myna. **Field Characters*:** A plain grey-brown bird with a black cap, and orange-yellow ring round eye, legs and bill. Female paler and more ashy, with brown cap. Singly or loose parties, in foothills forest. **Distribution:** Practically all peninsular India south from Mount Abu and the Vindhyan hills; Ceylon. Five Indian races, and one Ceylonese, on details of coloration and wing formulae. **Habits:** Resident of well-wooded hills to about 5000 ft elevation, wandering down into plains during winter. Often seen in groves and jungle in the neighbourhood of towns and villages. Hops about on the ground turning over and flicking aside dry leaves in search of insects and windfallen fruit. Also feeds in trees on drupes and flower nectar. During winter only utters a sharp, high-pitched *kree-ee* and throaty *chuck-chuck-chuck*. In the breeding season, male has a loud, rich, melodious song with perfectly mimicked calls of other birds, interwoven in it. Flight swift and direct without pause in wing beats. **Nesting:** *Season* — May to August. *Nest* — typical of all blackbirds, a deep cup of moss, rootlets, etc., copiously intermixed with wet mud, lined with fern stems and root hairs; in trees usually under 10 ft up. *Eggs* — 3 to 5, pale greenish white blotched with ruddy-brown, densely at broad end.

* These refer chiefly to the Blackcapped Blackbird (*T. m. nigropileus*).

PLATE 55

217

218

♀

♂

219

220

PLATE 56

INS

221. Blueheaded Rock Thrush. *Monticola cinclorhynchus* (Vigors)
HINDI NAME :
Handbook Vol. 9

Size: Bulbul. **Field Characters:** Head, chin and throat blue. Upper parts blue and black; rump and underparts chestnut. A white patch on wing conspicuous, particularly in flight. Female plain brown above with barred rump and brown-and-white scaly patterned underside. Singly, in light forest. **Distribution:** In winter more or less throughout India and Pakistan excepting Sind and the Punjab plains; particularly common in the Western Ghats country. Parts of Burma. Not Ceylon. **Habits:** Affects light deciduous and bamboo jungle (October-April). Also moister localities, but seldom if ever within dense evergreen forest. Partial to cardamom and coffee plantations in S. India. When disturbed, flies up silently into an overhanging branch and sits motionless. Silent in its winter quarters. Breeding males have a loud, clear and rich though rather monotonous whistling song. **Nesting:** Breeds throughout the Himalayas chiefly between 3000 and 6000 ft. *Season* — April to June. *Nest* and site similar to the Blue Rock Thrush's. Sometimes placed under exposed roots of a tree. *Eggs* — normally 4, pinkish white, closely stippled with pale reddish brown, heavily at the larger end.

222. Blue Rock Thrush. *Monticola solitarius* (Linnaeus)
HINDI NAME :
Handbook Vol. 9

Size: Bulbul. **Field Characters:** Male bright indigo blue. Female grey-brown above, whitish below cross-barred with dark brown, and with a pale wing-bar. Solitary, on boulders, ruins, stone quarries, etc. **Distribution:** In winter practically throughout the Indian Union; Bangladesh; Pakistan; Ceylon; Burma. Chiefly the Himalayan breeding race *pandoo*. One other race occasionally straggles in just across our northern borders. **Habits:** Sedentary. Frequents boulder-strewn hillsides, rock scarps, ruins of forts and ancient buildings, and even occupied dwellings in towns and villages from October to April. Keeps to the same neighbourhood day after day, and even in successive seasons. Perches bolt upright, bows jerkily and flirts tail in manner of Redstart. Sallies down to ground to pick up an insect. If too large to dispose of on the spot, flies back and whacks it against the perch before swallowing. Mostly silent, but the male's sweet whistling song sometimes heard just before the birds depart for their breeding grounds. In silhouette, during flight and while alighting, may look confusingly like Brown Rock Chat (*Cercomela fusca*). **Food:** Mainly insects; also berries. **Nesting:** *Season* — in Kashmir, Garhwal, etc., the Indian race *pandoo* breeds between 6000 and 9000 ft, April to June. *Nest* — a rough pad of grass, moss and leaves in holes in cliffs or banks, or amongst piled-stone parapet walls. *Eggs* — 3 to 5, pale blue speckled with brownish red.

223. **Malabar Whistling Thrush.** *Myiophonus horsfieldii* (Vigors)

HINDI NAME : *Kāstūra*

Handbook Vol. 9

Size: Myna + ; Pigeon — . **Field Characters:** A blue-black thrush with patches of glistening cobalt blue on forehead and shoulders, and black bill and legs. Sexes alike. Singly or pairs, on rocky hill streams. The closely related Himalayan form *M. c. temminckii*, found also in Assam and Burma, lacks the cobalt shoulder-patches and has a yellow bill. **Distribution:** Western Ghats, Pachmarhi (Madhya Pradesh), Sambalpur (Orissa), Shevaroy Hills. Not Ceylon. **Habits:** A denizen of well-wooded rocky hill streams, both near and away from human habitations. Silent in winter except for a sharp *kree-ee* uttered in flight. In breeding season male has a rich and remarkably human whistling song, rambling aimlessly up and down the scale, whence the bird gets its popular name of ' Idle Schoolboy '. It is one of the earliest and latest diurnal bird songs. **Food:** Chiefly aquatic insects, snails and crabs. The latter are purposefully battered on the rock to remove their shells. **Nesting:** *Season* — February to August, varying with locality. *Nest* — a large, compact pad of roots and grasses reinforced with mud. Placed on a shelf or ledge of precipitous rock flanking a hill torrent. *Eggs* — 3 or 4, pale buff or greyish stone, blotched and speckled with greyish brown and lavender. Both sexes share parental duties.

224. **Whitethroated Ground Thrush.** *Zoothera citrina* (Latham)

HINDI NAME :

Handbook Vol. 9

Size: Myna. **Field Characters:** A plump, short-tailed, long-legged thrush with yellowish brown head, neck and underparts. Rest of upperparts slaty blue. A large white patch on wing conspicuous in flight. Throat and sides of head white, banded obliquely with black. Female has the slaty blue portions suffused with olive-green. Singly, on ground in light forest, flying up silently into branches when disturbed. **Distribution:** Two races mainly concern us: the orange-headed north Indian *citrina* and the white-throated peninsular *cyanotus* (illustrated). The former breeds up to about 5000 ft along the Himalayas and spreads out in winter mainly over northern India and down to Ceylon. The latter is resident in peninsular India where it moves about a great deal locally, particularly during the monsoon. **Habits:** Mainly terrestrial. Affects forest, both deciduous and evergreen, and partial to overgrown ravines and nullahs. Digs in the mulch for insects and windfallen berries. Silent in winter except for the sharp *kree-ee* typical of the thrushes. Breeding males have a rollicking whistling song of several rich notes, often repeated, into which imitations of other birds' calls are cleverly interwoven. **Nesting:** *Season* — May/June for northern race; June/July for southern. *Nest* — a shallow cup of moss, roots and grass sometimes mixed with a little mud, in a tree 4 to 15 ft up. *Eggs* — 3 or 4, pale bluish or creamy white, blotched and freckled with pale reddish, more densely at the broad end.

225. Pied Bushchat. *Saxicola caprata* (Linnaeus)
HINDI NAME : *Kālā piddā*
Handbook Vol. 9

Size: Sparrow. **Field Characters:** Male black, with white patches on rump, abdomen and wings, the last particularly conspicuous in flight. Female earth-brown with pale rusty coloured rump. Separated pairs, on bush-tops etc., in open country. **Distribution:** Patchy. Resident or winter visitor throughout the Indian Union: Bangladesh; Pakistan; Ceylon; Burma. Plains and hills up to about 7500 ft. Four races, on size of bill and extent of white on underparts. **Habits:** Affects sparsely scrubbed country and hillsides, commonly in the neighbourhood of cultivation and villages. From an exposed perch on a stake or bush-top darts down to the ground to pick up insect prey. Sometimes springs up into the air or makes short sallies after winged insects. Utters a harsh *chek, chek* ending in a subdued *trweet*. In breeding season male delivers a pretty whistling song resembling Indian Robin's or Crested Bunting's from a perch or during the display flight with ' delayed action ' wing-beats as in a pigeon ' clapping '. Song also uttered as threat to rival male with tail depressed and neck craned forward menacingly, white rump fluffed out and wings drooped, flaunting the white shoulder-patches. **Nesting:** *Season* — mostly between February and May. *Nest* — a pad of grass lined with hair or wool, in hole in ground, or earth-cutting. *Eggs* — 3 to 5, usually pale bluish white, speckled and blotched with reddish brown. Only female incubates, but male occasionally helps in building nest, and shares in feeding young.

226. Collared Bushchat. *Saxicola torquata* (Linnaeus)
HINDI NAME : *Khǎr piddā*
Handbook Vol. 9

Size: Sparrow. **Field Characters:** Male with black head, orange-brown breast, and prominent white patches on sides of neck (the ' collar '), shoulders, and above root of tail. Female like that of the Pied Bushchat but dark-streaked on upperparts. Separated pairs, in open country, about cultivation and reedy marshes. **Distribution:** In winter throughout the Indian Union; Bangladesh; Pakistan; Burma. Plains and hills. Not Ceylon. Of the four races occurring here, only one breeds within our limits, in the Himalayas between about 2000 and 9000 ft. **Habits:** Seen in its winter quarters between September and April. Singly or pairs in open country, fallow land, reedy margins of tanks and marshes, and among mangroves and sea-holly patches bordering tidal creeks on the coast. Food and feeding habits similar to the foregoing. Constantly flicks open tail, and up and down, as it watches for insect prey from a bush-top or reed stem. Utters *chek, chek* but the pretty breeding song of the male is also occasionally heard while the birds are with us. **Nesting:** *Season* — in the Himalayas April to July. *Nest* — like the Pied Bushchat's, a pad of grass, hair, and wool in a hole in an earth-bank or under a stone. Often placed among the piled stone boundary walls of hillmen's fields. *Eggs* — 4 to 6, not markedly different from those of the last.

11

227. Redstart. *Phoenicurus ochruros* (S. G. Gmelin)
HINDI NAME : *Thirthirā*
Handbook Vol. 8

Size: Sparrow. **Field Characters:** A slim active black and orange-chestnut bird, constantly shivering its tail (orange-chestnut) and dipping forepart of body. Female brown and paler generally, also with orange-chestnut tail. Singly, in stony sparsely scrubbed country and groves of trees. **Distribution:** In winter more or less throughout the Indian Union; Bangladesh; Pakistan; Burma. Plains and hills. Not Ceylon. Two races visit us, the more widely spread (*rufiventris*) having crown and upperparts less grey-fringed. **Habits:** Met with between September and April around villages and cultivation, in groves of trees, stony hummocks and dry scrub jungle. Flits from perch to perch on rooftop, boulder or branch, ceaselessly shivering its tail. **Food :** Insects and spiders etc., usually picked off the ground. Winged insects sometimes captured in the air like a flycatcher. Usual call a sharp, mousy *whit* .... *whit* .... *whit* etc. reminiscent of a squeaking unoiled bicycle wheel revolving at moderate speed. In the breeding season the male utters a pleasant little song. **Nesting:** *Season* — in the Himalayas between 10,000 and 17,000 ft, and beyond from Iran to Mongolia, May to August. *Nest* — a loose cup of grass, moss, hair, wool and feathers, in hole in earth-bank, under a rock or amongst piled stone boundary walls and chortens. *Eggs* — 4 to 6, from white to pale blue-green, unmarked.

228. Whitebrowed Bulbul. *Pycnonotus luteolus* (Lesson)
HINDI NAME :
Handbook Vol. 6

Size: Redvented Bulbul. **Field Characters:** Uncrested, sober brownish olive-green, with pale underparts and conspicuous white forehead and eyebrows. Sexes alike. Unobtrusive, skulking pairs in scrub-and-bush jungle. **Distribution:** Peninsular India south of a line from about Baroda to Midnapur (Bengal); Ceylon. Plains and foothills. Two races. Ceylonese race differs from Indian in being smaller and darker. **Habits:** Frequents shrubbery in dry, open scrub-and-bush country. Occasionally enters rambling jungly gardens and compounds. Normal note, a subdued *churr*, but every now and again the male explodes in loud, abrupt snatches of rattling song, quite unmistakable when once heard. **Food:** Banyan and peepul figs, berries (such as *Zizyphus* and *Lantana*), insects and flower nectar. All species of bulbuls, being predominantly fruit and berry eaters, play an important role in the dispersal of seeds and dissemination of plant life over the countryside. **Nesting:** *Season* — principally March to September; February to April in Kerala and Ceylon. *Nest* — typical bulbul structure, but rather flimsy cup of rootlets etc., in a bush normally under 5 ft. *Eggs* — 2 or 3, like the Redvented Bulbul's, but less richly marked.

114

PLATE 57

226

♀

♂

227

♀

228

225

♂

INS.

PLATE 58

229. Yellowcheeked Tit. *Parus xanthogenys* Vigors
HINDI NAME :
Handbook Vol. 9

Size: Grey Tit (= Sparrow). **Field Characters:** A black and yellow tit with prominent pointed black crest, and black band down centre of yellow underparts. Sexes alike in north Indian race; in the peninsular and south Indian races ventral band of female olive-green. Female of latter race moreover dimorphic, sometimes with black sometimes with olive-green crown. **Distribution:** Throughout the Indian Union; Bangladesh; Pakistan. Four races recognized on size and coloration details. Absent in Ceylon. An allied species, *P. spilonotus*, with bright yellow forehead, in Burma. **Habits:** Similar to those of the Grey Tit. Affects hill forests and wooded plateau country. Usually keeps in family parties, hunting insects in company with other small insectivorous birds in the foliage canopy. Active and restless. Utters a lively *chee-chee* while in quest of food. During the breeding season the male has a loud, clear, whistling song: *cheewit-pretty-cheewit* etc., delivered with crest erect and wings drooping at sides. **Nesting:** *Season* — varies somewhat with local conditions, between April and September. *Nest* — like the Grey Tit's, a pad of moss, hair, wool or feathers inside a hole in a tree-stem, or crack in a wall or earth-bank. *Eggs* — 4 to 6, white or pinkish white lightly spotted and blotched with reddish or purplish brown. Both sexes share parental duties.

230. Chestnutbellied Nuthatch. *Sitta castanea* Lesson
HINDI NAMES : *Siri, Kătphoriyā*
Handbook Vol. 9

Size: Sparrow — . **Field Characters:** A short-tailed bird with relatively long heavy pointed bill. Slaty blue above, deep chestnut below. Underparts of female paler. Singly, or pairs, creeping along trunks and branches of trees like a mouse. **Distribution:** The Indian Union; Bangladesh; Burma. Not Ceylon. Five races, distinguished on size of wing and bill and coloration of underparts. **Habits:** Affects forest and well-wooded tracts; also groves of old mango and other trees on the outskirts of villages. Usually in association with hunting parties of mixed insectivorous birds. Scuttles jerkily up and down or sideways and around trunks and branches of trees, clinging to the undersurface of a bough and running along it back downwards with surprising agility. Actions and behaviour a combination of woodpecker, tit, and mouse. **Food:** Spiders, grubs and insects lurking in holes and crevices in the bark; occasionally also kernels of seeds and nuts. **Call:** A feeble mousy *chilp-chilp*. **Nesting:** *Season* — overall, between February and May. *Nest* — a tree-hollow lined with leaves, moss, wool, etc., and walled up with mud plaster, leaving a small neat and round entrance hole. *Eggs* — 2 to 6, white, speckled with red. Both sexes share parental duties.

231. Velvetfronted Nuthatch   *Sitta frontalis* Swainson
HINDI NAME : *Kātphoriyā* (all nuthatches)
Handbook Vol. 9

Size: Sparrow — . **Field Characters:** Like the Chestnutbellied Nuthatch, but purplish blue above, greyish lilac below. Forehead velvety jet black. Chin and throat whitish. Female differs from male (illustrated) in lacking the black stripe above and behind eye. Pairs or family parties in forest, creeping up and around branches of trees. **Distribution:** Ceylon and the better wooded portions of the Indian Union and Bangladesh; plains as well as hills up to about 7500 ft. elevation. The birds occupying the lower Eastern Himalayas, Assam, Burma and Malaysia are slightly smaller. **Habits:** Though the two are frequently found in the same localities, this species prefers moister and better wooded tracts than the Chestnutbellied Nuthatch. No appreciable difference in habits. Most commonly met with amongst the mixed hunting parties of small birds that rove the forest, of which the usual members are tits, flycatchers, minivets and warblers. **Call:** A loud, cheeping whistle, rather of the volume of a sunbird's. Also a variety of mousy cheeps. **Nesting:** *Season* — about February to April in South India; April to June in the north. *Nest* — as in the foregoing species. Old woodpecker and barbet holes commonly utilized, the original entrace partially blocked up with mud plaster. *Eggs* — 3 to 6 white, densely speckled and blotched with red or purplish. Both sexes partake in parental duties. Incubation period 13/14 days.

232. Jungle Babbler.   *Turdoides striatus* (Dumont)
HINDI NAMES : *Sāt bhāi, Ghonghāi*
Handbook Vol. 6

Size: Myna — . **Field Characters:** An earthy brown frowzled and untidy looking bird with a longish tail which gives the impression of being loosely stuck into body. Sexes alike. Invariably in flocks of half a dozen or more, whence its popular names *Sāt bhāi* in Hindi, ' Seven Sisters' in English. **Distribution:** Throughout the Indian Union, Bangladesh, Pakistan, and SW. Ceylon; plains and hills up to about 5000 ft elevation. Several races, on differences in coloration. **Habits:** Inhabits outlying jungle, well-wooded compounds, gardens and groves of trees about towns and villages. Flocks or ' sisterhoods' hop about on the ground rummaging amongst the fallen leaves and mulch for moths and other insects. They usually form the nucleus of the mixed hunting parties of birds in forest. The flock keeps up a constant conversational chatter and squeaking which sometimes develops into loud discordant wrangling. Sociable even while paired off and nesting, feeding in flocks and banding together to ward off attack by predatory hawk or cat. **Food:** Spiders, cockroaches and other insects, and larvae; wild figs, berries, grain and nectar of flowers of Coral, Silk Cotton and other trees. **Nesting:** *Season* — irregularly throughout the year. *Nest* — a loosely built cup of twigs, rootlets and grass in the fork of a leafy branch 8 to 10 ft up. *Eggs* — 3 or 4, turquoise blue. Parental duties shared by both sexes and more or less communally. Nests commonly parasitized by the Pied Crested and Common Hawk-Cuckoos.

(See also LAUGHING THRUSHES, pp. 135, 136.)

233. Yellowheaded Wagtail. *Motacilla citreola* Pallas
HINDI NAMES : *Pāni ka pilkyā, Pān pillākh*
Handbook Vol. 9

Size: Sparrow $\pm$. **Field Characters:** In summer dress (illustrated) male's bright yellow head diagnostic. Female, and male in winter, have crown and back grey, underparts yellowish white. Differentiated at all times from other similar coloured wagtails by presence of broad yellow supercilium and more or less yellow forehead. Scattered parties, sometimes large swarms, on marshland and grassy tank margins.
Distribution: In winter all India north of about Mysore; Bangladesh; Pakistan; Burma. Not Ceylon. Three races, difficult to differentiate in winter plumage. **Habits:** More gregarious than 234 and essentially a water wagtail, inseparable from marshland and grassy jheels. Numbers often seen on floating lotus leaves and vegetation on a tank, tripping along lightly in search of tiny insects, sometimes springing up into the air, and launching sprightly sallies in pursuit of escaping midges and other quarry. General habits typical of the family.
Nesting: Hodgson's Yellowheaded Wagtail (*M.c.calcarata*), the black-backed race, breeds in Kashmir between 5000 and 12,000 ft. *Season* — May/June. *Nest* — a cup of grass in the centre or at the foot of a tuft of coarse grass or small bush in a marsh, or on wet ground near an upland stream. *Eggs* — 3 to 5, variable but not unlike those of the Grey Wagtail. Both sexes share the domestic duties.

(See also YELLOW WAGTAIL, p. 78.)

234. Grey Wagtail. *Motacilla caspica* (Gmelin)
HINDI NAME : *Pilkyā*
Handbook Vol. 9

Size: Sparrow $\pm$. **Field Characters:** A sprightly, slim long-tailed bird chiefly grey and yellow, running about singly on ground near rocky streams and trickles in wooded country and forest glades. Sexes alike in winter; chin, throat and upper breast black in summer.
Distribution: In winter throughout the Indian Union; Bangladesh; Pakistan; Ceylon; Burma. Plains and hills. **Habits:** Runs about briskly in spurts chasing tiny insects, turning and twisting with agility in their pursuit and often springing up into the air to capture winged ones. The tail is incessantly and characteristically wagged up and down. Flight, a series of long undulating curves, produced by alternate quick flapping and closing of the wings. A sharp *chicheep, chicheep,* etc., is uttered on the wing. The male has a pretty little song in the breeding season. **Nesting:** Within our limits breeds only in the Himalayas between 6000 and 12,000 ft elevation. *Season* — May to July. *Nest* — a cup of grass, rootlets and wool under a stone or among the roots of a bush or tree near a stream, preferably on a small islet. *Eggs* — 4 to 6, yellowish grey or greenish, freckled with reddish brown, more densely at the broad end. Both parents tend the young.

117

235. White Wagtail. *Motacilla alba* Linnaeus
HINDI NAME : *Dhobăn*
Handbook Vol. 9

Size: Same as the Grey Wagtail (= Sparrow ±). **Field Characters:** In non-breeding or winter plumage the black bib (illustrated) is much reduced or wanting, the chin and throat being white like the underparts. Sexes alike. Scattered parties or flocks running about and feeding on open grassland. **Distribution:** In winter the greater part of the Indian Union, Bangladesh and Pakistan. Occasional straggler to Ceylon (*dukhunensis*). The two races common over most of this area are the Indian *dukhunensis*, and the Masked *personata*. Both very similar, but the former has white ear-coverts at all seasons as against black in *personata*. A third race, the NE. Siberian *ocularis*, with a black streak running backward through eye, visits Assam and Burma. **Habits:** Winter visitor arriving about September/October; departing March/April. Runs about swiftly, wagging tail incessantly up and down, to pick up tiny insects on ploughed fields, fallow land, golf links, maidans and lawns even in the midst of populous towns. Roosts at night in large mixed gatherings with other wagtails and swallows in reed-beds, sugar cane fields, and leafy trees. General habits and food typical of the family. **Nesting:** Within our limits only *personata* breeds in Kashmir and NW. Pakistan between 6000 and 12,000 ft. *Season* — May to July. *Nest* — a pad of rootlets, moss, hair, etc., placed in a hole in a ruined wall or amongst a pile of stones. *Eggs* — 4 to 6, white, freckled and spotted with reddish brown.

236. Large Pied Wagtail. *Motacilla maderaspatensis* Gmelin
HINDI NAMES : *Māmulā, Khănjăn*
Handbook Vol. 9

Size: Bulbul ± . **Field Characters:** A large wagtail of black-and-white plumage, resembling in pattern that of the familiar Magpie-Robin, but with a prominent white eyebrow. In the female the black portions are duller and browner. Pairs, at streams, tanks, etc.

May be confused with the somewhat smaller HODGSON'S PIED WAGTAIL (*M.a.alboides*), where both are found together in winter. But this has an entirely white forehead whereas in *maderaspatensis* the black of the crown extends in a point over the forehead to base of bill.

Distribution: Resident throughout the Indian Union, excepting Assam, from about 2000 ft in the Himalayas. Also Sind in Pakistan. Not Ceylon or Burma. **Habits:** Affects clear, shingly or rocky smooth-running streams with diminutive grass-covered islets here and there. Also village tanks and irrigation reservoirs. Usually tame and confiding. Has a number of loud, pleasant whistling calls. During the breeding season, the male sings sweetly from a rock or house-top. Song somewhat reminiscent of Magpie-Robin's. Food and general habits like other wagtails'. **Nesting:** *Season* — elastic, chiefly March to September. *Nest* — a cup-shaped pad of rootlets, hair, wool, and dry algae, etc., under a projecting rock, among rafters of a dwelling house, or under girders of a bridge — always near water. *Eggs* — 3 or 4, greyish-, brownish-, or greenish white, blotched and streaked with various shades of brown. Both sexes share the domestic duties.

PLATE 59

234

236

233

235

INS

PLATE 60

♂

240

♀

238

♂

♀

237

♂

♀

239

INSE

237. Tickell's Flowerpecker. *Dicaeum erythrorhynchos* (Latham)
HINDI NAME : *Phoolchūki*
Handbook Vol. 10

Size: Sparrow — ; smaller than sunbird. **Field Characters:** A diminutive, restless, olive-brown bird with greyish white underparts — like a female sunbird in general effect — with short, slender, slightly curved, *flesh coloured* bill. Sexes alike. Singly, on *Loranthus* clumps in mango orchards and thin deciduous forest. **Distribution:** The Indian Union, excepting the arid portions; Bangladesh; Ceylon, and perhaps Burma. Two races, the Indian (*erythrorhynchos*) being paler than the Ceylonese (*ceylonense*). **Habits:** Affects orchards, forest plantations and groves near villages. Its staple food is the berries of the noxious plant parasites *Loranthus* and *Viscum* belonging to the mistletoe family. The ripe berries are swallowed entire and the sticky slimy seeds excreted on to another branch of the same host tree or of a neighbouring one where they adhere and sprout within a few days, spreading the infestation. Utters an almost incessant sharp *chick-chick-chick* while flying across from one mistletoe clump to another, and as it hops restlessly among the parasite clusters. Has a twittering song besides. **Nesting:** *Season* — chiefly February to June. *Nest* — a hanging oval pouch with lateral entrance hole, rather like a sunbird's nest but smaller and neater and minus the exterior drapery of rubbish. Of soft fibres and vegetable down with the texture of felt. Suspended on twig 10 to 40 ft up. *Eggs* — 2, white. Both sexes share in building the nest and feeding the young.

(See also THICKBILLED FLOWERPECKER, p. 126.)

238. Firebreasted Flowerpecker. *Dicaeum ignipectus* (Blyth)
HINDI NAME : *Phoolchūki*
Handbook Vol. 10

Size: Same as 237. **Field Characters:** Glistening greenish black above, creamy buff below with a scarlet patch on breast. Female olive grass-green above with a contrasting yellow rump; buff below. Wings and tail black. Singly, or twos and threes, on clumps of mistletoe (*Loranthus*) parasitizing trees in wooded Himalayan country. **Distribution:** Himalayas between 5000 and 12,000 ft from the Sutlej Valley to NE. Assam; Burma. **Habits:** Entirely arboreal and not different from those of Tickell's Flowerpecker except that it ascends to higher elevations than perhaps any other flowerpecker. Its restricted distribution would not entitle it to a place in this book, were it not so common where it occurs. It is met with at most Himalayan hill-stations. Inseparable from the loranthus tree parasite, living largely on its berries. It disseminates the sticky seeds from tree to tree and is responsible for the spread of this harmful plant. Also eats nectar, small spiders and insects. Call notes practically indistinguishable from those of Tickell's Flowerpecker. **Nesting:** *Season* — March to June. *Nest* — similar to that of 237. *Eggs* — 2 or 3, white.

239. Purplerumped Sunbird. *Nectarinia zeylonica* (Linnaeus)
HINDI NAME : *Shăkărkhorā*
Handbook Vol. 10

Size: Purple Sunbird (241). **Field Characters:** Upperparts and breast glistening metallic crimson, green, and purple; lower parts yellow. Rump metallic bluish purple. Breeding and non-breeding plumages alike. Female very similar to that of 241, but with chin greyish white and rest of lower parts brighter yellow. Pairs in wooded country. **Distribution:** Ceylon and peninsular India north to Bombay, east to Calcutta. In Tamil Nadu not recorded north of Godavari Valley. **Habits:** Similar to the Purple Sunbird's. In quest of nectar it is responsible for cross-pollinating numerous species of flowers, one of great economic harmfulness being the pernicious tree-parasite *Loranthus*. The male sings excitedly while pivoting on his perch from side to side and opening and closing his wings and tail: *tityou, tityou, tityou, trr-r-r-tit* and so on. **Nesting:** *Season* — not well defined. *Nest* — an oblong pouch of soft grasses, rubbish and cobwebs, draped with pieces of bark, woody refuse and caterpillars' droppings, with a projecting portico above the lateral entrance hole. Suspended from the tip of a branch of bush or creeper at moderate heights, often adjacent to an occupied bungalow. *Eggs* — 2, also similar to those of 241. Female alone builds and incubates; male helps to feed the young.

240. Yellowbacked Sunbird. *Aethopyga siparaja* (Raffles)
HINDI NAME : *Shăkărkhorā* (as for all sunbirds)
Handbook Vol. 10

Size: Sparrow — . **Field Characters:** A brilliantly coloured glistening purple, green and crimson sunbird with long, pointed, metallic green tail and a distinctive yellow rump. Female short-tailed as in the Purple species, but dusky olive-green above, dull ashy green below. Pairs in well-wooded country. **Distribution:** Patchy, over the greater part of the Indian Union in moist-deciduous and evergreen forest biotope, up to between 5000 and 8000 ft elevation in the Himalayas and peninsular hills. Also Bangladesh and Burma. Not Ceylon or Pakistan. Several races, of which two chiefly concern us: the Himalayan *seheriae* of continental India, and *vigorsii* of the Western Ghats country. In the latter the scarlet-crimson breast is boldly streaked with yellow. **Habits:** Flits about restlessly like a gem in the sunshine among blossoming shrubs and trees, hanging upside down and in other acrobatic positions to probe into the flower tubes for nectar. Also eats insects and spiders. **Call:** A sharp, harsh *chichwee*, reminiscent of the Blacknaped Blue Flycatcher (205). **Nesting:** *Season* — overall April to October. *Nest* — a felted, pear-shaped pouch typical of the sunbirds, suspended from a low bush on a ravine bank etc., in forest. *Eggs* — 2 or 3, creamy whitish, minutely flecked with brown.

241. Purple Sunbird. *Nectarinia asiatica* (Latham)
HINDI NAME : *Shākărkhorā*

Handbook Vol. 10

Size: Sparrow — ; (= White-eye). **Field Characters:** Male in non-breeding plumage like female — brown to olive-brown above, pale dull yellow below — but with darker wings and a broad black stripe running down middle of breast. Pairs in open lightly-wooded country.

LOTEN'S SUNBIRD (*Nectarinia lotenia*) also occurs in peninsular India south of a line from Bombay to about Madras, and in Ceylon. The male is like the Purple in breeding plumage (illustrated) but with unglossed underparts, longer bill, and a maroon band across breast.

Distribution: Throughout the Indian Union; Bangladesh; Pakistan; Ceylon; Burma. Three races, based on details of size and coloration. **Habits:** Affects gardens, groves, cultivated and scrub country as well as light deciduous forest. **Food:** Insects and spiders, and very largely flower nectar. Its slender curved bill and tubular tongue are admirably adapted for probing into flower tubes and sucking the nectar; in doing so the bird helps to cross-pollinate the blossoms. **Call:** A sharp monosyllabic *wich, wich* uttered as it flits about. The breeding male sings excitedly from exposed perches, *cheewit-cheewit-cheewit* etc., raises and lowers his wings displaying the brilliant yellow and scarlet tufts of feathers under the ' armpits '. **Nesting:** *Season* — elastic, mostly March to May. *Nest* — typical of sunbirds, an oblong pendulous pouch of soft grasses etc. as described under 239. *Eggs* — 2 or 3, greyish- or greenish white marked with various shades of brown and grey. Only the female builds and incubates, but male assists in feeding the young.

242. White-eye. *Zosterops palpebrosa* (Temminck)
HINDI NAME : *Baboona* (?)

Handbook Vol. 10

Size: Sparrow — . **Field Characters:** A tiny, square-tailed greenish yellow and bright yellow bird with a conspicuous white ring round eye and slender, pointed, slightly curved bill. Gregarious; in trees in gardens and wooded country. **Distribution:** Practically throughout the Indian Union; Bangladesh; Pakistan; Ceylon and Burma, excepting actual desert. Resident and locally migratory. Five geographical races in the above, based on details of size and coloration. **Habits:** Arboreal. Flocks of 5 to 20 or more hunt energetically among the foliage of trees and bushes for insects, often clinging upside down and peering into likely nooks and crannies in the manner of tits. They also subsist largely on flower nectar and on the fleshy pulp of fruits and berries. Feeble jingling conversational notes keep the members of a flock together. In the breeding season the male delivers a pleasing, tinkling song reminiscent of the Verditer Flycatcher's. It commences almost inaudibly, grows louder and presently fades out as it began. **Nesting:** *Season* — principally April to July. *Nest* — a tiny cup of fibres neatly bound with cobwebs — a miniature Oriole's nest — slung hammockwise in the end fork of a thin twig, normally between 5 and 10 ft up. *Eggs* — 2 or 3, pale blue, sometimes with a cap of deeper blue at the broad end. Both sexes share the domestic duties.

243. Blackbellied Finch-Lark. *Eremopterix grisea* (Scopoli)
HINDI NAMES : *Diyora, Dūri, Jothauli, Deoli*
Handbook Vol. 5

Size: Sparrow — . Field Characters: A small, squat, thick-billed crestless lark. Male sandy brown above, black below, with ashy crown and whitish cheeks. Female rather like the hen House Sparrow. Pairs or small flocks, in open plains country. Distribution: All India from the Himalayas to Kanyakumari, east to about Calcutta. Also Pakistan and Ceylon. Resident, and locally migratory. Habits: Affects open cultivated country and semi-barren waste land. Squats close to the ground and shuffles along in zigzag spurts in search of seeds and insects. Very obliteratively coloured and matches sandy soil to perfection. Flies by a series of rapid wing beats as in hovering. The male performs a remarkable aerobatic display. He shoots up vertically on quivering wings, a hundred feet or so, then nosedives perpendicularly some distance with wings pulled in at sides. Using the momentum he suddenly turns about to face the sky and with a few rapid flaps and wings again closed, shoots up a few feet once more. At the crest of the wave he reverses and repeats the nosedive, and so on in descending steps till when near the ground he flattens out and comes to rest on a clod or stone. A pleasant little ' wheeching ' song accompanies these extravagant proceedings. The whole mano-euvre is soon repeated. Nesting: More or less throughout the year. *Nest* and *Eggs* — 2 or 3, very like those of the Rufoustailed Finch-Lark (244). Apparently female alone builds nest, but male assists in incubation and care of the young.

244. Rufoustailed Finch-Lark. *Ammomanes phoenicurus* (Franklin)
HINDI NAMES : *Ăggiā, Rētăl*
Handbook Vol. 5

Size: Sparrow + . Field Characters: A squat, dark rufous brown stout-billed lark with a bright rufous tail ending in a black band. Sexes alike. Pairs or small flocks, in dry open country. Distribution: The greater part of peninsular and continental India, north to the Ganga river. Not Assam. Absent also in Ceylon and Burma. Only the nominate race *phoenicurus* concerns us here. Habits: Affects open, stony scrub-and-bush country, ploughed fields, fallow land and the neighbourhood of cultivation. Zigzags on the ground in short spurts picking up grass and weed seeds, paddy and other grains, as well as insect food. Stampedes insects out of their hiding in the little un-evennesses of the ground by rapidly flicking open its wings. Pleasant rollicking notes, uttered chiefly during the spectacular aerial display similar to that of the Blackbellied Finch-Lark, described above. Nesting: *Season* — principally February to May. *Nest* — a cup of grasses etc., in a slight depression in the ground — usually in a freshly ploughed field — under shelter of a clod of earth or tiny bush. *Eggs* — 3 or 4, creamy white, freckled and spotted with reddish brown or inky purple, more densely at the broad end.

PLATE 61

242

♂

♀

241

♀

♂

243

244

PLATE 62

♀ 246

♂

♀

♂ 245

248

247

INS

245. Baya Weaver Bird. *Ploceus philippinus* (Linnaeus)
HINDI NAME : *Bāyā*
Handbook Vol. 10

Size: Sparrow. **Field Characters:** Female, and male in non-breeding plumage, rather like the hen House Sparrow: dark-streaked fulvous brown above, plain whitish fulvous below. Stout conical bill; short square-cut tail. Flocks, about open cultivation. **Distribution:** Throughout the Indian Union; Bangladesh; Pakistan; Ceylon; Burma. Resident and locally migratory. Three races, on size and details of coloration. **Habits:** Flocks, sometimes of considerable size, glean paddy and other grain in harvested fields. Occasionally damages ripening crops. Roosts in enormous numbers in reed-beds bordering tanks etc. Its seasonal local movements are largely governed by paddy and cereal cultivation which provide both nesting material and food. Also eats insects. **Call:** A sparrowlike *chit-chit-chit*. In breeding season males follow these up by a long-drawn joyous *chee-ee* uttered in chorus, accompanied by flapping of wings in unison while weaving their nests in a colony. **Nesting:** *Season* — May to September, coincident with the SW. monsoon and paddy cultivation. *Nest* — a swinging retort-shaped structure with long vertical entrance tube, compactly woven out of strips of paddy leaf and rough-edged grasses, suspended in clusters from twigs usually over water. Blobs of mud, collected when wet, are stuck inside the dome near the egg-chamber. *Eggs* — 2 to 4 pure white. Male alone builds; female alone incubates. Each male has several nests and females at the same time.

246. Streaked Weaver Bird. *Ploceus manyar* (Horsfield)
HINDI NAME : *Bāmăni băyā*
Handbook Vol. 10

Size: Sparrow. **Field Characters:** Differs from the Baya in having the breast fulvous, boldly streaked with black in both sexes and at all seasons. Crown of head in breeding males yellow; in females and non-breeding males brown. Flocks, in swampy tall reed-beds. **Distribution:** Patchily more or less throughout the Indian Union; Bangladesh; Pakistan; Ceylon; Burma. Two races, on details of coloration. **Habits:** Similar to the Baya's, except that it is more partial to tall coarse grassland and swampy reedy tank margins. In addition to the normal *chit-chit-chit*, the breeding male has a pretty song: *tililili, tililee-kiti-tilileekiti*, etc., uttered in courtship chase and in invitation to a female to an available nest. **Nesting:** *Season* — February to September, varying with local conditions. *Nest* — similar to the Baya's but not so free swinging. Usually also smaller and with shorter entrance tube. Attached directly to tips of several arching bulrush (*Typha*) or grass blades. Small colonies in marshy reed-beds. *Eggs* — 2 to 4, pure white.

(See also BLACKBREASTED WEAVER BIRD, p. 125.)

123

247. Whitethroated Munia. *Lonchura malabarica* (Linnaeus)
HINDI NAMES : *Chắrchắrā, Sar mūniā*

Handbook Vol. 10

Size: Sparrow — ; same as 248. **Field Characters:** A plain earthy brown, thick-billed little finch with pointed black tail, white upper tail-coverts and whitish underparts. Sexes alike. Parties or flocks, in dry open scrub country. **Distribution:** The drier parts of all India to about 6000 ft elevation in the Himalayas; Ceylon; Pakistan. Not Bangladesh, Assam or Burma. **Habits:** Inhabits dry, open, cultivated as well as sparse scrub-and-bush country, and avoids the more humid tracts. Its food, call notes and general behaviour do not differ appreciably from those of other munias. **Nesting:** *Season* — practically all year, varying locally. *Nest* — a large globular structure of coarse grasses, lined with softer flowering grass. In cotton-growing districts, cotton wool filched from neighbouring fields is largely employed. Old baya nests are also habitually utilised for laying in. *Eggs* — 4 to 6, pure white. Both sexes share domestic duties. Disused nests serve as family dormitories.

248. Whitebacked Munia. *Lonchura striata* (Linnaeus)
HINDI NAME : *Shắkắri mūniā*

Handbook Vol. 10

Size: Sparrow — . **Field Characters:** A small black and white finch with heavy bluish conical bill and wedge-shaped tail. White rump and white abdomen conspicuous in flight. Sexes alike. Parties, in open cultivated country. **Distribution:** The greater part of peninsular India and a wide sub-Himalayan belt east of Garhwal; Bengal; Bangladesh; Assam; Ceylon; Burma; Andamans & Nicobars. Four races, chiefly on details of coloration. **Habits:** Goes about in family parties of 6 or 7 or larger flocks. Feeds on grass seeds etc., on the ground or off the feathery tufts or ears, in and around cultivation. Utters feeble chirruping notes. The flocks fly in a disorderly undulating rabble. **Nesting:** *Season* — practically all year, varying locally. *Nest* — large, untidy, globular, of feathery flowering grasses with a lateral entrance hole, sometimes like a short tube or tunnel. In low dense bushes, 5 to 10 ft up. *Eggs* — 5 or 6, pure white. Both sexes share domestic duties. The nests are used as dormitories by the family till long after the young have flown.

(See also GREEN MUNIA, p. 125. RED MUNIA, SPOTTED MUNIA, p. 127. BLACKHEADED MUNIA, p. 128.)

249. **Blackbreasted Weaver Bird.** *Ploceus benghalensis* (Linnaeus)
HINDI NAMES : *Sarbo băyā, Shor băyā, Kăntăwălā băyā*
Handbook Vol. 10

Size: Sparrow. **Field Characters:** Male in breeding plumage has brilliant golden yellow crown, white throat and a black band separating it from the fulvous-white underparts. In non-breeding male (illustrated), and female, crown brown like rest of upper plumage; black pectoral band less developed. A prominent supercilium, a spot behind ear, and narrow moustachial streaks, pale yellow. Flocks about cultivation and around reedy margins of tanks and jheels, or extensive tall grass areas. **Distribution:** Northern India east to Assam (common in the Himalayan terai); south to Gujarat. Bangladesh; Pakistan. Patchy and local. **Habits:** Polygynous; colonial; on the whole similar to those of the Baya and Streaked weavers (245, 246). In courtship bows low before visiting female, presenting golden crown at her. Flaps wings deliberately and sings softly *tsi-tsisik-tsisik-tsik-tsik* like chirp of cricket or subdued squeaking of unoiled bicycle wheel. **Nesting:** *Season* — June to September. *Nest* — similar to the Streaked Baya's; somewhat smaller and normally with shorter entrance tubes. Built in reed-beds in marsh with some of the growing reeds incorporated into the dome as support. Singly or in scattered groups of 4 or 5; sometimes larger colonies. *Eggs* — 3 or 4, white, indistinguishable from those of the other two weavers.

250. **Green Munia.** *Estrilda formosa* (Latham)
HINDI NAMES : *Hări mūniă, Hări lāl*
Handbook Vol. 10

Size: Sparrow — . **Field Characters:** Very like the Red Munia (253) but light olive-green above, yellow below, the flanks barred with greenish brown and white. Tail black, rounded (not pointed). Bill deep scarlet. *Female* similar but much paler. Flocks in open deciduous forest and stony scrub jungle, to about 3000 ft elevation. **Distribution:** A broad belt of central India between a line from Sirohi (Rajasthan) to Hazaribagh (Bihar) in the north, and Khandesh (Maharashtra) to Visakhapatnam Ghats (Andhra) in the south. Local and patchy. **Habits:** Sociable. Similar to those of the Red Munia (253), but is less dependent on damp localities. Lantana scrub country is widely favoured. Flocks of 20 or more birds not uncommon, flying about in the characteristic disorderly undulating rabble and uttering feeble cheeps. **Food:** Chiefly grass seeds. **Nesting:** Curiously enough very little known. *Season* — ill-defined; October to January, and July, mentioned. *Nest* — globular, of coarse grass lined with finer grasses. Placed in a growing sugar cane plant with some of the leaves interwoven into the structure for support. The lateral entrance hole is prolonged to a short neck. Several nests built in close proximity. *Eggs* — 5 (?), white. Both sexes recorded as building the nest and incubating the eggs.

251. Thickbilled Flowerpecker. *Dicaeum agile* (Tickell)
HINDI NAME :
Handbook Vol. 10

Size: Sparrow — ; smaller than sunbird. **Field Characters:** Ashy olive-brown above; greyish buffy white below, faintly brown-streaked. Stout *bluish* finch-like bill readily distinguishes it from Tickell's Flowerpecker (237). Sexes alike. Singly, on mistletoe-laden trees in open wooded country. **Distribution:** Indian race *agile* found practically throughout India (barring the arid NW. portions) up to 5000 ft in Himalayas; Bangladesh. Ceylon has an endemic race, *zeylonense*. **Habits:** Similar, in general to Tickell's Flowerpecker. Feeds largely on ripe berries of *Loranthus* and *Viscum* plant parasites, but unlike Tickell's does not normally swallow them entire. The edible pulp is stripped off by manipulating berry in bill, the viscous seed being wiped on to a neighbouring branch. Thus it spreads the infestation among branches of the same tree rather than to distant ones. Also eats peepul figs, lantana berries, and other fruit. **Call:** A sharp metallic *chik-chik-chik* distinct from Tickell's. Spreads stumpy tail and screws it restlessly from side to side while perched. **Nesting:** *Season* — January to June. *Nest* — an oval felted pouch of vegetable down, similar to Tickell's, brown in colour, and well camouflaged. *Eggs* — 2 or 3, pinkish white, blotched and speckled with brick-red.

252. Pied Myna. *Sturnus contra* (Linnaeus)
HINDI NAME : *Ăblăk mynā*
Handbook Vol. 5

Size: Bulbul + ; Common Myna — . **Field Characters:** A trim black and white myna with orange orbital skin, and deep orange-and-yellow bill. Sexes alike. Parties and flocks about villages and cultivation. **Distribution:** India east of a line from Ambala (Haryana) to Hyderabad and Masulipatam (Andhra); Bangladesh; Burma. The two races that chiefly concern us are the nominate *contra*, and the NE. Assamese *sordidus*. They are differentiated on details of coloration. **Habits:** Rarely met with away from the neighbourhood of villages, towns, and cities where refuse dumps afford attractive feeding. Commonly seen in attendance on grazing cattle, particularly on moist or marshy environs of village tanks. **Calls:** A number of pleasant high-pitched notes, some reminiscent of snatches from the flight song of the finch-larks. **Nesting:** *Season* — March to September. *Nest* — large, untidy, globular, of twigs, leaves, grass and rubbish, with a lateral entrance. In branch of mango or similar tree 15 to 30 ft up, sometimes 3 or 4 nests in the same tree. *Eggs* — 4 or 5, glossy blue. Both sexes share in building the nest and care of the young.

PLATE 63

252

250

249

251

PLATE 64

254

255

253

256

♂

♀

INS

253. Red Munia or Waxbill. *Estrilda amandava* (Linnaeus)
HINDI NAMES : *Lāl, Lāl mūniā*
Handbook Vol. 10

Size: Sparrow — . Same as of the other munias. **Field Characters:** Male in non-breeding plumage, and female, brownish sparsely stippled with white, with red bill and crimson rump. Tail rounded at tip. Flocks among reeds and herbage, on wet grassland. **Distribution:** Throughout the Indian Union from about 2000 ft in the Himalayas almost to Kanyakumari. Up to 6000 ft elevation in the peninsular hills. Also Bangladesh, Pakistan, and Burma, Not Ceylon. The Burmese race differs from the Indian in details of coloration. **Habits:** Typical munia, with a preference for damp localities. Has feeble but musical chirruping call notes. Breeding males utter a low, continuous, twittering song. A popular cage bird, always to be seen in bird markets. **Nesting:** *Season* — chiefly the monsoon, June to October. *Nest* — a small globular structure of grass, lined with finer grasses and feathers, usually within 2 ft of the ground, in a coarse grass tussock or bracken bush. *Eggs* — 4 to 7, pure white. Both sexes share domestic duties.

254. Spotted Munia. *Lonchura punctulata* (Linnaeus)
HINDI NAMES : *Telia mūniā, Sinéwāz*
Handbook Vol. 10

Size: Sparrow — . Same as 247. **Field Characters:** In breeding plumage upper parts chocolate-brown; lower white, speckled with black. In non-breeding and immature plumage, more or less plain brown. Sexes alike. Flocks, about open cultivation. **Distribution:** All India (excepting the arid portions of Rajasthan and Punjab, up to 6000 ft in the Himalayas. Assam; Bangladesh; Ceylon; Burma. Not Pakistan. Three races, on details of coloration. **Habits:** Typical munia. Flocks, sometimes of up to 200 individuals or more, hop about gleaning grass seeds etc. The birds occasionally also devour winged termites emerging from the ground, and when disturbed fly up into trees and bushes, uttering feeble chirrups. They fly in the same disorderly closepacked undulating rabbles as other munias. **Nesting:** *Season* — chiefly July to October. *Nest* — a globular structure of grass blades like the other munias', about 8 inches across, and with a lateral entrance hole near the top. Built in a low thorny bush or tree, sometimes several nests together. *Eggs* — 4 to 8, pure white. Both sexes share domestic duties.

255. Blackheaded Munia. *Lonchura malacca* (Linnaeus)
HINDI NAME : *Nākăl nōr*
Handbook Vol. 10

Size: Sparrow — . Same as of the other munias. **Field Characters:** A small chestnut, black and white munia with typical short, heavy, conical bill. Head, neck and upper breast, vent, thighs and under tail-coverts black. Abdomen white. Sexes alike. Flocks, on marshy tall grassland. **Distribution:** Peninsular India south of about Madhya Pràdesh, and Ceylon. Not Bangladesh, Pakistan or Burma. **Habits:** Partial to swampy low-lying and ill-drained areas with feathery grass and reeds, and the vicinity of wet paddy cultivation in forest. Otherwise not different in habits, food or voice from the other munias described. **Nesting:** *Season* — principally the monsoon, June to October, varying with local conditions. *Nest* — a large ball of coarse grasses, lined with finer grass, with a lateral entrance hole. Built in low bushes or amongst coarse grass stems. *Eggs* — 5 to 7, pure white.

256. Rosefinch. *Carpodacus erythrinus* (Pallas)
HINDI NAMES : *Tūti, Lāl tūti*
Handbook Vol. 10

Size: Sparrow + . **Field Characters:** Both in the rose coloured male and the brownish female the heavy conical finch bill and the slightly forked tail are noticeable features. Flocks, in wooded country and about cultivation. **Distribution:** The Indian race *roseatus* which chiefly concerns us, breeds at 10,000 ft and higher in the Himalayas from Kashmir to eastern Tibet. In winter it spreads out practically all over the Indian Union, Bangladesh, Pakistan, and Burma. Not Ceylon. **Habits:** Found south of the Himalayas between September and May. Keeps in flocks to wooded country, feeding on lantana and other berries, wild figs and flower buds, bamboo seeds, linseed and cereals. Flower nectar of *Butea*, *Erythrina* and other flowers is also relished, and the birds do service in cross-pollinating them. Ordinary call note: a musical, whistling, interrogative *tooee? tooee?*. Just before departure for breeding grounds a loud, pleasant song sometimes heard. **Nesting:** *Season* — June to August. *Nest* — a cup of grass lined with fine roots and hair, placed in a wild rose or similar bush, 2 to 6 ft up. *Eggs* — 3 or 4, blue, spotted and speckled with blackish and light red. Both sexes share domestic duties.

257. House Sparrow. *Passer domesticus* (Linnaeus)
HINDI NAME : *Gauriyyā*
Handbook Vol. 10

Size: Bulbul — ; (6 inches). **Field Characters:** Undoubtedly our most familiar bird. Female ashy grey-brown above, streaked with blackish and rufous, and with a pale fulvous supercilium; fulvous ashy white below. Inseparable from human habitations. **Distribution:** Practically world-wide. Throughout India normally to about 7000 ft in the Himalayas. Bangladesh; Pakistan; Ceylon; Burma. Apparently absent in the Andamans and Nicobars. Two races; the Kashmiri and north-western being larger. **Habits:** A confirmed hanger-on of man, in hills and plains alike, whether in a bustling noisy city or outlying forest hamlet. Omnivorous; eats grain, insects, fruit buds, flower nectar and kitchen scraps. Sometimes collects in enormous flocks and does damage to ripening crops and in market gardens. Non-breeding birds have favourite community roosts in leafy trees, where large numbers foregather with much noise every evening. Chirping call notes too well known. ' Song ' of breeding male a loud, monotonous *tsi, tsi, tsi,* or *cheer, cheer, cheer* uttered *ad lib* as he fluffs out his feathers, arches his rump, droops his wings and struts about arrogantly, twitching his partly cocked tail. **Nesting:** *Season* — practically all year, the most favoured months varying with locality. *Nest* — a collection of straw, rubbish and feathers in a hole in ceiling, niche in wall, inverted lamp shade, and every conceivable site within or without an occupied building. *Eggs* — 3 to 5, pale greenish white, stippled and blotched with brown. Several successive broods are often raised.

258. Yellowthroated Sparrow. *Petronia xanthocollis* (Burton)
HINDI NAME : *Jăngli chiri*
Handbook Vol. 10

Size: Sparrow. **Field Characters:** A pale earth-brown sparrow with a conspicuous chestnut shoulder-patch, two whitish bars in the wing, and a lemon-yellow ' thumb impression ' on the throat. Female lacks the yellow on throat, and her chestnut shoulder-patches are paler. Pairs or flocks, in open thinly-wooded country. **Distribution:** Practically all India from about 4000 ft in the Himalayas to Kanyakumari and from Sind to Bengal. Also Bangladesh, Pakistan, Ceylon and parts of Burma. Resident and marked seasonal local migrant. Two races: a paler and a darker. **Habits:** Often found in the neighbourhood of towns and villages, but not so closely associated with man as the House Sparrow. Keeps to open scrub country and light deciduous forest. Gleans paddy grains and grass seeds in stubble fields and on cross-country cart tracks. Also feeds on berries, flower nectar, and moths and other insects. Chirpy call notes similar to the House Sparrow's but pleasanter. Forms into large flocks in winter. **Nesting:** *Season* —April to June. *Nest* — a collection of grass, wool, feathers and rubbish stuffed inside a tree-hole between 8 and 40 ft from the ground. Old woodpecker and barbet nest-holes are commonly appropriated. *Eggs* — 3 or 4, pale greenish white, spotted, blotched and streaked with dingy brown. Both sexes share domestic duties.

259. **Blackheaded Bunting.** *Emberiza melanocephala* Scopoli
259A. **Redheaded Bunting.** *Emberiza bruniceps* Brandt
HINDI NAME : *Gǎndǎm* (both)
Handbook Vol. 10

Size: Sparrow + . **Field Characters:** Slender yellow sparrowlike birds with longer, noticeably forked tail. Female of Blackheaded pale fulvous brown above with the rump tinged chestnut; of Redheaded Bunting ashy brown with the rump tinged yellow. Lower plumage in both pale fulvous, washed with yellow. Large flocks about cultivation, commonly of both species together. When massed on green trees, look like clusters of yellow blossoms in distance. **Distribution:** Winter visitors to Pakistan and the greater part of peninsular and continental India. The Blackheaded confined chiefly to the western side south to Belgaum; the Redheaded extending east to Chota Nagpur, south to Coimbatore. **Habits:** The birds arrive September/ October and depart again March/April. They keep in enormous flocks or ' swarms ' to open cultivation of jowari, wheat, etc., particularly where the fields are interspersed with bush and babool jungle, and may do considerable local damage to the ripening crops. Call note in winter quarters a musical *tweet*. The loud, pleasant, whistling song of the males is sometimes heard before they depart for their breeding grounds. **Nesting:** The Blackheaded Bunting nests in W. Asia and E. Europe. The nearest breeding ground of the Redheaded species is in Baluchistan. *Season* — May/June. *Nest* — cup-shaped, of weed stalks and fibres lined with goat's hair. Well concealed in bushes, 2 to 4 ft up. *Eggs* — normally 5, pale greenish white, speckled and spotted with dark brown, lavender, and grey.

··260. **Crested Bunting.** *Melophus lathami* (Gray)
HINDI NAME : *Pathar chiria* (?)
Handbook Vol. 10

Size: Sparrow. **Field Characters:** A black-and-chestnut, crested, sparrow-like bird with rather the colour scheme of the Crow-Pheasant. Female dark brown with cinnamon colour in wings and tail; also with prominent pointed crest. Singly, pairs or small scattered parties, on stony scrub-covered hillsides and about forest cultivation. **Distribution:** Found locally and patchily throughout the lower Himalayas, up to about 5000 ft from Kashmir to E. Assam; Mount Abu, Rajasthan and central India south to about Satara, east to Bihar. Also portions of Burma. Seasonal local migrant.

The STRIOLATED BUNTING (*E. striolata*) rather like the female Crested Bunting, but smaller and without crest, is also found locally and capriciously in many parts of India excepting the south.

Habits: Gleans grass seeds and grain on the ground, flying up into bushes when disturbed. Partial to recently burnt, charred stony patches in dry grass and pole forest. Utters *pink, pink* like a munia, but louder. Song of breeding male rather like Pied Bushchat's: *which ..which..which-whee-whee-which* (accent on second *whee*). **Nesting:** *Season* — April to August, varying locally. *Nest* — a deep cup of grass lined with fine rootlets, in a pocket in earth-cutting or under a stone or grass tuft on a hillside. *Eggs* — 3 or 4, pale greenish grey, freckled with purplish brown, densely at broad end. Both sexes share in nest building and feeding young.

259 A

259

257

258

♀

260

♂

INS

PLATE 66

261

262

2 IN

0   50 MM

264

263

3   4   6 IN

261. Indian Cliff Swallow. *Hirundo fluvicola* Blyth
HINDI NAME : *Năhăr ăbābeel*
Handbook Vol. 5

Size: Sparrow — . **Field Characters:** Very like Dusky Crag Martin, also with short square-cut tail, but glossy steel-blue above with pale brown rump and dull chestnut forehead and crown; whitish below boldly streaked with brown on throat and upper breast. Sexes alike. Large congregations hawking insects near water. **Distribution:** Pakistan plains (excluding Sind), and eastward through Jammu and S. Kashmir along the base of the Himalayas to Sikkim duars; southward throughout the Peninsula to about Coimbatore. Local and patchy. **Habits:** Keeps in large colonies near water — canals, tanks, moats, etc., e.g., along the Ganges and Jumna canals in U.P. Hawks midges and other tiny winged insects often close over water, usually in company with other swallows and House Swifts. Utters a sharp *trr-trr* in flight. On winter mornings long, close-packed lines sun themselves on telegraph wires, till the sun is well up, at one point suddenly ' exploding ', as to a given signal, and dispersing to fly about in a scattered rabble and feed. **Nesting:** *Season* — more or less all year; principally December to April and July to October. *Nest* — colonial: a large agglomeration of mud, like a disorderly honeycomb, sometimes with hundreds of ' pots ' fused together, each with a short tubular entrance (see Plate 75). Attached under bridges over canals, or under gateway arches etc., usually near water, often within a town. *Eggs* — 3 or 4, normally white, sometimes smudged with brownish.

262. Pied Flycatcher-Shrike. *Hemipus picatus* (Sykes)
HINDI NAME :
Handbook Vol. 6

Size: Sparrow $\pm$. **Field Characters:** A small black-and-white fly-catcher-like bird with a characteristic hunchbacked profile when perched. In female, black portions replaced by sooty brown. Pairs or small parties in evergreen and moist-deciduous forest country. **Distribution:** Himalayas from Garhwal to Assam (including Nepal, Sikkim, Bhutan), foothills and up to *c.* 7000 ft; Bangladesh. All peninsular India south of Narbada river, and Ceylon; foothills and up to *c.* 6000 ft. Three races: in northern *capitalis* male has black head, brown back; in southern *picatus* black head, black back. Females of the two indistinguishable: both brown-headed, brown-backed. In Ceylonese, *leggei*, both sexes like male *picatus*, with head as well as back black. **Habits** and behaviour resemble both wood-shrikes' (*Tephrodornis*) and flycatchers'. The members of a party follow one another from tree to tree searching among the leaves for their insect food and making nimble aerial sallies after winged quarry, turning and twisting in pursuit. **Call:** Feeble squeaky notes *whi-riri, whi-riri, whi-riri*, etc., frequently uttered. **Nesting:** *Season* — overall March to June with local variations. *Nest* — a shallow saucer of rootlets, moss, etc. bound on the outside with cobwebs and attached on the upper surface of a branch 10 to 25 ft up. *Eggs* — 2 or 3, pale greenish white, blotched with inky black and with underlying marks of grey.

131

263. Lesser Whistling Teal. *Dendrocygna javanica* (Horsfield)
HINDI NAMES : *Seelhi, Seelkāhi*
Handbook Vol. 1

Size: Domestic duck — . **Field Characters:** A small pale brown and maroon-chestnut coloured duck confusable with no other of the same size except the rarer Large Whistling Teal (*D. bicolor*). Uniformly chestnut upper tail-coverts distinguish it from the latter in which they are creamy white. Sexes alike. Feeble, flapping, jaçana-like flight accompanied by the constantly uttered shrill whistling notes proclaim its identity. Small flocks on vegetation-covered tanks. **Distribution:** Resident more or less throughout the Indian Union, Bangladesh, Pakistan, Nepal (terai), Ceylon, Andaman and Nicobar islands. Subject to local movements influenced by drought and floods. **Habits:** Rests on weed-covered tanks during daytime, flighting to flooded rice fields etc. to feed during the night. Walks well on marshland, often grazing like a goose, and is a good diver. Perches freely in trees. **Food:** Largely vegetarian — shoots and grain — but also eats small fish, snails, etc. **Call:** A shrill wheezy, whistling *seasick, seasick*, uttered on the wing. **Nesting:** *Season* — chiefly the monsoon, June to October; in Ceylon also December-January. *Nest* — normally a natural tree-hollow lined with twigs and grass; sometimes built on the ground among reeds. *Eggs* — 7 to 12, ivory white. Both sexes incubate and lead the young.

264. Indian Skimmer. *Rynchops albicollis* Swainson
HINDI NAME : *Pāncheera*
Handbook Vol. 3

Size: House Crow $\pm$. **Field Characters:** A very long and pointed-winged tern-like bird of pied plumage, chiefly blackish brown above, glistening white below, with a peculiar laterally flattened knife-bladelike orange-yellow bill and bright red legs. Sexes alike; female smaller. Seen singly or in small parties flying low over the water surface in rivers. **Distribution:** Fairly common on the larger rivers in northern India—Indus, Ganges, Brahmaputra systems, etc.—south to about the Kistna; Bangladesh; Pakistan. **Habits:** Rather tern-like. Hunts actively up and down the river in daytime as well as during moonlit nights. Skims with quivering wing-tips over placid water with tip of lower mandible immersed at an angle lightly ploughing the surface, the short upper mandible raised open in readiness to snap on any fish touching the edge and hold it in a vice-like grip. The quarry is jerked into position and swallowed head foremost. **Food:** Mainly fish. **Call:** Described as a shrill, chattering scream; also as a nasal *kap, kap*. **Nesting:** *Season* — chiefly February to April. *Nest* — an unlined depression in the sand in a dry river bed or sandy islet amid stream. *Eggs* — 3 or 4, pale pinky buff to pale salmon colour or greyish white, blotched and streaked with brown. Incubation apparently by female alone. When first hatched, bill of downy chick of normal shape, like young tern's, and horn-coloured.

265. Small Pratincole or Swallow-Plover. *Glareola lactea* Temminck
HINDI NAME: *Chhōta bābuibătăn* (?)
Handbook Vol. 3

Size: Sparrow +. **Field Characters:** A sandy grey riverside bird with pointed swallow-like wings and squarish (slightly forked) tail. Underparts rufous-tinged sooty brown, belly white. A black band from eye to bill. When flying overhead the whitish underparts, black winglining, and short black-tipped white tail are leading pointers. Gregarious habit and fluttering pipistrelle-like flight further help identification. Sexes alike. Small flocks or large loose concentrations on broad rivers and streams with dry shingle beds; also at large jheels and coastal swamps, e.g. the Sunderbans. **Distribution:** Resident, nomadic, and local migrant. Practicaly all India, Nepal, Pakistan, Bangladesh and Sri Lanka. Occasionally up to *c.* 1800 m on Himalayan rivers. **Habits:** Rather crepuscular, often hunting till well after dusk. Scattered flocks hawk insects high up in the air or close to the surface, zigzagging at great speed with abrupt turns and twists. In failing light easily mistakable for small insectivorous bats. On ground runs about in short spurts, stopping abruptly to pick up a morsel in typical plover style. **Food:** Insects. **Calls:** A gecko-like *tuck-tuck-tuck*; a soft *tiririt, tiririt, tiririt*, etc. when a flock is disturbed and flying about agitatedly. **Nesting** colonial. *Season* — February to April. *Nest* — a shallow scrape in a dry sandy riverbed. *Eggs* — 2 or 3, pale sandy grey spotted and blotched with some shade of brown, admirably camouflaged. Both sexes incubate and tend the young.

266. Nilgiri Wood Pigeon. *Columba elphinstonii* (Sykes)
HINDI NAME:
Handbook Vol. 3

Size: Pigeon+. **Field Characters:** A large reddish brown forest pigeon with grey head and prominent black-and-white 'chessboard' on hindneck. Sexes alike. **Distribution:** Resident, but wandering a great deal with fruiting seasons of forest trees. The Sahyadri or Western Ghats complex from Kerala to a little north of Bombay, including the Anaimalai, Nilgiri, Palni and western Karnataka hills, up to *c.* 2000 m. **Habits:** Affects evergreen and moist-deciduous forest (sholas etc.), singly or in small flocks. Chiefly arboreal but commonly forages among the mulch on the forest floor, picking up windfallen fruit and tiny snails etc. Flies at speed through the jungle, turning and twisting expertly to avoid tree trunks and branches. Settles quietly up in trees hidden among the foliage canopy, and is seldom seen except in dashing flight. **Food:** drupes and berries, some of inordinately large size. **Call:** A langur-like *who* followed by 3 or 4 quick-repeated deeper *who-who-who*. **Nesting:** *Season* — chiefly April to June. *Nest* — a flimsy stick platform as typical of the pigeons, through which the contents are often visible from below. Placed in a moderate sized forest tree. *Egg* — a singleton, pure white.

267. **Painted Spurfowl.** *Galloperdix lunulata* (Valenciennes)
HINDI NAME: *Chhoti jāngli mūrghi*
Handbook Vol. 2

Size: Grey Partridge; same as 68. **Field Characters:** Coloured differently but otherwise similar to Red Spurfowl. Cock (illustrated) has buff-coloured breast with black spots. Hen chiefly dark olive-brown and chestnut above, with black crown. Pale olivaceous brown below; yellowish on breast with chestnut-mottled buff throat. **Distribution:** Wide but patchy; in many areas overlapping range of Red Spurfowl. Up to *c.* 1000 m elevation. Rare or absent in Rajasthan, Gujarat and coastal belt of Western Ghats. Affects bamboo jungle and thorn scrub in drier, rockier country than Red. **Habits:** Very similar to Red Spurfowl q.v. Is also a great skulker, trusting to its legs for swift escape on the slightest alarm, and reluctant to fly unless hard pressed. **Food:** Seeds, berries, drupes, insects (especially termites). **Call:** Described as a fowl-like cackling, but needs verification. **Nesting:** *Season* — principally February to May. *Nest* — a scrape in the ground lined with dry leaves, among rootstocks of a bamboo clump or under a boulder in thorn scrub, carefully hidden. *Eggs* — 3 or 4, pale buff, like small eggs of domestic fowl.

268. **Painted Bush Quail.** *Perdicula erythrorhyncha* (Sykes)
HINDI NAME: *Kōkni lowwā*
Handbook Vol. 2

Size: Grey Quail. **Field Characters:** A darkish brightly coloured quail with deep red bill and legs, eyecatching even in flight. *Female* has brick-red underparts and lacks the white throat and head stripe. Coveys in broken foothills grassland at edge of jungle. **Distribution:** Resident; local and parochial. Practically all continental and peninsular India and Bangladesh, up to *c.* 2000 m. Not Sri Lanka. Two subspecies. **Habits:** Very similar to Jungle Bush Quail (67) q.v. Keeps in coveys of 6 to 10. Comes out in open grassy patches, or on forest roads and cart tracks to feed and dust-bathe in the mornings and evenings. When flushed the birds 'explode' with a loud whirr of wings and scatter in all directions. But the covey soon reunites by the constant calling of the members to one another. **Food:** grain, grass-seeds, and insects. **Call:** Runs of soft whistles for rallying the scattered covey. A pleasant, oft-repeated triple note *kirikee, kirikee,* etc. by cocks in the breeding season. **Nesting:** *Season* — varying locally, but practically all year. *Nest* — a scrape in the ground at the root of a bush or grass clump, sometimes thinly lined with grass. *Eggs* — 4 to 7, creamy buff to *café-au-lait*, indistinguishable from Jungle Bush Quail's. Incubation by female, 16-18 days.

PLATE 67

266

268

265

267

JPIrani

0   3   6   9   12   15 cm

Plate 68

9 cm

6

3

0

269

270

271

272

269. **Nilgiri Laughing Thrush.** *Garrulax cachinnans* (Jerdon)
HINDI NAME:
Handbook Vol. 7

Size: Myna ±. **Field Characters:** An olive-brown and rufous laughing thrush. Crown and nape slaty, with a prominent white supercilium. Distinguished from Kerala Laughing Thrush (270) by its rufous, not grey, breast. Sexes alike. **Distribution:** Resident. Very common in its curiously restricted range — the Nilgiri Hills of South India, from *c.* 1200 m up to the summits. Affects dense undergrowth and lichen-covered trees in shola forest, freely entering hillstation gardens and roadside shrubbery. **Habits** reminiscent of Jungle Babbler, q.v. Parties of 6 to 12 birds often in association with mixed hunting flocks which are such a feature of the south Indian sholas. The birds hunt in the low trees, often descending to the ground to rummage among the fallen leaves. It is a great skulker and will creep away silently through cover on the least alarm, or climb up into trees hopping along the boughs, and from branch to branch, with great agility. **Food:** Insects and berries, especially wild raspberry (*Rubus* spp.) and hill guava (*Rhodomyrtus*). **Calls:** A spirited 'laughing' oft-repeated *pee-ko-ko* etc. frequently uttered in concert. Also an assortment of squeaks and squeals. Normally very noisy. **Nesting:** *Season* — February to July, chiefly May-June. *Nest* — cup-shaped, of grass, rootlets, moss and lichens, in a bush or small tree. *Eggs* — 2 or 3, pale blue spotted and blotched with reddish brown. Commonly brood-parasitized by Pied Crested Cuckoo.

270. **Kerala Laughing Thrush.** *Garrulax jerdoni fairbanki* (Blanford)
HINDI NAME:
Handbook Vol. 7

Size: Myna ±. **Field Characters:** Similar to 269 but throat and breast grey, not rufous. Sexes alike. **Distribution:** Resident. Common in the hills of N. Kerala and western Tamil Nadu (Madurai dist.) — Cardamom, Kanan Devan and Palni; High Wavy Mountains. From *c.* 1200 m to the summits, coincident with occurrence of brambles (*Rubus* spp.). Affects wild raspberry and bracken thickets at edge of sholas and along streams through tea gardens etc. Also shrubbery near hillmen's settlements and at hillstations. Two other subspecies are found in this restricted area: l. *G. j. jerdoni* (western Karnataka — Coorg and Brahmagiri Hills) which has a black chin; 2. *G. j. meridionale* (South Kerala — Ashambu Hills) which has a shorter white supercilium and grey of breast running down centre of belly. **Habits, Calls, Food, Nesting,** etc. similar in all three subspecies; same as those of Nilgiri Laughing Thrush.

271. **Wynaad Laughing Thrush.** *Garrulax delesserti* (Jerdon)
HINDI NAME:
Handbook Vol. 7

Size: Myna. **Field Characters:** An uncrested babbler, chiefly slaty grey and chestunt-brown above, ashy grey and chestnut below. Pure white throat, and broad black streak through eye. Sexes alike. Has one far-flung subspecies (*gularis*) in the eastern Himalayas, with yellow throat instead of white. **Distribution:** Resident; locally common. The Sahyadri (Western Ghats) hill complex from Goa and Belgaum south through western Karnataka, Kerala and western Tamil Nadu (Nilgiris, Palnis, etc.). Foothills and up to *c.* 1500 m. Affects humid rain forest with dense undergrowth of *Strobilanthes*, thorny cane brakes, and cardamom sholas. **Habits:** Typical of laughing thrushes. A great skulker. Noisy flocks or 'sisterhoods' of 6-10 rummage among the mulch on the forest floor, turning over or flicking aside the dry leaves in search of insects. **Food:** Insects and berries. **Calls:** Shrill chattering cackles and squeals, and discordant 'laughter' in concert. **Nesting:** *Season* — chiefly the monsoon, between April and September. *Nest* — a bulky semi-domed cup of rootlets and creeper stems etc. in a bush or sapling. *Eggs* — 3 or 4, white, unmarked.

272. **Rufous Babbler.** *Turdoides subrufus* (Jerdon)
HINDI NAME:
Handbook Vol. 6

Size: Myna —. **Field Characters:** An olive-brown and rufous babbler with deep grey forehead. Sexes alike. **Distribution:** Resident. The Sahyadri or Western Ghats complex from about Mahableshwar (Maharashtra) south through the Nilgiri, Palni, and associated hills, and Kerala. Also Shevaroy Hills in northern Tamil Nadu. Foothills and up to about 1100 m. Evergreen or moist-deciduous secondary jungle with dense scrubby undergrowth and tall grass and bamboo brakes. The Kerala population *T. s. hyperythrus* is more richly coloured than the adjacent nominate *T. s. subrufus* to the north of it. **Habits:** A skulker like the rest of its tribe. Keeps in parties of 6-8 which rummage for food on the ground among the mulch and humus. The birds clamber up among the bamboo clumps and scuttle away on alarm through the spiky tangles with the agility of a rat. **Food:** Insects, berries and flower nectar. **Calls:** A continuous shrill whistling *tree...tree...tree* in long runs, punctuated now and again by typical harsh babbler squeaks. **Nesting:** *Season* — mostly February to May. *Nest* — a rough bulky cup of dry leaves and grass, placed in a bush or small tree in abandoned overgrown clearings etc. *Eggs* — normally 4, unmarked dark blue.

273. Nilgiri Verditer Flycatcher. *Muscicapa albicaudata* Jerdon
Neelākkili (Malayalam)
Handbook Vol. 7

Size: Sparrow ±. **Field Characters:** Very like the wintering Himalayan Verditer(202) but duller coloured — more indigo-blue than bluish green — with a white patch at base of tail. *Female*: dull greenish grey, also with the distinctive white tail-patch. **Distribution:** Common resident in the hills, from *c.* 600 m to the highest summits. Southern section of the Sahyadri (Western Ghats) complex (including the Nilgiri, Palni and associated hills) southward through Kerala to the Ashambu Hills. Affects sholas, cardamom and coffee plantations, and forest glades; also gardens and roadside trees at hillstations. **Habits:** Typical flycatcher. Met with singly, often in association with Greyheaded Flycatcher (211). Launches graceful aerial sorties to capture winged insects. Perches rather upright, and switches tail up and down while calling. **Food:** Flies and gnats etc. **Call:** A series of 4 or 5 *chip*s. Song reminiscent of Pied Bushchat's; of general pattern of Verditer Flycatcher (202). **Nesting:** *Season* — chiefly March-April. *Nest* — a largish cup of moss etc. placed in hollows or holes in earth banks, walls or tree-trunks; sometimes under eaves in occupied bungalows. *Eggs* — 2 or 3, pale creamy pink freckled with reddish.

274. Whitebellied Blue Flycatcher. *Muscicapa pallipes* Jerdon
Kāttūneeli (Malayalam)
Handbook Vol. 7

Size: Sparrow ±. **Field Characters:** *Male* rather like Nilgiri Verditer (273) but with white belly. *Female*: Above, pale brown with chestnut tail; below, throat and breast orange-rufous; belly white. Distinguished from somewhat, similar Redbreasted Flycatcher (210) by *chestnut* tail instead of black-and-white. **Distribution:** Resident, fairly common in the hills of the Sahyadri (W. Ghats) complex (Nilgiri, Palni, High Wavy, etc.) from a little north of Bombay (Bhimashankar) to S. Kerala. Foothills and up to *c.* 1700 m; in evergreen biotope— sholas, cardamom ravines, dank undergrowth of seedlings, *Strobilanthes*, etc. **Habits:** Typical flycatcher, but comparatively sluggish and retiring, thus often escaping observation. Keeps singly, frequently in association with the itinerant mixed hunting flocks. Perches bolt upright, spreads tail and screws it from side to side rather like Thickbilled Flowerpecker (251). **Food:** Chiefly insects. **Call:** A low *tsk-tsk*. Song, sweet and rich though somewhat squeaky, divided into phrases of several notes. **Nesting:** *Season* — February to September. *Nest* — a rough untidy cup of grass, rootlets, moss, etc. placed on a fairly low ledge of rock or in a hole in a dead tree stump or earth bank. *Eggs* — normally 4, pale sea-green or yellowish, blotched with dark brown.

137

275. **Black-and-Orange Flycatcher.** *Muscicapa nigrorufa* (Jerdon)
Mēnippākshi
Handbook Vol. 7

Size: Sparrow —. **Field Characters:** English name adequately descriptive. *Female* similar to male (illustrated), but with the orange paler, and the head less black. **Distribution:** Resident, fairly common. Restricted to the hills of Tamil Nadu, Karnataka and Kerala (Nilgiris, Palnis, Anaimalais, etc.) south to the Ashambu Hills. From c. 1000 m to the summits; commoner above 1500 m. Evergreen biotope — dense undergrowth in sholas, at edge of coffee plantations, in dank ravines, etc. **Habits:** A 'non-conformist' flycatcher. Not shy, but unobtrusive and difficult to locate except by its soft chittering calls from depth of shrubbery. Keeps singly or in pairs hopping quietly on the ground or among the low stems and rootstocks, and flitting from bush to bush. Very parochial, frequenting the same thicket day after day. Swoops to the ground to pick up an insect and back again, very like a bushchat. Like it also switches expanded tail up and down, sometimes jerking it up to half-cocked position with wings partially drooped at sides. Rarely makes the typical flycatcher sallies to capture insects in the air. **Food:** tiny insects and caterpillars. **Call:** A high-pitched soft *chee-ri-ri-ri* and *tui-tui-tui* with variations. Song (♂), a soft whistling *whi-chee-ree-rirr*. **Nesting:** *Season* — chiefly April to June: *Nest* —a friable untidy ball of loosely put-together sedge blades(*Carex* sp.) and bamboo leaves etc. in a low bush or seedling. *Eggs* — almost invariably 2, pale greyish or buffy white freckled with reddish, more densely and in a ring round the broader end.

276. **Fairy Bluebird.** *Irena puella* (Latham)
Pana-kara-kūrūvi (Tamil); *Lalita* (Malayalam)
Handbook Vol. 6

Size: Myna+. **Field Characters:** *Female* differs from male (illustrated) being a dull blue-green all over with blackish lores. **Distribution:** Resident, subject to seasonal wandering. Humid, heavy-rainfall areas of SW. India, mainly the Sahyadri hill complex, from about Ratnagiri southward through Kerala; plains level to c. 1800 m. Disjunctly also the eastern Himalayas, and Andaman and Nicobar islands. Affects evergreen and moist-deciduous biotope — shola forest, coffee plantations, and deep jungle. **Habits:** Arboreal. Small parties of 6 to 8 birds, often in association with green pigeons, hornbills and other frugivorous birds among large fruiting trees; sometimes descending into berry-laden bushes. **Food:** Chiefly fruits, berries and flower-nectar. Also insects. **Call:** A 2-noted percussive liquid whistle *whit-tu* or *peepit* repeated every few seconds with a sharp jerking of the tail. **Nesting:** *Season* — not well defined; mainly February to April. *Nest* — distinctive; a rough platform of thickish straight twigs overlaid by green moss, leaf-ribs and rootlets. Placed in the fork of a densely foliaged tree in forest, from about 5 m up. *Eggs*—normally 2, olive-grey with irregular blotches of brown all over, more densely and in a ring round the broad end.

PLATE 69

273

276

274

275

0   3   6   9 cm

JPIrani

PLATE 70

JPIrani 1976

280

278

279

277

277. Yellowbrowed Bulbul. *Hypsipetes indicus* (Jerdon)
HINDI NAME: *Hāldi bulbūl*
Handbook Vol. 6

Size: Bulbul (Myna —). **Field Characters:** Uncrested. Olive-yellow above, lemon-yellow below, with bright yellow forehead and eyebrow (supercilium). Sexes alike. **Distribution:** Resident, locally common. The Sahyadri (W. Ghats) hill. complex, including Nilgiri, Palni, Cardamom, etc., from south of Bombay (Mahableshwar) to south Kerala. Also Sri Lanka. From *c.* 900 m to the summits; commonest between 1000 and 1500 m. Evergreen biotope — sholas, shade trees in coffee and cardamom plantations, edges of moist jungle, etc. Three subspecies on shades of coloration. **Habits:** Arboreal. In noisy parties of 5 to 7; sometimes gatherings of 50+ where food is plentiful. Often forms the nucleus of the mixed feeding bird flocks. Forages among lofty fruit-laden trees as well as low bushes; winged insects flushed in the process seized in the air. **Food:** Mainly drupes and berries; also insects, spiders, and flower-nectar. **Call:** A clear mellow double whistle, frequently uttered. **Nesting:** *Season —* February to May. *Nest —* unconventional for bulbul; more like oriole's: deep round cup slung hammockwise in a horizontal fork of twigs, 2 or 3 m up in a sapling in thick cover. *Eggs —* 2 or 3, pale creamy pink freckled and blotched with red, more densely at broad end.

278. Black Bulbul. *Hypsipetes madagascariensis* (P.L.S. Müller)
HINDI NAME:
Handbook Vol. 6

Size: Bulbul (Myna —). **Field Characters:** A slaty grey, black-crested bulbul with slightly forked tail and bright red bill and legs. Sexes alike. **Distribution:** Resident, with local movements. The Sahyadri (W. Ghats) hill complex, including Nilgiri, Palni, and other hills in Karnataka and Kerala, from near Bombay (Matheran) southward. Also Shevaroy Hills (Tamil Nadu). From *c.* 700 m to the summits. Affects evergreen and moist-deciduous forest, hillstation gardens, etc. Besides the South Indian subspecies (*ganeesa*) there are 3 others differing in details, respectively in the Himalayas, Assam hills and Sri Lanka. **Habits:** Arboreal. Noisy boisterous parties of 6 to 10, sometimes large flocks, in the foliage canopy of lofty forest trees, flying in rabbles from tree to tree, commonly keeping company with the mixed hunting flocks. Seldom descends to bushes. Often launches short twisting sallies from treetops to capture insects in the air. **Food:** Mainly fruits and berries; also insects and flower-nectar. **Call:** An assortment of loud sharp squeaky whistles *chirp, chee-chee-chee* or *whew whé* etc. **Nesting:** *Season—* chiefly May-July. *Nest —* a neat but flimsy cup of grass, dead leaves, moss, lichen bound with cobwebs and lined with rootlets, fine grass, etc., 10 m or more up in the fork of a horizontal branch. *Eggs —* 2 to 4, pale pink covered all over with tiny blotches of red- or purple-brown and grey.

139

279. Whitebellied Tree Pie. *Dendrocitta leucogastra* Gould
Kātu nāli (Malayalam)
Handbook Vol. 5

Size: Myna, + with long tail. **Field Characters:** Distinguished from the common Tree Pie (183) by chestnut back and pure white hindneck, rump and underparts. A large white patch on the black wings, and long graduated grey-and-black tail conspicuous in undulating flight. Sexes alike. **Distribution:** Resident; local and patchy. The Sahyadri (W. Ghats) heavy-rainfall strip from Goa and Belgaum southward‚through W. Karnataka, Nilgiri Hills and Kerala; foothills and up to *c.* 1500 m. Not Sri Lanka. Confined to evergreen biotope: dense forest, cardamom sholas, secondary jungle on abandoned forest clearings, etc. **Habits:** Very similar to those of the more familiar Tree Pie (183). Pairs or family parties, commonly associated with the mixed itinerant bird flocks; almost unfailingly with Racket-tailed Drongo. **Food:** Omnivorous. Fruits, large insects, small birds and rodents, and other living things. **Call:** Various notes, harsh as well as musical. In courtship a throaty *chuff-chuff-chuff* with ludicrous bowing and jumping stiffly up and down on the perch like a clockwork toy, forepart of body depressed and tail half-cocked. **Nesting:** *Season* — February to April. *Nest* — a stick platform like a crow's, the inner cup lined with soft rootlets etc. *Eggs* — 4 or 5, very variously coloured: creamy, reddish white or greenish white, blotched and streaked with shades of brown and lilac, the markings often confined to the broader end in a ring or cap.

280. Bluewinged Parakeet. *Psittacula columboides* (Vigors)
HINDI NAME: *Mădăngour tota* (bird dealers)
Handbook Vol. 5

Size: Myna + with long pointed tail. **Field Characters:** Similar to Blossomheaded Parakeet (137), but greyish green rather than yellowish green, with a brilliant bluegreen and black collar. Conspicuous blue wings and tail, the latter with yellow (*v.* white) tips. No maroon-red shoulder-patch. *Female* lacks verditer collar behind black neck-ring. **Distribution:** The Sahyadri (W. Ghats) complex, including Nilgiri, Palni and associated hills, from a little south of Bombay to south Kerala; chiefly between *c.* 500 and 1500 m. Not Sri Lanka. Evergreen and moist-deciduous biotope — foothills woodland, and around hillmen's cultivation. **Habits:** Keeps in noisy parties of 4 or 5 or small flocks. Abandoned forest clearings with relict trees and secondary jungle are among its favourite haunts. Flight and general ecology as of Blossomheaded Parakeet which is addicted to a dry-deciduous forest habitat. **Food:** Grain and fruits, especially wild figs (*Ficus*); also flower-petals and nectar. **Call:** A harsh, distinctive double-noted cry *che-chwé*, rather reminiscent of Paradise Flycatcher's but much louder and shriller; uttered chiefly on the wing. **Nesting** *Season* — January to March. *Nest* — a woodpecker- or barbet-hole in a tree trunk in forest, 6 to 30 m up. *Eggs* — normally 4, white, spherical.

281. **Mottled Wood Owl.** *Strix ocellata* (Lesson)

HINDI NAME:

Handbook Vol. 3

Size: Pariah Kite ±; dumpier and shorter tailed. **Field Characters:** A medium-sized vermiculated reddish brown owl without ear-tufts. Facial disc white with fine concentric black bars. Throat white-stippled chestnut and black. A white half-collar on foreneck. Sexes alike. Large amount of yellowish buff in wings conspicuous in flight. Singly or pairs in ancient leafy trees. **Distribution:** Practically all India from the Himalayas to Kerala and Punjab to Bengal. Not Assam or Sri Lanka. **Habits:** Crepuscular and nocturnal. Keeps to lightly wooded plains country. Partial to mango topes and groves of tamarind, banyan, etc. on village outskirts and in cultivation. Is of great ecomic benefit as destroyer of rodent pests. **Call:** A loud, somewhat eerie but pleasant quavering *chūhūaaa*. Also a single mellow hoot from time to time during night. **Food:** Rats, mice and squirrels; lizards, crabs, beetles, other large insects, etc. **Nesting:** *Season* — November to April. *Nest* — a natural unlined hollow in an ancient tree trunk. *Eggs* — 2, sometimes 3, roundish, creamy white. Incubation by both sexes; period unknown.

282. **Brown Hawk-Owl.** *Ninox scutulata* (Raffles)

HINDI NAME: *Chūghǎd bǎsra*

Handbook Vol. 3

Size: Pigeon ±. **Field Characters:** Very hawk-like in appearance and movements. Dark greyish brown above, white below barred with reddish brown. Throat and foreneck brown-streaked fulvous. Sexes alike. **Distribution:** Practically the entire subcontinent from the outer Himalayan foothills in Pakistan eastward to Assam and Bangladesh southward to Kerala and Sri Lanka. Also Andaman and Nicobar islands. Four subspecies. Plains and up to *c.* 1500 m elevation, in forest and well-wooded country with groves of trees along streams and nalas, often close to habitation. **Habits:** Crepuscular and nocturnal, spending the daytime in shady trees. *Flight* — rapid wing-beats and glides strikingly hawk-like. **Call:** Distinctive and diagnostic. Rather soft, musical *oo...ūk...oo...ūk*, etc. in runs of 6 to 20 repetitions. Very vocal during breeding season. **Food:** Large insects, frogs, lizards, mice, small birds, etc. **Nesting:** *Season* — overall January to July, varying locally. *Nest* — a natural hollow in a tree trunk. *Eggs* — 3 or 4, white, roundish. Incubation evidently by both sexes: period once recorded 24 days.

283. Greyheaded Fishing Eagle. *Ichthyophaga ichthyaetus* (Horsfield)

HINDI NAME: *Mădhuya*

Handbook Vol. 1

Size: Kite+. **Field Characters:** A dark brown eagle with grey head and neck. Belly, flanks and tail white, the last with a broad black terminal band. In overhead flight shortish black-ended white·tail, and white belly and vent, diagnostic. Sexes alike. In well watered, well wooded plains country. **Distribution:** All India from the Himalayan tarai south to Kerala, east to Assam and Bangladesh. Absent in Pakistan and semi-desert areas of NW. India. A smaller endemic subspecies in Sri Lanka. **Habits:** Affects perennial forest streams and pools, lakes, and tidal lagoons. Keeps singly or in widely spaced pairs, sitting bolt upright on boughs overhanging a stream or waterhole. Captures fish from near the surface by pouncing from the lookout post or swooping from the air, not by plunging like osprey. **Call:** A weird clanging scream or shout, uttered singly or in quick succession. **Food:** Fish, birds and small mammals. **Nesting:** *Season*— chiefly November to March. *Nest* — a huge stick platform in a large tree, usually near water. *Eggs* — 2 or 3, rarely 4, white, unmarked. Both sexes share the domestic chores. Incubation period 28-30 days.

284. Pied Harrier. *Circus melanoleucos* (Pennant)

HINDI NAME: *Pahātai*

Handbook Vol. 1

Size: Kite – ; slimmer. **Field Characters:** A slim and elegant long-winged raptor of contrasting black-and-white plumage. Female dark brown above with whitish rump; rufous below. Confusable with other female harriers in the field. Usually met with in widely separated pairs. **Distribution:** Winter visitor chiefly to the eastern side of the subcontinent — Assam, Bengal, Orissa, Bangladesh, etc. Also Sri Lanka, and sporadically elsewhere in the Peninsula. Affects open grassland, plain and hill, and paddy stubbles. **Habits:** Very similar to the Pale (cf. 48) and other harriers of the genus. **Call:** Not heard in its winter quarters. **Food:** As of other harriers — lizards, frogs, field mice, grasshoppers, etc. **Nesting:** Mainly extralimital (Siberia, Mongolia, N. China, etc.); occasionally and sparsely also breeds in Manipur and Cachar. *Season* — April to July (?). *Nest* —a rough pad of grasses on the ground in open grassland. *Eggs* — 4 to 6, white, sometimes with faint reddish flecks.

PLATE 71

281

282

283

284

♂

♀

PLATE 72

285

♂

286

♀

287

288

KRJADAV

285. Great Stone Plover. *Esacus magnirostris* (Cuvier)

HINDI NAME: *Băda kărwānăk*

Handbook Vol. 3

Size: Domestic hen. **Field Characters.** An enlarged edition of Stone Curlew (101): greyish sandy above, white below. Stout black-and-yellow upturned bill, and enormous yellow 'goggle' eyes. In flight the peculiar arched profile of the back, and round white wing-patch diagnostic. Sexes alike. **Distribution:** Mainly resident with some local movements. All India, Nepal, Pakistan, Bangladesh, Sri Lanka. Rocky river-beds and their dry environs: sometimes sea beaches, tidal estuaries and salt pans. **Habits:** As of Stone Curlew (101). Largely crepuscular and nocturnal. Pairs or small parties of 4 or 5; sometimes small flocks. A fast runner: also swims on occasion, riding water high like duck. **Food:** Mainly crabs from under stones prised up with the specially adapted bill. Also other small animals found in its habitat. **Call:** Quite unlike Stone Curlew's: a single harsh creaking note. **Nesting:** *Season* — February to June/July. *Nest* —a shallow scrape in an exposed sandy river-bed: sometimes even lays on bare sheet rock. *Eggs* — very cryptically coloured like Stone Curlew's: pale buff to olive green, blotched with brownish or purplish. Both sexes incubate and tend the young.

286. Kora or Watercock. *Gallicrex cinerea* (Gmelin)

HINDI NAME: *Kora, Kāngıra*

Handbook Vol. 2

Size: Partridge +. **Field Characters:** A rail-like swamp bird. In non-breeding plumage both sexes like the smaller female. Breeding male black, with a bright red fleshy 'horn' above crown, and bright red legs and eyes. **Distribution:** All India south of the Himalayas from Pakistan to Assam and Bangladesh and south to Kanyakumari and Sri Lanka. Also Andaman and Nicobar islands. **Habits:** Marsh haunting; rail-like. Keeps singly or pairs. Largely crepuscular, emerging cautiously into open at dusk or dawn, and in cloudy overcast weather. Saunters to feed at edge of shrubbery, and scuttles into cover on least alarm. Male highly pugnacious in breeding season. **Food:** Largely vegetarian — seeds, and green shoots of rice etc.; also insects and molluscs. **Call:** A series of hollow metallic booming *ūtūmb-ūtūmb-ūtūmb* etc. rapidly repeated. Also others. **Nesting:** *Season* — chiefly SW. monsoon, June to September. *Nest* — a deep cup-shaped pad of sedges, grass, etc. in a flooded ricefield or reedy marsh. *Eggs* —3 to 6 or 8, like coot's eggs, varying from white or pinkish to brick-red, longitudinally blotched and spotted with reddish brown. Details of incubation etc. unknown.

287. Slatylegged Banded Crake. *Rallina euryzonoides*
(Lafresnaye)

HINDI NAME:

Handbook Vol. 2

Size: Partridge –. **Field Characters:** A marsh-haunting rail, largely rufous brown. Throat and underparts (below breast) white, the latter conspicuously barred with black. Sexes alike. **Habits:** Crepuscular and partly nocturnal. Usually seen singly on the edge of shrubbery in a marsh, sauntering about with upright carriage and high-stepping gait, wings partly drooping at sides, tail slightly cocked and twitched from time to time. Runs to cover on the slightest alarm. Swims jerkily like moorhen for short distances. **Food:** Insects, molluscs, shoots and seeds of marsh plants. **Call:** A double note *kek-kek* persistently repeated during night. Also various other calls. **Nesting:** *Season* — SW. monsoon, June to September. *Nest* — an untidy cup-like pad of grasses etc. in a bamboo clump or tangle of creepers up to a metre or so from the ground in dense undergrowth or scrub jungle. *Eggs* — 4 to 8, creamy white, fairly glossy. Both sexes incubate and tend the young. Incubation period unrecorded.

288. Baillon's Crake. *Porzana pusilla* (Pallas)
HINDI NAME: *Jhilli*

Handbook Vol. 2

Size: Quail ±. **Field Characters:** A typical marsh-dwelling rail. Dwarf size, rufescent olive-brown back streaked with blackish and spattered with narrow white paint-like smears, and unspotted grey breast, diagnostic. Sexes alike. **Distribution:** Breeds abundantly in Kashmir and probably elsewhere within our limits. Widespread in the subcontinent including Sri Lanka and Andamans. Affects reedy marshes and jheels. **Habits:** Keeps singly or in pairs. Trips lightly over floating vegetation in search of food or swims across narrow channels, twitching up the stub tail from time to time like moorhen. A great skulker like its other relations, but tame and confiding where undisturbed. **Food:** Mainly seeds of water plants; also insects and molluscs. **Call:** A single loud, high-pitched *krek* followed by a rapid succession of *kreks* in rising tempo, reminiscent of the trilling of a dabchick. **Nesting:** *Season* — May to August. *Nest* — a pad of grass at the base of a bush in a swamp or flooded rice field. *Eggs* — 5 to 8 or 9, olive or pale brown, streaked and flecked reddish brown. Both sexes incubate. Period 20-21 days.

289. **Maroonbacked Imperial Pigeon.** *Ducula badia* (Raffles)
HINDI NAME: *Dūkūl* (Nepal)
Handbook Vol. 3

Size: Jungle Crow. **Field Characters:** A large arboreal forest
pigeon: dull olive-brown or copper-brown above, with greyish
head, neck and underparts. Sexes alike. In heavy moist forest.
Distribution: Disjunct. East · Himalayan duars and foothills up
to *c.* 2300 m; Kerala, W. Karnataka, W. Tamilnadu (Nilgiris,
Palnis to *c.* 2000 m). 3 subspecies. **Habits:** Pairs or small flocks
in tall forest trees, usually hidden in foliage canopy. Seen mostly
on the wing. Flight swift, but leisurely-looking, rather crowlike in distance. Has a spectacular switchback aerial courtship
display, reminiscent of both Blackbellied Finch-Lark (243) and
Roller (139). **Food:** Exclusively fruit, chiefly banyan and other
wild figs, nutmegs, etc. Gullet and gape enormously extensible,
capable of swallowing very large drupes. **Call:** A deep, far-carry-
ing, booming *ūk-ōok...ōok.* **Nesting:** *Season*—March to August
(north); January to May (south). *Nest* — sketchy platform of
twigs in small tree, usually hidden among tangled creepers.
Eggs — a singleton (rarely 2) white, glossy. Incubation by both
sexes. Period undetermined.

290. **Greyfronted Green Pigeon.** *Treron pompadora* (Gmelin)
HINDI NAME: *Hǎriǎl* (for all green pigeons)
Handbook Vol. 3

Size: Pigeon –. **Field Characters:** Very like Common Green
Pigeon (107) but smaller, and with red legs instead of yellow.
Sexes dissimilar: male with prominent chestnut mantle. **Distribution:** Wide: five subspecies within our limits of which the
peninsular *affinis* here illustrated and described. Southwestern
India from a little north of metropolitan Bombay to Kerala.
In lowland forest and well-wooded country, and up to *c.* 1200
m in the Ghats. The endemic subspecies, *pompadora,* of Sri
Lanka has the forehead yellow. **Habits:** As of other green
pigeons. Small flocks of a dozen or so in fruiting trees such
as banyan and peepal, effectively camouflaged among the foliage
and gorging themselves, often in company with barbets, mynas
and other frugivorous birds. **Food:** Exclusively fruit and berries; wild figs specially favoured. **Call:** Musical mellow whistles
up and down the scale, very like those of the Yellowlegged
(107) but somewhat higher in key. **Nesting:** *Season* — December
to March. *Nest* — a flimsy platform of twigs in a moderate-
sized tree. *Eggs* — 2, white. Both sexes share all domestic
chores.

291. Haircrested Drongo. *Dicrurus hottentottus* (Linnaeus)

HINDI NAME: *Kishenrāj, Kesrāj*

Handbook Vol. 5

Size: Myna ±, with longer tail. **Field Characters:** A glossy, spangled, blue-black drongo with longish slightly forked tail, outwardly upcurled at the ends. Sexes alike. **Distribution:** Practically the entire subcontinent—except Pakistan, the dry NW. portions and Sri Lanka — from the Himalayan tarai and foothills south to Kerala; in suitable moist-deciduous forest country, plains and foothills, rarely even up to *c.* 2000 m (E. Himalayas). **Habits:** Keeps singly or in pairs and small parties. Forest-haunting, arboreal and largely nectar-eating, the long and noticeably curved bill specially adapted for the function. Local movements largely governed by the flowering seasons of its favourite blossoms such as Silk Cotton or Semal (*Bombax*). **Food:** Flower-nectar and large insects. **Call:** A subdued musical metallic clanging note, constantly uttered. Is also a good mimic of other birds' calls. **Nesting:** *Season*—April to June (north), March-April (south). *Nest* — typical drongo's: a deep flimsy-bottomed saucer of grass, rootlets, etc. in a horizontal fork at the end of a branch. *Eggs* — 3 or 4, variable, creamy to salmon pink, minutely freckled with reddish. Both sexes share all domestic chores. Incubation period unrecorded.

292. Caspian Tern. *Hydroprogne caspia* (Pallas)

HINDI NAME:

Handbook Vol. 5

Size: Jungle Crow+. **Field Characters:** Our largest tern, recognized also by its very large, stout coral-red bill, and black legs and feet. In winter plumage head largely white, streaked on crown with black. Sexes alike. **Distribution:** Chiefly winter visitor, but breeds sparingly also in Pakistan and Sri Lanka. Affects sea coast, estuaries and large lakes, e.g. Chilka. **Habits:** Not very different from other terns' (cf. 88, 104). Usually seen in twos and threes in company with other species. Sometimes alights on water like a gull, but normally rests on ground. **Food.** Fish, prawns, swimming crabs, etc. captured by plunging from air. **Call:** A loud, raucous *krake-kra*, **Nesting:** Colonial, on islands off Makran coast and sandbanks off Mannar (Sri Lanka), along with other terns. *Season* — May-June. *Nest* — a shallow scrape in sand. *Eggs* — 2 or 3, very variable, pale yellowish to dark greyish stone colour, blotched with blackish and grey. Both sexes incubate; period *c.* 20-22 days.

Plate 73

289

290

291

292

0   1   2   3   4   INCHES

K.R.JADAV

Plate 74

293

295

♂

♂

294

♀

♀

296

♀

0 1 2 3 4 5 INCHES

K.P.JADAV

293. **Small Greenbilled Malkoha.** *Rhopodytes viridirostris*
(Jerdon)

HINDI NAME: *Kappra, Popiya*

Handbook Vol. 3

Size: House Crow – ; slimmer, with longer tail. **Field Characters:** A greenish ashy grey non-parasitic cuckoo with suffused rufous underparts. Bright green bill; naked blue patch round eye; long, broad, graduated, conspicuously white-tipped tail. Sexes alike. Singly or pairs skulking in dry thorn jungle. **Distribution:** Resident; locally common. Peninsular India from Gujarat to Orissa and south to Kanyakumari. Keeps to rather dry scrub-and-bush, plains and broken foothills country with euphorbia and lantana thickets, up to *c.* 1000 m elevation. **Habits:** Reminiscent of Crow-Pheasant. Creeps through thickets and clambers actively among branches of low trees, rarely descending to the ground. Is a poor flier, seldom seen on the wing except when making from one thicket to another. **Food:** Caterpillars, large insects (grasshoppers, mantises, etc.), lizards and other small animals; probably also some berries. **Call:** Usually silent. A low croak, *kraa,* sometimes heard. **Nesting:** *Season*—chiefly March to May, but also other months. *Nest*—an untidy platform of thorny twigs like a dove's nest, at moderate height in a euphorbia bush, bamboo brake and the like. *Eggs*—Normally 2, chalky white, roundish. Period of incubation and share of the sexes undetermined.

294. **Southern Trogon.** *Harpactes fasciatus* (Pennant)

HINDI NAME: *Kufni chidi* (?)

Handbook Vol. 4

Size: Myna ± , with longer tail. **Field Characters:** A brilliantly coloured arboreal forest bird with relatively long, broad and curiously truncated graduated tail. Sexes dissimilar. Singly or widely separated pairs in evergreen or moist-deciduous forest and mixed foothills bamboo jungle. **Distribution:** Peninsular India south of Gujarat and Khandesh, chiefly the more humid tracts of the Western and Eastern Ghats, and Sri Lanka. Locally up to *c.* 1800 m. **Habits:** Perches bolt upright and motionless for long periods on tree stumps and low branches, making occasional agile sallies after winged insects. **Food:** Caterpillars, beetles, cicadas and other insects. Also some leaves and berries. **Call:** A throaty musical *cue* or *mew* usually repeated in unhurried runs of 3 or 4. **Nesting:** *Season*—overall February to June. *Nest*—an unlined natural hollow in a low tree stump in deep forest. *Eggs*—2-4 roundish, glossy ivory white. Incubation by both sexes; period unrecorded.

295. Heartspotted Woodpecker. *Hemicircus canente* (Lesson)

HINDI NAME:

Handbook Vol. 4

Size: Sparrow +. **Field Characters.** A small, squat black-and-buff woodpecker with a short thin neck, large crested head, and a strikingly stumpy rounded tail. Sexes dissimilar. Pairs in deciduous forest. **Distribution:** Peninsular India from Kerala north to Gujarat and Khandesh, and east to west Bengal, Assam and Bangladesh. Plains and foothills up to *c.* 1300 m. Affects moist-deciduous biotope; partial to teak and bamboo forest. **Habits:** Pairs frequently seen with the mixed hunting parties of insectivorous birds, jerkily creeping along the terminal twigs of trees and tapping on them to dislodge lurking insects. Often perches crosswise on a branch like a passerine bird or its relative the Wryneck. **Food:** Ants, termites, grubs, etc. **Call:** A characteristic harsh but not unpleasant trill of 7 or 8 *twee, twee, twee* notes. A sharp double *tchlik-tchlik* in flight. Also drums on branches during the breeding season. **Nesting:** *Season*—chiefly November to April. *Nest*—a tiny hole drilled in a dead branch 3 or 4 m up; sometimes higher or lower. *Eggs*—3, sometimes 2, white, unmarked. Incubation period and share of the sexes unrecorded.

296. Small Yellownaped Woodpecker. *Picus chlorolophus* Vieillot

HINDI NAME:

Handbook Vol. 4

Size: Myna +. **Field Characters:** A medium-sized yellowish green woodpecker with golden yellow nuchal crest. Sexes dissimilar. In secondary jungle. **Distribution:** The lower Himalayas (including tarai, bhabar and duars) from Punjab eastward to Assam. Southward practically the entire Peninsula to Kerala; moist-deciduous and semi-evergreen biotope, locally up to *c.* 2100 m. Partial to foothills country. Three subspecies in India, and a fourth in Sri Lanka. **Habits:** Typical woodpecker. Usually met with in pairs, often among the mixed hunting parties of drongos, minivets, babblers, flycatchers and other insectivorous birds. Commonly descends to the ground to pick ants etc. **Food:** Ants, termites, beetle larvae, etc. Occasionally berries. **Call:** A single long-drawn nasal scream—*cheenk*—by both sexes, repeated monotonously at several seconds' interval for prolonged periods at a time. Also other vocalizations and drumming on wood as characteristic of the family. **Nesting:** *Season*—overall January to July, chiefly April-May. *Nest*—a hole excavated by the birds in the trunk or branch of a forest tree, 3 to 7 m up. *Eggs*—2, white, blunt ovals. Incubation period, and share of the sexes, undetermined.

SOME NESTS AND NESTING BEHAVIOUR

IN the Introduction I said that ' For the safety of their eggs and young, birds build nests which may range from a simple scrape in the ground, as of the Lapwing, to such elaborate structures as the compactly woven nest of the Weaver Bird '. To complete the picture, it may be added that most birds incubate their eggs with the heat of their bodies by brooding them, and show considerable solicitude for their young until they are able to fend for themselves. In this chapter I shall consider the main types of nests built by Indian birds and deal briefly with the nesting behaviour of some of the builders.

Nesting seasons

Broadly speaking, the majority of our resident birds have more or less well-marked seasons in which they lay their eggs and rear their young. The periods favoured by different species vary somewhat in the different portions of their distribution, depending upon geographical position and local climatic conditions. The season in India as a whole is perhaps nowhere as clearcut as in the Temperate and Arctic zones. In the lower Himalayas and the country about their base, most species commence their nesting operations with the advent of Spring, which may be put down as the beginning of March. The farther south one moves towards the Equator the more equable does the climate become, so that the most important seasonal change in those parts is the one brought about by the monsoons, particularly the South-west Monsoon. Birds that nest in tree-holes, as well as the ground-nesting species, must be discharged of their parental duties before the onset of the SW. Monsoon in June. In North India it is of vital importance for such birds as nest on sandbanks in the larger rivers to have finished their activities before the rivers swell in summer due to melting of the Himalayan snows. Therefore, March and April are the principal months in which to look for the eggs of river birds.

The SW. Monsoon — June/July to September/October — is the time when the annual vegetation is at the height of its luxuriance and insect life at its peak. In these respects the season corresponds to Spring in the more northerly latitudes. A large section of Indian birds of diverse families and species find optimum conditions for bringing up families during this period of plenty. By about mid October the majority of young birds of the monsoon-breeding species have left their nests. The raptors, or birds of prey, commence their nesting activities about this period and are busy throughout the winter months up till about the end of February. It is often quite late in March or even the middle of April before the young of some of the larger forms — vultures and eagles — have launched into the world. Young raptors have astonishingly healthy appetites. The continuous supply of animal food the parents are obliged to procure for them makes the choice of this season a happy one; young birds are then plentiful and easily hunted, and their numbers are augmented by vast hordes of winter immigrants from beyond our borders.

Territory, courtship and song

Individual breeding pairs usually occupy a ' Territory ' in the surroundings of their nest which is treated as their special preserve and
into which intrusion by other members of the same species is regarded
as an unfriendly act, to be actively resented. The acquisition of breeding territories is a fairly general practice among birds, but not universal.
Their existence is particularly noticeable in the more aggressive species,
like the Black Drongo. Territory is acquired by the male. In migrant
species this accounts in a measure for the fact that on Spring passage
when journeying to their breeding grounds, the males usually precede
the females. Having arrived in the breeding locality, the male proceeds
to stake out and establish possession of an area, usually more or less
definable and varying in extent according to species and to the density
of its avian population. In the process it may have to fight for ownership with another male already in occupation, or in defence of its
territory against an interloper. Once in secure possession, the male
awaits the arrival of the body of females and advertises his presence
and the availability of a nesting site by singing full-throatedly from
exposed situations. The song serves not only to attract likely females,
but also as a warning to rival males to keep off. Having secured a
female, in the process of which again there is often much active hostility
between rival males, courtship displays commence. These take numerous forms; fluffing out of the ornamental plumage, fanning and
erecting the tail and dancing or posturing in front of the female, as
in the Peacock and many pheasants, being some of the more spectacular. The extravagant aerial contortions of shooting skywards and
nose-diving to the accompaniment of raucous screams indulged in
by the Roller or ' Blue Jay ' in love are a familiar sight at the commencement of the hot weather. There is an infinite variety of courtship
behaviour ranging from the sublime to the ridiculous. Again, Song —
which reaches the climax of its intensity in the breeding season — plays
a predominating part in the courtship ceremonials of certain birds,
the skylark and thrush for example. All this feverish activity is indulged in either by one partner or by both, and has for its ultimate
object the rousing of the necessary physiological response for successful
breeding.

In birds where the sexes differ in coloration it is the male who is the
more showy and who takes the initiative in the display and courtship
ceremonials (except in the case of polyandrous species where the
normal conditions are reversed). In birds where the sexes are outwardly alike, as in larks and pipits, they apparently recognise each
other's sex only by the mutual response to each other's behaviour.

Coloration of eggs

The colour patterns of birds' eggs are almost as varied as the birds
themselves, or as the architecture of their nests. Egg-coloration
suggests an advanced stage of evolution; the ancestors of birds —
the Reptiles — lay only white eggs. Birds that nest in tree-holes or
earth-tunnels also lay white eggs since, as in reptiles, the required

Redwattled Lapwing and nest

PLATE 75

Photo: *Auth*

Mixed heronry of Cormorants, Painted Storks and White Ibises

PLATE 76

protection is afforded them by the situation. It cannot be denied that in the main the coloration of eggs is a protective device and in a general way bears a direct relation to the types of nests in which they are laid. The eggs of the Yellow-wattled Lapwing deposited on barren, open wasteland, and of the Tern in a sandy river bed are convincing examples. They match the soil and blend with their surroundings to such perfection that they are quite invisible at a few feet's distance even when diligently looked for. The eggs of the Pheasant-tailed Jaçana, often laid directly upon floating singāra (*Trapa*) leaves, resemble the surrounding olive-brown vegetation so closely as to be completely obliterated from view (pl. 80). Anomalies, however, are not wanting. Thus the eggs of the Rain Quail laid in grassland are obliterative, whereas those of the Bush Quail, laid in not much more sheltered sites, are white!

Types of nests

The following are the main types of birds' nests found in India:

1. Simple scrapes in the ground sparsely lined with grass and leaves, e.g. quail, junglefowl and other game birds, or with no semblance of lining, e.g. tern and lapwing (pl. 75). Protection is secured by the eggs and young of such birds through their remarkably obliterative coloration.

2. Twig nests like platforms with a cup-like depression in the centre usually lined with softer material — grass, tow, feathers, etc. This type, built in trees or on buildings or cliffs, is common to a large number of birds of different families, e.g. crow, kite, dove, vulture, cormorant, stork (pl. 76), etc.

3. Nests in tree-holes either excavated in living or decayed wood, or in natural hollows, and either with a sparse lining of soft material or unlined, e.g. tits, Yellowthroated Sparrow, woodpeckers, barbets, hornbills (pl. 78), owls, some mynas and most of our resident ducks (pl. 81). The holes are in the first instance cut by woodpeckers, parakeets or barbets and subsequently appropriated in rotation by many other species. Nesting in natural tree hollows is a common habit among our resident ducks, all of whom breed during the SW. Monsoon. The raised situation gives security against sudden rise of water level in the jheels due to cloud-bursts or the swelling of streams flowing into them. The ducklings reach the water by tumbling out of the nest and are not carried down by the parents as has sometimes been asserted.

4. Nests in excavated tunnels in earth-banks, or in clefts of buildings, rock cliffs, etc., e.g. bee-eaters, kingfishers, hoopoe. The tunnels are driven horizontally into the side of an earth-cutting or bank of a stream, the bird using its bill to dig and its feet to kick back the loose earth. The tunnels are from a few inches to several feet in length and usually bent near the extremity where they widen into a bulbous egg chamber.

5. Nests built entirely of mud or in which mud predominates, e.g. Whistling Thrush, blackbirds, swallows (pl. 83),

martins. The wet mud is commonly collected at rain puddles. It is mixed with a certain amount of saliva in the case of swallows. There is a marked increase in the size of the salivary glands of these birds and swifts during the breeding season. Swallows' nests have perforce to be built very gradually, pellet by pellet, so that not too much of the material is daubed on at one time before the underlying layer is sufficiently dry.

6. Cup-shaped nests of grass and fibres in crotches or forks of branches, usually well plastered over with cobwebs, e.g. Iora, fantail and other flycatchers, orioles (pls. 77, 79, 82), white-eye, minivets, reed warblers, cuckoo-shrikes, etc. Cobwebs are very extensively employed as cement in bird architecture, for binding the material compactly and neatly together. It is collected by being twisted round and round the bill and is then unwound and attached on the exterior of the nest, or used in securing the nest into position.

7. Domed or ball-shaped nests of twigs, grass or rootlets with a lateral entrance hole, e.g. munias, Rufousbellied Babbler.

8. Pendant nests, e.g. weaver birds (woven), sunbirds, flowerpeckers. The sunbird's nest is a vertical oblong pouch suspended from the tip of a thin outhanging twig, usually not high above the ground. It has an entrance hole at the side with a little projecting porch over it. The exterior is draped untidily with pieces of bark, caterpillar droppings, and spiders' egg-cases which give it an effective camouflage. The flowerpecker's nest is a hanging pouch of the same general pattern, but made entirely of seed- and vegetable down worked into a felt-like fabric.

9. Woven oblong purse—loofah-like—attached to stems of tall grass or low bushes, e.g. wren-warblers (alternative to the next type).

10. Nest in leaves stitched together in the form of a funnel, e.g. Tailor Bird (pl. 79), Franklin's Wren-Warbler, Ashy Wren-Warbler.

There are yet other nests of less conventional design. The edible-nest swiftlets which breed in vast colonies, attach their half-saucer shaped nests made entirely of the birds' saliva or with an admixture of straw and feathers, to the sides of the rock in dark grottoes and caves on islands in the sea. The Palm Swift makes a rather similar nest but with more feathers reinforcing it, attached to the leaves of the Palmyra palm and usually well concealed among the furrows. The Rufous Woodpecker makes its home in the carton-nests of certain tree ants, and seems to live on terms of amity with the insects.

A distinction must be made between birds that nest in individual pairs in usually well-recognised territories, like the Black Drongo for example, and those that nest in colonies. Some familiar examples of the latter are the weaver birds, cliff swallows, common and edible-nest swifts, and water birds such as storks, cormorants and herons.

Whatever its pattern, the nest is always true to the type of the species that builds it, and is primarily the outcome of instinct fixed and inherited through countless generations of builders. That a young Baya in its first season builds a nest exactly like the one in which it was

Photo: Christina Loke

Paradise Flycatcher (sub-adult male) at nest

PLATE 77

Malabar Pied Hornbill (*Anthracoceros coronatus*)

Male feeding young in nest

(Note the diagnostic all-white outer tail feathers)

PLATE 78

Tailor Bird and nest

PLATE 79

Photo: Loke Wan Tho

Pheasant-tailed Jacana and floating nest

PLATE 80

Nakta duck at nest in tree trunk

PLATE 81

Golden Oriole and hammock nest

PLATE 82

Colony of mud nests of Cliff Swallow

Photo: *Author*

PLATE 83

'Flamingo City'—Great Rann of Kutch

PLATE 84

born is neither the result of training by its parents nor of intelligence as we understand it. The architecture may be improved and perfected with practice, but the design will remain constant. Experiments have shown that birds hatched in an incubator who can therefore have no idea of the sort of nest built by their kind, will, at the appointed time, build nests after their own specific pattern. A great deal of the other seemingly intelligent behaviour of nesting birds, such as solicitude or love for their offspring, and the ' broken wing ' trick practised by many different species to draw off an intruder from the nest or young, prove upon analysis to be largely, if not wholly, the working of a blind and unreasoning instinct.

This chapter would be incomplete without special mention of the remarkable nesting habits and behaviour of four of our Indian birds.

The Hornbills

The first of these is the hornbill whose prodigious beak at once makes him unmistakable. His nesting habits are in keeping with his unusual get-up. All our hornbills, as far as is known, share this peculiar behaviour. Their commonest representative, the Grey Hornbill (p. 78), may be taken as the type.

At the appointed season, after the courtship and pairing ceremonials have been duly performed, the female hornbill betakes herself to a natural hollow in some tree-trunk, the same perhaps as has served for nursery to numerous previous hornbill generations. She incarcerates herself within this hollow, using her droppings as plaster and the flat sides of her enormous bill as trowel to wall up the entrance. merely leaving a narrow slit through which to receive the food brought in by the male. This walling-up process occupies 2 or 3 days and it is doubtful if the male assists her at all in the work, except presumably in fetching the mud. For it is now ascertained that besides the female's own excrement there is a considerable proportion of mud or clay mixed in the cement. The plaster sets so hard that no ordinary predatory animal can get at the occupant within. From this self-imposed confinement the female does not free herself until after the young — 2 or 3 in number — hatch out and are about a fortnight old. All the time she is within, the male assiduously brings her food — banyan and peepul figs varied occasionally by a lizard or some other tit-bit. The heavy labour of foraging for his spouse wears him down to a skeleton, while she thrives exceedingly on this life of ease and plenty and is said to grow enormously plump. In the case of the closely related Great Indian Hornbill it is believed that during her incarceration the female moults her flight quills, so that the imprisoning wall gives her protection from predators at a time when she is most helpless. This question of moult, however, and the manner of its taking place needs further investigation. When the young are about a fortnight old the female breaks down the wall by hammering away patiently at it, and releases herself. After her exit the wall is usually built up once more and thenceforth father and mother slave to fill the hungry maws of the voracious squabs until such time as they are old enough to be let out to fend for themselves.

153

The Baya

The Baya Weaver Bird is a cunning polygamist with a system of his own. At the onset of the rainy season, the males, now in their handsome breeding dress, commence to build their wonderful retort-shaped pendant nests, chiefly on babool trees or date palms preferably standing in or overhanging water. The building parties which may consist of from 10 to 50 birds or more are comprised exclusively of cocks. A great deal of noisy, joyous, chirruping choruses and fluttering of wings accompanies the work. After the strands of the initial attachment are wound and twisted round and round the selected twig till a firm support is secured, the bird proceeds to work the loose strips dangling from it into a transverse oblong loop. This is the skeleton of the structure. Porches are built over the upper part on either side of this loop and continued down, one bulging out lower into the egg chamber, the other less bulgy being produced to form the entrance tube. When the nests have reached the crucial ' bell ' or ' helmet ' stage, there is a sudden visitation from a party of prospecting hen Bayas who have been completely absent from the colony hitherto. They hop about from nest to nest, deliberately entering to inspect the interior, seemingly indifferent to the amorous prancing, strutting and chittering advances of the cocks around them. If a hen is satisfied with a particular nest she calmly ' adopts ' it and moves into possession. Thenceforth she and the builder are wife and husband. He works assiduously to complete the nest while she busies herself mainly with tidying the egg chamber. As soon as this nest is completed and the hen settled on eggs within, the cock commences to build himself another nest on a nearby twig. In course of time this too, if approved, is similarly appropriated by a second prospecting female who then becomes Wife No. 2. The process may be repeated until the cock finds himself the devoted husband of 3 or even 4 wives and the fond father of as many families, all at once!

The Bustard-Quail

The normal condition among birds is that where the sexes differ in coloration, it is the male who is the brighter coloured and more showy. He displays his splendour before the female, courts her and if need be fights furiously with rival males for her possession. In the Bustard-Quail, however, the role of the sexes is reversed. Here it is the female who is the larger and more brightly coloured and who takes the initiative in affairs of the heart. She decoys eligible males by a loud drumming call, courts them sedulously, displaying all her charms before them, and engages in desperate battles with rival Amazons for the ownership of the favoured one. As soon as the husband is secured, the preliminaries over and the full complement of eggs laid, she leaves him to his own devices and wanders off in search of fresh conquests. The unfortunate husband is saddled with the entire responsibility of incubating the eggs and tending the young which, to his credit, he discharges admirably and with great solicitude. By feminine artifice the roving hen manages to inveigle another unattached cock, who is likewise landed with family cares. And she is once again in the

Flying Silhouettes

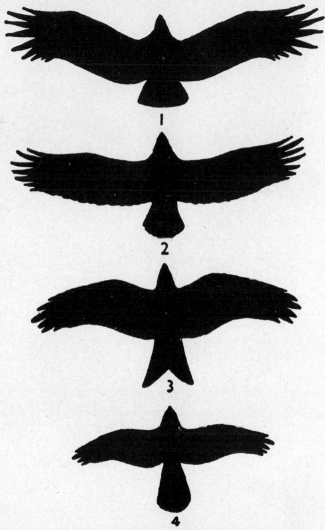

1. Vulture 2. Eagle 3. Kite 4. Kestrel

Plate 85

1. Gull 2. Pelican 3. Crane 4. Duck

Plate 86

market, for a third husband! In this manner each hen may lay several clutches of eggs during a single season which, accordingly, is much prolonged. The Painted Snipe is another Indian species which is similarly polyandrous, while the two jaçanas are yet others.

The Parasitic Cuckoos

A large section of the cuckoo family is known as the Parasitic Cuckoos on account of their disreputable habit of building no nests of their own but utilising those of other birds for laying in, and foisting their parental responsibilities upon the dupes. Familiar examples of our parasitic cuckoos are the Brainfever Bird and the Koel. The former commonly lays in the nests of babblers, often removing one of the rightful eggs to make room for its own. The Koel habitually parasitizes the House and Jungle Crows and leaves to them the task of incubating its eggs and rearing its young. The eggs of parasitic cuckoos usually bear a remarkably close resemblance to those of their hosts or fosterers. It is believed that this similarity has been brought about gradually by the discrimination exercised by the fosterer, i.e. by its rejecting, generation after generation, such eggs as differed glaringly in size or coloration from its own. There is good evidence that even among parasitic cuckoos of the same species there are distinct strains or ' gens ' which are as a rule constant in their selection of fosterers. Thus Plaintive Cuckoos in Hyderabad City (Deccan) habitually lay in the nests of the Ashy Wren-Warbler while those in the surrounding country favour nests of the Tailor Bird. Now, the eggs of the wren-warbler and those of the tailor bird are markedly unlike, but those of the respective strains of the plaintive cuckoos have evolved through Natural Selection to match the eggs of their normal fosterers in either area.

We have still a great deal to learn about the breeding biology of even some of our commonest birds. Egg-collecting alone is not enough. Some of the points on which detailed information is desirable are (1) The share of the sexes in nest-building, incubation and care of the young, (2) Periods of incubation, (3) Interval between the laying of each egg in a clutch (this varies among species and groups), (4) Nature of food and quantity fed each day to the young, (5) Behaviour of parents and young.

Those interested in the nesting habits of Indian birds should read BIRDS AT THE NEST by Douglas Dewar which, though written over 40 years ago, contains some useful indications of what still remains to be done in this country. For the serious student there is nothing more comprehensive than the four volumes by E. C. Stuart Baker — NIDIFICATION OF BIRDS OF THE INDIAN EMPIRE. His subsequent CUCKOO PROBLEMS is a mine of information on questions relating to Indian parasitic cuckoos.

FLIGHT

EVEN persons who may know nothing else about birds except that some are good to eat, know this much that birds fly. Indeed so snugly is this notion fixed in the popular mind that it is sometimes not easy to convince people that everything that flies is not a bird. Witness the widespread confusion that exists over the natural position of the bats.

Up to a point the criterion of flight is perhaps justifiable since this type of locomotion is not enjoyed in the same degree of perfection by any other class of animals. The only other backboned animal that flies is the bat, but the structure of the bat's wing is comparatively clumsy. An elastic membrane of skin stretches between its enormously elongated fingers, and the whole organ lacks the perfection of the bird's wing. While perfect flight is certainly the bird's most outstanding qualification, it must not be forgotten that there exist a number of birds — such as the ostrich and the penguin — that do not fly at all. Recent anatomical research suggests controversially, that ostrich-like birds never possessed the power of flight. But in the penguin this is certainly the result of disuse of the wings as flying organs by countless generations through thousands of years. In lesser degree a similar result of disuse can be observed in the case of our domestic poultry — geese, ducks and fowls — whose wild ancestors are strong fliers even today.

The wing of a flying bird combines strength with lightness and flexibility in a manner that can scarcely be improved upon. The structure of the bones of the hand and forearm, and the arrangement of the flight feathers upon it — opening out when required, and folding up one beneath its neighbour like the blades of a fan when not in use — is the most efficient and economical that can be conceived. The bones of the wing are kept in place by a ligament or elastic band running along the front of both the upper and lower arms. This prevents the joints being completely extended and the wing from turning inside out like an old umbrella in a gale, when extra pressure of the air exerts along the fore-edge. Details of the structure of the flight quills themselves do not concern us here; they combine strength, elasticity and lightness unequalled by any other similar device in nature. When extended in flight they overlap in just the right proportions, with one broad and one narrow vane, to attain the maximum efficiency in supporting and propelling a bird in the air with the minimum expenditure of its energy. Equipped with these quill feathers — the Primaries chiefly for locomotion, the Secondaries for lift — the bird's wing is so built and attached to the body that as a unit it can be moved freely in every plane. The primaries (better termed ' hand-quills ' in the German) usually number 10-12 in each wing. The secondaries (' arm-quills ') vary from 6 as in humming-birds and swifts to 20 in pelicans and up to 40 in albatrosses, depending upon the respective style of flight.

The motive power operating the wings is supplied by the strongly developed pectoral muscles. The sternum or breast bone is provided with a deep keel or ridge — the carina — to the edge of which most of these muscles are attached. Among them are some that help to depress the wing and provide the propelling stroke, and others working by means of a tendon, in rope-and-pulley fashion, to raise the wing in preparation for the next power stroke. The position of these enormous muscles — *below* the point at which the wing is inserted into the body — is a noteworthy feature since it makes for stability in flight. Like the engines of the modern aeroplane they form a considerable proportion of the bird's total weight. For example, in the snipe, a bird well known for its speed and dexterity on the wing, they weigh as much as a quarter of its entire weight.

To withstand the stresses and pulls exerted by the powerful breast muscles a rigid framework is obviously essential, combining strength with lightness. Such a framework is admirably provided by the various adaptations in the bird's skeleton. The hard hollow bones (' tubular construction ') make for lightness, and the fusions in the vertebral column (' welded joints ') effect rigidity in sections of the back where the strain is greatest. The pelican, a heavy-looking water bird weighing about 25 lb., has a skeleton of rather under $1\frac{1}{2}$ lb.

The flying bird has excited Man's imagination and envy throughout his long history, and many have been his unsuccessful attempts from time to time to emulate it. I have already referred elsewhere to the estimate that for a man, to be able to lift himself off the ground on wings on the bird model, he would have to develop his pectoral muscles till they projected at least 4 feet beyond his chest. The angels and cherubim of holy portraiture must indeed be hard put to it to keep themselves aloft without such monstrous outgrowths!

The wing actions of a bird in flight are actually less simple than the up and down flapping they appear to be. They involve a number of complex principles of aerodynamics which have been more intensively studied and are better understood since the invention and development of the aeroplane and the glider. Modern aircraft design owes a great debt to the careful analyses of the principles involved in the flight of birds. The improvements continually being made in flying machines keep pace with our knowledge of the mechanics of bird flight. A remarkable and comparatively recent example of how flying man has profited from the flying bird was the invention of the Handley-Page ' slotted-wing ' safety device now almost universally used in aeroplanes. A well-known principle of aerodynamics is that the heavier a plane the faster it must fly to keep itself in the air and prevent ' stalling '. The use of the slotted-wing device enables heavy aircraft to land safely at relatively slow speeds without crashing. It has not only helped to avert innumerable accidents, but also made possible the enormous increase in the size and weight of the planes we see today: the largest modern passenger plane, the Boeing-747, weighs over 350 tons. Briefly, by regulating the pressure and angle of the air upon the wings of an aeroplane this contrivance produces what may roughly be described as a parachute or helicopter effect and enables the machine to fly comparatively slowly and land gently. The device is clearly an application of the same feature as is seen in the splayed fingerlike wing-tips of heavy flying birds with relatively broad wings, such as eagles, vultures and storks. If one of the outer primary feathers of a vulture is examined it will be seen that there is a conspicuous narrowing, or ' emargination ' as it is known, on the outer portion of the vane, i.e. on the outer web. The gaps or slots between the outspread primaries (or 'fingers') of a soaring vulture are formed not only by the normal spreading of the primaries but they can be further considerably widened by these emarginations. A clever friction surface on the web prevents the feathers from splaying beyond a certain limit. By manipulating the slots between the primaries, so as to offer varying and controlled resistance to the air, rather in the manner of venetian blinds or shutters, the heavy bird is enabled among other advantages to soar in comparatively still air. It also permits accurate landing at a speed which would ordinarily be unable to withstand the pull of gravity, and bring the bird crashing to earth, unless it steadied itself by flapping.

The bird's tail is an important accessory of flight and assumes a variety of shapes and sizes, e.g. the short rounded tail of the eagle and the vulture, the deeply forked tail of the swallow, the tern and the kite, and the long graduated tail of the tree pie. Its primary function is that of balancing and steering. If accidentally lost, the bird's movements in the air are considerably hampered; but it is not rendered completely helpless since much of the steering, balancing and braking is also done by the wings. The tail further helps in regulating height in the air, and of course serves as a brake in checking momentum. It is noticeable that the alighting or landing of a bird is invariably preceded by an upward tilt of the long axis of its body accompanied by a vigorous flapping of wings and a depressing and expanding of the tail.

No better example can be given of the perfect muscular control over wings and tail and the co-ordinated efficiency of the various special adaptations of the flying bird (viz. streamlining, flexibility of neck, sideways position and rapid focusing of eye, etc.) than the Alpine Swift (p. 68). Cruising at speeds which may be anything up to 250 km p.h., this bird is capable of shooting directly and with effortless grace up into the narrow fissure of a rock cliff that holds its nest. The ease and skill with which the parent Baya flies into the narrow entrance tube of its swaying pendant nest with no hesitation or slackening of speed; the stooping of a Pariah Kite upon a dead rat lying in the middle of a congested city bazaar, and its dexterous turns and twists to avoid the traffic below and the tangle of telephone wires overhead — are sights familiar to every bird watcher, and such as never cease to thrill.

It is useful to be able to recognise the style of flight adopted by various groups and species of birds and their sundry little mannerisms on the wing since these are points that may assist materially in field identification. A familiarity with the wing action and outline of a bird high up in the heavens, or when silhouetted against the darkening sky, is particularly helpful in observations relating to migrating birds. The three main types of flight to be differentiated are:

1. The normal **F l a p p i n g** flight which may be roughly compared to swimming breast-stroke. In this the wings move upward and forward, downward and back (under the plane of the body) and then upward again, in a sort of rotary motion. The upstroke is very rapid, but owing to the curvature on the wing surface (the camber), the partial folding of the wing and the set of the feathers, a minimum amount of resistance is created. The free movement of the wing makes this upstroke resemble the 'feathering' of an oar when rowing. The wing tips do not work simply up and down but they roughly describe a

Speedflash: *Loke Wan Tho*

Hoopoe leaving nest-hole

PLATE 87

Photo: J. N. Unwalla

Brownheaded Gulls
(Note white 'mirrors' on black wing-tips)

PLATE 88

figure of 8. The downstroke (or power stroke) is made with the wing fully outstretched exerting its maximum push on the air. It helps both to lift the bird and propel it forward. The crow and most of the Passerine or Perching birds may be cited as examples of flapping fliers. The wing-beats vary according to size of bird and speed of flight: while the sparrow has about 13 strokes per second, the pelican has only 1 to $1\frac{1}{2}$! A short, rounded wing (as, for example, in the Jungle Babbler or Spotted Owlet) is the mark of a weak flier or a more or less sedentary bird. Long, pointed wings indicate strong sustained flight, often against heavy head-wind, and are possessed by pigeons, falcons, swifts and all birds that undertake long migratory journeys, e.g. sandpipers, wagtails, etc.

2. **G l i d i n g** involves sailing on outstretched motionless wings taking advantage of wind currents. It may be compared to 'freewheeling' or coasting downhill on a bicycle. Unless launched from a cliff or other elevated position the bird requires a certain amount of initial flapping to produce the required momentum. And if momentum is not renewed from time to time by further wing-beats, loss of height results. Gliding is best seen in gulls circling effortlessly round a ship looking for scraps thrown overboard. Typical gliding birds have rather narrow and long tapering wings without outspreading 'fingers' at the tip.

3. **S o a r i n g** is perhaps the most spectacular style of bird flight. It differs little from gliding except that ascending air currents, or thermals, play a predominant part in it. By various manipulations of its outstretched wings and tail, the soaring bird takes advantage of every current and eddy to gain height. The upward soaring of vultures and storks is achieved in loose, wide spirals like the coils of a spring. As the bird glides downwind it gains in momentum but loses somewhat in height. By a slight tilt of the body axis as it wheels round to face upwind, the bird is lifted upward without effort, and gradually gains height, spiral upon spiral, until it soon becomes a speck in the heavens. Since soaring depends largely upon ascending currents it is seen at its best in warm regions of the globe such as ours, and here only between the hours of sunrise and sunset when the heated air rushes up to higher levels.

Birds that habitually soar, such as vultures, eagles, storks, pelicans, etc., have relatively broad wings with rounded or squared wing-tips terminating in a finger-like spread of the outer primaries — the 'slotted-wing device'.

Besides these three main types of flight one must learn to recognise their variations and combinations. For instance a woodpecker or wagtail flies by a succession of rapid wing-beats followed by a short pause in which the wings are pressed to the sides of the body. This results in a forward dip and a slight loss of height, and produces the well-known *undulating* effect so characteristic of these species. In other birds, e.g. partridge, shikra, brainfever bird, rosy starling, etc., a succession of rapid wing-beats is followed by a short glide on outstretched motionless wings — free wheeling — in which the bird does not lose height; its flight is *direct* and not undulating.

The *hovering* flight of certain birds needs special mention. Its foremost exponents among our Indian species are certainly the Kestrel and the Pied Kingfisher, but harriers, the Blackwinged Kite, fishing eagles and some other birds also frequently indulge in it. Hovering enables the bird to poise itself stationary in mid-air and survey the ground or water below for its prey. It is really a variant of the normal flapping flight but always attained head-to-wind and with an upward tilt of the body axis so as to offer maximum resistance to the lateral current of air. The wings or wing-tips are flapped rapidly to ' tread ' the air as it were, and the bird thus remains suspended for many seconds at a time. Hovering flight on rapidly vibrating wings is also seen in the sunbirds as they probe into flower tubes for nectar or search for insects poised in front of a flower. It has reached its perfection among the humming-birds of the New World. In some of these, scarcely larger than a bumble-bee, the wing strokes have been ascertained to be between 20 and 50 per second (1200-3000 per minute!).

Whether it be the effortless, leisurely soaring of the vulture in the firmament or the swishing lightning stoop of the falcon upon its quarry, the loud whirring flush of the startled partridge in the corn-field or the silent ghostly glide of the questing owl in the gloaming, it is all the manifestation of the same remarkable process of evolution that has culminated in the flying bird, raising it as if by a magic wand from the lowly cold-blooded reptile to this bundle of superabundant energy — a graceful and buoyant creature with a mastery of the air that Man, with all his ingenuity and cunning, is never likely seriously to challenge.

BIRD MIGRATION

No resident in India who is even moderately observant can fail to notice the great influx of birds that takes place annually between September and November, or to remark upon their abundance during winter in places where none were to be seen a couple of months before. The species eagerly sought after by the man with the gun — the snipe, duck, geese, cranes and others — together with the hosts of smaller fry that interest him less or not at all — the sandpipers, leaf warblers, larks, wagtails and pipits — all seem to pop up suddenly from nowhere. While this transformation is magical enough to be felt by all, it is doubtful if five persons in a hundred ever stop to ask themselves what brings it about, and how. To the man in the street the birds come at this season simply because it is in the nature of things that they should. Whence they come is not his concern, while why or how they do it is clearly the birds' own affair!

Yet, the subject of Migration is one of the most enthralling branches of the study of bird life. The magnitude of the movements and the regularity and orderliness of their occurrence are no whit less than the cycle of the seasons; they have aroused the wonderment of Man through the ages. The Red Indians of the Fur Countries actually named their calendar months after the arrival of migrant birds. A realistic scientific approach is now helping to dispel some of the more fanciful notions, but it must be admitted that many of the phenomena involved continue to remain a mystery and are unlikely to emerge from the realm of speculation.

Until not so long ago there was a widely prevalent belief that small birds such as the swallow, nightingale and cuckoo hibernated like mammals and reptiles to get over unfavourable weather conditions. This notion had held ground since the days of Aristotle, and even that excellent naturalist Gilbert White of Selborne was not immune from the belief that swallows passed the winter buried in mud at the bottom of ponds, whence they emerged with the first signs of returning spring.

What is bird migration ?

Landsborough Thomson, an eminent authority, describes bird migration as " Changes of habitat periodically recurring and *alternating in direction*, which tend to secure optimum environmental conditions at all times ". The italics are important since it is just this *back and forth* movement that is the crucial feature of the migration of birds. The periodic movements of locust swarms for example, loosely referred to as migrations, are really overflow movements and do not entail a return to the starting point. Thus they differ markedly from the seasonal return traffic of birds. The ' pendulum-swing ' movement is noticeable in some other groups of animals as well, but it has reached its rhythmical climax among birds.

Its extent and advantages

On account of their special attributes — warm-bloodedness, feather covering and unparalleled powers of flight — the phenomenon of

14.

migration finds its highest development in birds. Although directly they are the least affected of all animals by extremes of heat and cold, it is the difficulties connected with food-getting under adverse winter conditions that compel them to change their quarters or perish. Migration enables birds to inhabit two different areas at the respective seasons most favourable in each. It involves a swing from a breeding or nesting place — the bird's home — to a feeding or resting place — its winter quarters. It is an axiom of nature that birds always nest in the colder portion of their migratory range. Thus, in the Northern Hemisphere their breeding grounds lie nearer the Arctic or Temperate Zone and their winter quarters nearer the Equator. In the Southern Hemisphere the case is reversed. Although some migration takes place from east to west, its general direction as a whole may be considered as North and South. The movement may vary from no more than a few miles — such as from the north Indian plains to a couple of thousand feet up in the Himalayan foothills — to several thousand miles either way as is the case with many of our wintering wildfowl. The longest known migratory journey is performed twice each year by the Arctic Tern (*Sterna macrura*) which from the Arctic winter travels south, right across the world to the Antarctic summer and back again — a distance of over 11,000 miles each way!

A consideration of the various theories to explain the origin of this ' Racial Custom ' of migration among birds would here be out of place. But it is worth while to take stock of some of the more obvious as well as the more bewildering facts concerning it. The resultant advantages of migration to birds are self-evident. Absence from high latitudes during the winter enables: (a) avoidance of cold and stormy weather, (b) avoidance of short daylight hours available for search of food, and (c) avoidance of those conditions that bring about a scarcity of food supply, such as freezing of water and snow enshrouding the ground.

The advantages of a return to high latitudes in summer are: (a) availability of suitable and uncongested nesting territories, (b) availability of long hours of daylight for search of food when food is most required for the young, and (c) availability of an abundant food supply following on the luxuriant growth of spring vegetation.

What stimulates a bird to migrate ?

The urge to migrate at the appropriate seasons is evoked by both external and internal stimuli. Experiments point to the assumption that one of the primary external stimuli is the variations in day length. The internal stimulus seems to be provided by the state of the reproductive organs which, in the laboratory, can be brought to known stages of maturity by artificial manipulation of day length. The nonexistence of the migratory instinct in sterile birds is consistent with this view. Readers interested in the details of Prof. W. Rowan's ingenious experiments on the causative aspects of bird migration are referred to his remarkable book THE RIDDLE OF MIGRATION (1931). Subsequent research has resulted in some modification of the original thesis.

What determines the goal of a migratory journey ?
How do birds find the way to this goal ?

These are two of the many problems to which satisfactory answers are difficult to find. And the great mass of experimental and obser-

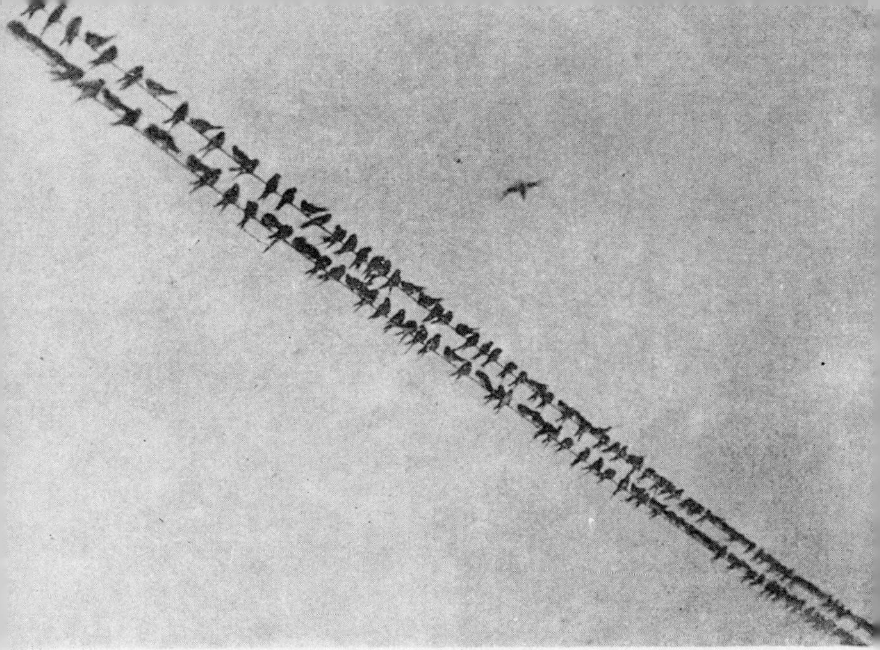

Photo: *Author*

Swallows collecting on migration

PLATE 89

Photo: Author

A migrator swarm of Rosy Pastors

PLATE 90

vational data that has accumulated within recent years does not advance our knowledge much beyond the stage of conjecture.

In the spring the adult males are the first to arrive on their breeding grounds. They are followed by the adult females, while immature birds that will not breed till the following year bring up the rear. In autumn the order of departure is reversed; the southward journey is performed more leisurely with many stop-overs on the way. The young birds, in many cases not more than a couple of months old, form the vanguard, the adults following later. Now comes the mystery. The young birds have had no previous experience either of the route or the destination, often thousands of miles away, yet they accomplish the journey without undue mortality through accidents and misadventure, and with amazing accuracy. Of the various hypothetical explanations suggested the most convenient seems to be that this prescience of the goal and route is the expression of an inborn racial custom inherited through countless generations of migrants journeying back and forth year after year, between their breeding grounds and their winter quarters. It is on a par with other vital urges such as building at the appointed season, without previous experience or training, of nests in accordance with the traditional pattern of the species, howsoever complicated their architecture.

Many speculations have been put forward from time to time as to how migratory birds orientate themselves. But it is only within the last few years that ingenious experiments have indicated that day-flying migrants maintain their course from the angle the sun makes with the earth at the appropriate season, while nocturnal migrants are guided by the major constellations of stars. Probability is lent to these findings by the commonly observed fact that in cloudy weather when the sky remains obscured for prolonged periods migrating birds often lose their way.

Accuracy and regularity of returns

Birds not only return to the same general locality for breeding year after year, but often also to the identical nesting site. Once the goal is roughly reached there seems every likelihood that landmarks, imprinted on the senses in some way as the result of previous experience and association, may play their part in guiding old birds to their former haunts with such astonishing precision. The ringing or banding method has now established that in Europe swallows often return not only to the same locality but even to the same building for nesting purposes year after year, covering distances of 6000 miles or more each way during the interval. This is the case with many other true migrants as well. And not only do individuals return to the same nesting sites, but they often also come back to the same restricted locality in their winter quarters, year after year.

The great regularity and punctuality, almost to the day, with which migrant birds arrive in a given locality is seen even from the few published records kept over several years by observers residing in different parts of this country. This is all the more amazing, when the enormous distances over which many of the species have to travel are taken into account. A ringed Grey Wagtail (*Motacilla caspica*) was found to return, presumably from its Himalayan breeding grounds at least 2000 km distant, to a particular lawn in Greater Bombay — no bigger than a badminton court — on almost the exact date in September for five years running. Incoming Orphean warblers (*Sylvia hortensis*) ringed in Kathiawar in September one year were retaken in nets on the self-same acre or two in the same month, almost to the date, in the following year; in one case even in each of three successive years!

Varying status of winter visitors

The status of every migrant to India varies in the different portions of its winter habitat. Take any locality — say Bhopal in central India. A large number of species coming in from across our northern and NW. frontiers in autumn touch Bhopal on the south-bound journey to their winter quarters in peninsular India and Ceylon. Some of these stay behind and may be seen in that neighbourhood throughout the cold weather. These will be classed here as true winter visitors. Other species make their appearance for a few days at the commencement of the season and then perhaps are not seen again till they are returning northwards at the beginning of the hot weather. These are the passage migrants. Others again may be seen on their southward journey in autumn but not on the return, since some species habitually travel to and from their winter quarters by different routes. Thus, while these are autumn passage migrants in Bhopal, they are spring passage migrants in another part of the country. Similarly some species may pass over Bhopal only on their northward journey in spring and may have the status of autumn passage migrants elsewhere. Again there are birds which though true winter visitors may yet have their numbers vastly augmented by waves of passage migrants from the north or south at the appropriate seasons. The status of these species will therefore be a combination of winter visitor and passage migrant.

Local migration

In addition to these very extensive movements of migrant birds from beyond our frontiers, there are movements of a similar but perhaps less spectacular kind ceaselessly going on amongst our resident bird populations. The periodical appearances and disappearances of the Paradise Flycatcher, Golden Oriole, and Pitta must be obvious to any one with an eye for birds. In northern India and along the base of the Himalayan foothills where the changes of the season are more pronounced than nearer the Equator, these local migratory movements are especially noticeable. The seasonal arrivals and departures of local migrants are no less regular in their cycle than those of the true migratory birds. In some portions of the country one species may be a summer visitor, in another a rains visitor, while in a third locality it may be found only during the winter months. Apart from these regular seasonal shiftings other movements of an even more parochial character are constantly taking place. They are governed by local conditions of heat, drought, or floods, and by their resultant effect upon the available food supply: the flowering season of certain plants, the ripening of certain fruits, and the fluctuation of insect populations.

164

Under stress of abnormal natural conditions birds are frequently driven out of their accustomed habitats in search of a living and are then met with as stragglers far beyond their normal range.

Thus, practically no square mile of the Indian subcontinent is static for any length of time as regards its bird population, and there is an unending chain of comings and goings of species and individuals.

Altitudinal migration

Lastly, mention must be made of altitudinal migration which is particularly marked among species living in the Himalayas. In winter, high elevation birds are forced to descend to lower levels by exigencies of the weather and the descending snow line. With the return of spring when the snow melts and the snow line recedes upwards they re-ascend to breed in the higher hills. These altitudinal movements are not confined to high-elevation birds only, but are indulged in also by species resident at lower altitudes.

Velocity and altitude of migratory flight

Modern devices such as radar, the aeroplane, speed indicators, altimeters and other instruments used in aviation and anti-aircraft gunnery have made it possible to discard the almost fabulous notions formerly held and to arrive at fairly accurate estimates of the speed and height at which migrating birds fly. Velocities naturally vary with species of bird and prevailing meteorological conditions. The average cruising speed of ducks and geese, for instance, has been found to be between 40 and 50 miles per hour. Under favourable weather conditions it may reach 55-60 m.p.h. or slightly more. A bird's flying day (or night) ranges from 6 to 11 hours, and the following figures are of interest as showing the average mileage known to be covered in a ' hop ': Coot 160 miles; Stork 125 miles (6 hours); Woodcock 250-300; Plover 550 (11 hours).

Non-stop flights of at least 2000 miles across open sea are undertaken by the Eastern Golden Plover (*Pluvialis dominica fulva*) which is a winter visitor to India also. This bird breeds in western Alaska and NE. Siberia and is a regular visitor to the Hawaiian islands. Also the Snipe *Capella hardwickii*, which breeds only in Japan and spends the winter in E. Australia and Tasmania, must habitually fly 3000 miles non-stop over the sea since it has never been met anywhere in between. There are others, especially among the shore birds or waders, that cover enormous stretches without halting for rest or food. A probable example of such a long distance flier in India is the Woodcock (*Scolopax rusticola*) whose nearest breeding place is in the Himalayas. It winters in some numbers in the Nilgiri and other hills of S. India, but is found nowhere in between except as the rarest accidental straggler. The least distance it must normally cover in a single hop, therefore, is about 1500 miles. The Pied Ground Thrush (*Zoothera wardii*) travelling by the Eastern Ghats route from the Himalayas to the Nilgiris and on to Ceylon probably covers equally long distances non-stop.

It has been believed in the past that migrating birds flew at stupendous heights and that in fact it was of some particular advantage for them to do so — for locating landmarks, minimizing air resistance and

165

in other ways. In actual practice, however, except where lofty mountain barriers have to be crossed, they fly chiefly under 400 m and only rarely over 900 m above the ground. Some species indeed habitually fly much lower, especially over the surface of the sea where they have no trees and similar obstacles to avoid. Nevertheless, that a considerable amount of migration does take place at unsuspected heights has recently been revealed by radar which has registered flocks of migrating birds at over 7500 metres without there being any apparent physical compulsion for them to fly at that great height.

Considering the gigantic scale on which bird migration takes place in India, the scantiness of our factual knowledge of every aspect of it is deplorable. Only the broad pattern is known, and that largely from rather disconnected observational records aided by reasonable conjecture. The major traffic from and to northern lands (E. Europe, northern and central Asia) in autumn and spring each year seems to take place at both ends of the Himalayan chain mainly through the valleys of the Indus and Brahmaputra rivers. The migrational streams of land birds converge down the two sides of the Peninsula weakening in species as well as numbers as they advance southward, and trickle over into Ceylon, which virtually forms the terminal. But evidence procured by individual mountaineers and successive Himalayan expeditions indicates that many species, particularly of ducks and geese, also fly directly across the mountain barrier often at heights of 3000 to 5200 m, and even to 6000 m, thereby shortening their journeys very considerably.

That birds *can* fly at immense heights if necessary with little inconvenience from the rarefied air is evident from the fact that one of the Everest Expeditions met crows and mountain finches about their camp at 7000 m and Griffon Vultures and Lämmergeier between 6 and 7 thousand metres, while choughs followed the climbers, quite effortlessly and with capacity for flight undiminished, even up to 8200 m, an altitude at which the atmosphere is reduced to only one third its supporting power! On his successful Everest climb in 1953 Sir Edmund Hillary saw a chough following him at 8500 m — presumably one of the several birds that scavenged daily round their camp at 7900 m.

Bird ringing

Apart from the purely observational method of bird migration study, which to be of real scientific value entails an unbroken continuity of careful records over prolonged periods, the method of ' ringing ' birds has in recent years been very extensively and profitably employed in Europe and America for collecting factual data. Bird ringing — or ' banding ' as it is called in the U.S. — consists of fastening a light aluminium ring of appropriate size, stamped with a number and return address, to the instep region or tarsus of a trapped or netted bird, or of a young bird before it leaves the nest. A detailed record is kept in a special register, and the bird is then released. A small percentage of these ringed birds are subsequently shot or recaptured in distant places, and the rings returned or their inscription communicated to the marking station with data as to the exact locality where recovered, date, and other particulars. When a large number of such recovery

Photo: Author

Ringed Sparrow-Hawk ready to be released

PLATE 91

Vultures at a carcase

PLATE 92

records have been obtained, it is possible gradually to build up accurate knowledge of the routes followed on migration by different species, and a number of other important facts impossible to ascertain in any other way. Thus, the ringing of White Storks in West Germany and East Prussia has established that the East Prussian birds migrate to Africa by a south-eastern route through the Balkans, whereas the West German storks travel by a south-western route through Spain. It was by means of a German-ringed stork accidentally recovered in Bikaner that we now know that some at least of the White Storks that visit us in winter are ' Made in Germany '. Very little bird ringing had been done in India prior to 1958, and mainly of migratory ducks. The recoveries, meagre as they were, nevertheless furnished our only positive evidence for the central Asian and Siberian provenance of our winter visitors. Since 1959 the Bombay Natural History Society has conducted an organized field project for ringing other birds besides wildfowl, mostly small passerines. Its rings bear the legend ' Inform Bombay Nat. Hist. Society '. Apart from determining the geographical origins and routes of the various species, the object is to investigate whether, and to what extent, migratory birds are responsible for the dissemination of virus diseases of man and animals through the agency of ticks and other blood-sucking parasites. The few ring recoveries so far reported are of the greatest interest and significance since they indicate the routes followed by the birds to and from their breeding grounds. For example Yellow Wagtails (*Motacilla flava beema* and *M. f. thunbergi*) ringed in Kerala during winter were recovered on passage in Kabul, Afghanistan, the following spring, and at Bannu, NW. Pakistan, in the succeeding autumn. A Forest Wagtail (*M. indica*) ringed in Kerala in February was killed in the Chin Hills of Burma in April. Spanish and Turkestan Sparrows (*Passer hispaniolensis transcaspicus* and *P. domesticus bactrianus*) ringed in Bharatpur, Rajasthan, in early spring were recovered on their nesting grounds in Kazakhstan, Russian Turkestan, in summer. The end-paper map shows some of the more important recent recoveries.

The use of plastic rings of different colours by which individuals may be recognised at a distance without the necessity of recapture, has, in recent years, yielded valuable information concerning the life history and local movements of more or less resident or sedentary birds.

Those who would like to pursue the study of bird migration literature further, will find the following books in English useful and interesting:

1. PROBLEMS OF BIRD MIGRATION. By A. Landsborough Thomson (H. F. & G. Witherby, London, 1926, 18/-).

2. BIRD MIGRATION. By A. Landsborough Thomson (H. F. & G. Witherby, London, 1936, 5/-).

3. THE MIGRATION OF BIRDS. By Jean Dorst (Heineman, London, 1962, 50s.). The latest authoritative work collating and summarizing the most important European and American literature to date.

Two excellent periodicals, the first devoted chiefly to international ringing techniques, important recoveries, and general information, the second to research in bird migration, are:

THE RING, published quarterly by the Polish Zoological Society, Warsaw, and

BIRD MIGRATION, published twice a year by The British Trust for Ornithology, Oxford.

THE USEFULNESS OF BIRDS

It has been said that birds could exist without man but that man would perish without birds. This observation has been further amplified by the remark that ' But for the trees the insects would perish, but for the insects the birds would perish, but for the birds the trees would perish, and to follow the inexorable laws of Nature to the conclusion of their awful vengeance, but for the trees the world would perish '. An impartial scrutiny of the facts, shows that there is indeed little extravagance in either of these speculations.

As destroyers of insect pests

The variety, fecundity and voracity of insects are unbelievable. Over 30,000 forms have been described from the Indian Region alone — about fifteen times the number of bird species and races — and probably many still remain to be added to the list. Practically all living animals as well as plants furnish food for these incomputable hordes. Many estimates have been made of what a single pair of insects would increase to if allowed unchecked multiplication, and astounding figures have been reached rivalling in their stupendousness those which we associate with astronominal calculations. A Canadian entomologist has estimated that a single pair of Colorado Beetles or Potato Bugs (*Leptinotarsa decemlineata* — belonging to the prolific family Chrysomelidae of which over 20,000 species are known throughout the world, and which is well represented in India), would, without check, increase in one season to sixty millions. Riley computed that the Hop Aphis or Chinch Bug (*Blissus leucopterus*) very destructive to grasses and cereals in America, which develops 13 generations in a single year would, if unchecked, reach ten sextillion individuals at the end of the 12th generation. If this brood were marshalled in line end to end at the rate of 10 per inch, the procession would be so long that light, travelling at the rate of 184,000 miles per second, would take 2500 years to reach from one end to the other!

A caterpillar is said to eat twice its own weight in leaves per day. Certain flesh-feeding larvae will consume within 24 hours 200 times their original weight. It is reckoned that the food taken by a single silkworm in 56 days equals 86,000 times its original weight at hatching. Locusts are as notorious for their prolific reproduction as for their prodigious appetites. Their swarms are sometimes so thick as to obscure the sun, and such a visitation will, in the course of a few short hours, convert a green and smiling tract into a desolate waste with nothing but bare stems. The female locust lays its eggs in capsules underground, each capsule containing about 100 eggs, and several of these capsules are laid by each individual. On a farm in South Africa measuring 3300 acres no less than 14 tons of eggs have been dug up at one time, estimated to have produced 1250 million locusts. It is evident from their rate of increase that unless insect numbers were kept under constant and rigid check, it would not be long before all vegetation vanished completely from the face of the earth.

A large proportion of the normal food of birds consists of insects including many that are in the highest degree injurious to man and his concerns. Birds of many species not only take heavy toll of the marauding locust hordes all along their flight lines, but also scratch up and devour their eggs in vast quantities, as well as the different stages of the young locust after hatching. The White Stork is a well known locust destroyer, and the enormous nesting colonies of the Rosy Pastor live and feed their young exclusively upon these insects on their common breeding grounds in central Asia. An idea of the extent of good birds do in destroying insect pests may be had from the fact that many young birds in the first few days of their lives consume more than their own weight of food in 24 hours. A pair of starlings have been observed to bring food (caterpillars, grasshoppers, locusts, etc.) to their nest-young 370 times in a day, and according to Dr. W. E. Collinge, the well known British authority, House Sparrows bring food (caterpillars, soft-bodied insects, etc.) from 220 to 260 times per day. A German ornithologist has estimated that a single pair of tits with their progeny destroy annually at least 120 million insect eggs or 150,000 caterpillars and pupae. This warfare is waged not only when the insects are at the peak of their periodical abundance, but incessantly, relentlessly, and in all stages of the insects' lives. Therefore, where birds have not been unwisely interfered with, they constitute one of the most effective natural checks upon insect numbers.

As destroyers of other vermin

Owls, kestrels, hawks and the birds of prey generally — so often accused of destructiveness to poultry and game and slaughtered out of hand — are amongst the most important of Nature's checks upon rats and mice, some of the most fecund and destructive pests from which man and his works suffer. These vermin do enormous damage to crops and agricultural produce, and are, besides, the carriers directly or indirectly, of diseases often fatal to man. The ravages of the Sind Mole-Rat in the rice-growing tracts of the Indus Delta in Lower Sind have been estimated by a competent investigator as between 10 and 50 per cent of the entire paddy crop. This Mole-Rat breeds throughout the year. The number of young born in a litter is 5 to 10, but in October and November the litters are very large varying from 14 to 18 young each. Mice are equally fecund and destructive.

It has been computed that one pair of house rats having 6 litters of 8 young annually and breeding when $3\frac{1}{2}$ months old, with equal sexes and no deaths, would increase at the end of the year to 880 rats. At this rate the unchecked increase of a pair in 5 years would be 940,369,969,152 rats. Such calculations, of course, are purely theoretical and their results will never be approached in Nature, but they are not extravagant considering the capacity to reproduce, and are based on moderate and conservative estimates.

It will thus be seen that every pair of rats destroyed by birds means the annual suppression of a potential increase of 880 rats. Many of our owls and diurnal birds of prey feed largely on rats and mice; some of the former, indeed, live more or less exclusively on them. Two or three rats or mice apiece, or their remains, may frequently be found in the stomachs of Horned Owls, for example, and as digestion in birds is a continuous and rapid process it is conceivable that a larger number may be taken in the course of 24 hours. Since these birds are engaged in the good work from year's end to year's end, some estimate of their beneficial activities can be made.

As scavengers

Vultures, kites and crows are invaluable scavengers. They speedily and effectively dispose of carcases of cattle and other refuse dumped in the precincts of our villages — notoriously lacking in any organised system of sanitation — that would otherwise putrefy and befoul the air and become veritable culture beds of disease. The services of the birds are of special importance during famines and cattle epidemics when large numbers of domestic animals perish and at best are left by the wayside covered with a flimsy layer of earth to be exhumed by the first prowling jackal that happens on the spot. The speed and thoroughness with which a party of vultures will dispose of carrion is astounding.

As flower-pollination agents

While the importance of bees, butterflies and other insects in the cross-fertilization of flowers is well known, the large part played by birds in the same capacity has not been adequately appreciated. A large number of birds of divers families and species are responsible for the cross-fertilization of flowers, many of them possessing special adaptations in the structure and mechanism of their tongue and bill for the purpose of extracting honey from the base of the flower tubes. Flower-nectar is rich in carbohydrates and provides excellent nutriment, so much so that many of the most highly organised flower-birds subsist more or less exclusively on this diet. In trying to reach the nectar, the forehead or throat of the bird comes into contact with the anthers. The ripe golden pollen dust adheres to the feathers and is transported to the mature stigma of the next flower visited, which it thus fertilizes. It is little realised how largely responsible birds are for the success of the present-day safety match industry in India. Of all the indigenous softwoods that have been tried in the manufacture of matches that of the Silk Cotton tree has been found to be the most satisfactory as regards quality, abundance and accessibility. The large showy crimson flowers of this tree serve as a sign-post to invite the attention of the passing bird. They contain a plentiful supply of sugary nectar, which is eagerly sought by birds of many kinds — over 60 different species have been noted in one small area alone — and are mainly cross-pollinated through their agency. Birds thus contribute to the production of fertile seed and the continuance of healthy generations of the tree, and incidentally to the supply of raw material for your box of matches. A careful scrutiny would reveal that we are ultimately dependent upon birds in this House-that-Jack-built sort of way for many more of our every day requirements. The Coral tree (*Erythrina*), which is largely grown for shade in the tea and coffee plantations of South India, is also one whose flowers are fertilized chiefly, if not exclusively, by birds of many species.

Photo: *Author*

Jungle Myna sipping nectar from Coral blossoms

PLATE 93

Photo: Author

Thickbilled Flowerpecker eating *Loranthus* berries

PLATE 94

As seed dispersers

In the dissemination of seed and the distribution of plant life, birds play a predominant part. Their activities, unfortunately, are not always of a beneficial character from the economic point of view. No better instance of the extent of their seed-dispersing activities can be cited than that of the lantana weed. This pernicious plant of Mexican origin was first introduced into Ceylon for ornamental purposes a little over a century ago. It has since overrun thousands of square miles of the Indian subcontinent, and become the despair alike of agriculturist and forester. Its phenomenal spread within this comparatively short period would have been impossible without the agency of birds, numerous species of which greedily devour the berries which the plant everywhere produces in such overwhelming profusion. A Blackheaded Oriole has been observed swallowing 77 berries in the course of 3 minutes. The seeds pass through the birds' intestines unaffected by the disgestive juices, and out with the waste matter in due course. They germinate rapidly under favourable conditions and establish themselves.

Another noxious plant that is entirely bird-propagated is the *Loranthus* tree-parasite. It belongs to the Mistletoe family, well represented in this country, almost all of whose Indian members are more or less wholly symbiotic with sunbirds, flowerpeckers and other bird species, which both fertilize its flowers and disperse its seeds. Bulbuls and barbets are largely responsible for the dissemination of the seeds of the Sandalwood tree in South India and are welcome in sandalwood plantations. In the newly colonised canal areas of Punjab, the Mulberry owes its abundance mainly to propagation by birds. Experiments have shown that the seeds of such plants as grow on richly manured soil, after passing uninjured through a bird's intestine, actually produce stronger seedlings than those which are cultivated without such treatment.

As food for man

A feature of the larger dhands or jheels in Pakistan and northern India during the cold weather is the magnitude of the netting operations that go on throughout that season for supplying the markets of the larger towns, both near and distant, with wildfowl of every description for the table. The population of the neighbourhood of those jheels subsists during those months more or less exclusively on the flesh of water birds or on the traffic in them. Round every village near a dhand of any size in Sind may be seen little mounds of coot feathers which furnish an indication of the esteem which the bird enjoys as an article of diet. The wildfowl netting operations on the Manchar Lake alone involved, in pre-partition days, a turnover of several thousand rupees annually, besides providing the inhabitants of the neighbourhood with free or almost free sustenance for several months in the year.

Quails, partridges and other game birds are also netted or shot for eating purposes, and innumerable other species of every description are captured and sold in the bazaars to fanciers or exported, yielding substantial returns to those engaged in the trade.

Egret feathers

Until a few years ago egret-farming for the sake of the valuable plumes was a profitable cottage industry and largely practised on the various jheels in Sind. The dainty ' decomposed ' breeding plumes of the white egrets — ' aigrettes ' as they are known to the trade — were largely exported to Europe for ladies' head-dresses, tippets, muffs and for other órnamental purposes. They were almost worth their weight in silver, and brought in handsome profit to the farmers. With the change in ladies' fashions, the demand has happily dwindled considerably, and with it the prices. The working of the Wild Birds and Animals Protection Act of 1912 imposed a further check upon exports, and most of the egret farms have now disappeared.

Birds' nests

There are other minor products of birds which, if properly husbanded could be made to yield sizeable revenue in India. The saliva nests of the so-called Edible-nest Swiftlets (*Collocalia*), which breed in vast colonies in grottoes on rocky islands off the S. Burma coast were a source of considerable income to those engaged in the trade, and of royalty to government before that country was separated from India — and doubtless still are. These swiftlets also breed on certain islets off the Konkan coast (W. India), but the nests here are of poor quality; the trade in them, which was small even in former years, is now non-existent. The nests were exported to China as an epicurean delicacy, the better qualities fetching from Rs. 7 to 14 per lb. The value of nests imported into China during 1923, 1924 and 1925 exceeded Rs. 25 lakhs; a fair proportion of these came from the then British Indian Empire.

Guano

Guano which is really the excrement of sea birds such as gannets, cormorants and pelicans is another product of great commercial value. The fertilising properties of the phosphoric acid and nitrogen contained in fish were not recognised until guano became a stimulus to intensive agriculture. The real guano is found in vast stratified accretions on rainless islands off the coast of Peru, and although no deposits of like magnitude or value exist within our limits, yet the possibilities of the ' liquid guano ' of colonial-nesting water birds have not been seriously exploited in India.

From all that has been said it must not be assumed that birds are a wholly unmixed blessing. They are injurious to man's interests in a number of ways. They destroy his crops, and damage his orchards, flower beds and vegetable gardens; they devour certain beneficial insects and prey upon fish and other animals useful to man as food; they act as intermediate hosts of parasites and viruses that spread diseases among his livestock, and disperse them far and wide in the course of their migrations; they fertilize the flowers and disseminate the seeds of noxious plants and weeds. Yet, considering everything, there can be no doubt that the good they do far outweighs the harm, which must therefore be looked upon as no more than the labourer's hire.

The case for the protection and conservation of birds in a country like ours — so largely agricultural and forested and therefore at their mercy — is clear, and needs no eloquent advocacy. Quite apart from the purely materialistic aspect, however, it must not be forgotten that man cannot live by bread alone. By the gorgeousness of their plumages and the loveliness of their forms, by the vivaciousness of their movements and the sweetness of their songs, birds typify Life and Beauty. They rank beyond a doubt among those important trifles that supplement bread in the sustenance of man and make living worth while.

BIRD WATCHING

NEARLY every one enjoys birds: the beauty of their forms and colouring, the vivacity of their movements, the buoyancy of their flight and the sweetness of their songs. It is precisely on this account that as a pursuit for the out-of-doors, bird watching stands in a class by itself. Its strong point is that it can be indulged in with pleasure and profit not only by the man who studies birds scientifically, but also by one possessing no specialised knowledge. The latter, moreover, is enabled to share his profit with the scientist who for certain aspects of bird study has to depend entirely upon data collected by the intelligent watcher.

The appreciation of the beautiful and the novel is a characteristic latent in the human species. There is none in whom the seed of this faculty is entirely wanting. Environment may nurture and develop it in some, smother it in others. The fact of its existence is proved by the enquiries an ornithologist frequently receives concerning the identity of this bird with a green head or that with a red tail from persons of the most prosaic ' butcher, baker and candlestick-maker ' type who in the course of their day to day lives would never dream of going a step out of their way merely to look at a bird. It shows that even such a person, in spite of himself, cannot at one time or another help being struck by some peculiarity in the sight or sound of a bird which had not forced itself on his notice before.

It is amazing what tricks the imagination can play with undisciplined observation. A person who, for example, notices a male Paradise Flycatcher for the first time and is struck by its exquisite tail-ribbons fluttering in the breeze, will, as likely as not, and in all good faith, clothe his bird in multi-coloured hues of green and blue and yellow and red when describing it to you. The only real clue he furnishes is the ribbon tail. Some days later you have an opportunity of pointing out a Paradise Flycatcher to your enquirer with the suitable suggestion, whereupon you promptly learn that this indeed was the object of his ecstasy! Yet it is equally amazing what small effort is needed to discipline oneself to observe accurately. After a comparatively short period of intelligent bird watching one can often become so proficient that the mere glimpse of a bird as it flits across from one bush to another — some distinctive flash of a colour, a peculiar twitch of the tail — is enough to suggest its identity fairly reliably. If it is an unfamiliar species this fleeting impression will often suffice to puzzle it out with the aid of a bird book afterwards.

Apart from the joy and exhilaration it affords, careful and intelligent bird watching — considering that it can be indulged in by the many without special scientific training — widens the scope immensely for procuring data relating to the lives and behaviour of birds. Observations by people who habitually watch birds even merely for pleasure, are often of great value to the scientist trying to unravel some particular phase of bird life. Indeed, such observations — made as they are without knowledge of, or being swayed by this pet theory or that —

Photo: R. S. P. Bates

Camouflaged Ground 'Hide'

PLATE 95

Photo: E. H. N. Lowther

Machan 'Hide' against Blackbacked Woodpecker's nest-hole

PLATE 96

frequently carry the added advantage of being completely unbiased. As mentioned in a previous chapter the bulk of the work that now remains to be done on the birds of India concerns the *living* bird in its natural surroundings: How does the bird live and behave? In what way is it fitted or is fitting itself to its habitat? How is it influenced by or is influencing its environment? It is only satisfactory answers to questions like these — and their number is legion — that can lead us to a better understanding of that very real but strangely elusive thing called life.

One often hears it asserted that there are *no* birds in this locality or that. Such statements merely suggest that the observer may not know exactly where and how to look for them. For indeed it is difficult to imagine a single square mile of the Indian subcontinent entirely devoid of birds. Even in the midst of the scorching Rajasthan desert or amongst the high Himalayan snows, birds there are for those who know how to find them. They may be scarce and local, simply because their food happens to be scarce and local, but they are never entirely absent over areas of any size.

For the new arrival in this country and for the novice, some suggestions as to when and where to look for birds with success might prove helpful. First and foremost, although birds are on the move all day long, their activity is greatest in the early mornings; therefore early rising is a most important pre-requisite for successful watching. Most song is also heard during the early morning hours. Discovering the identity of a songster often entails patient watching, and the chances of tracking him down are naturally greatest in the early morning when the bird is most vocal.

Contrary to the popular notion, a forest, to the inexperienced, is usually a very disappointing place for bird watching. You may tramp miles without seeming to meet or hear a bird, and then just as you begin to despair you may round a bend in the path and suddenly find yourself confronted by a gathering that includes well nigh every species of the neighbourhood. There are birds on every hand: on the ground, among the bushes, on the trunks of the lofty trees and in the canopy of leaves high overhead. There are tits, babblers and tree pies, woodpeckers, nuthatches and drongos, flycatchers, minivets, and leaf warblers, and numerous other species besides. The scene is suddenly transformed into one of bustling activity. You have in fact struck what the books call a ' Mixed Hunting Party ', or ' Localised Forest Association '. These mixed assemblages are a characteristic feature of our forests, both hill and plain. Here birds do not as a rule spread themselves out uniformly, but rove about in co-operative bands of mixed species in more or less regular daily circuits. All the members of the association profit through the co-ordinated efforts of the lot. Babblers rummaging amongst the fallen leaves for insect food disturb a moth which is presently swooped upon and captured in mid-air by a drongo on the look-out hard by. A woodpecker scuttling up a tree-trunk in search of beetle galleries stampedes numerous winged insects resting upon the protectingly coloured bark or lurking within its crevices. These are promptly set upon by a vigilant flycatcher or warbler — and so on.

Banyan and peepul trees when in ripe fig attract a multitude of birds of many species from far and wide and offer excellent opportunities to the bird watcher. A lively scene presents itself as party after party arrives, all eager to gorge themselves on the abundance spread around. There is a great deal of noise and chatter as the visitors hop from branch to branch in their quest. Bickering and bullying are incessant, but no serious encounters develop since every individual is much too preoccupied with the main business in hand. Such gatherings are ideal for studying the natural dispositions and ' table manners ' of the various species.

Some of the most charming and enjoyable venues for bird watching are certainly afforded by the Silk Cotton, Coral Flower, or Flame-of-the-Forest (*Butea*) trees in bloom. Their particular attractiveness lies in the fact that the trees, or the branches bearing the gorgeous flowers, are bare and leafless at this season, allowing a clear and unobstructed view of the visitors. Almost every small bird of the surrounding countryside flocks to the blossoms for the sake of the sugary nectar which they produce in such abundance. Riot and revelry prevails throughout the day, but especially in the mornings, and there is constant bullying, hustling and mock fighting amongst the roysterers. A pair of good binoculars multiplies the pleasures of bird watching many-fold, and is indeed an indispensable item of the watcher's equipment.

Another favourable occasion is after the first few showers of rain have fallen and the winged termites — the potential queens and their numerous suitors — are emerging from their underground retreats for their momentous nuptial flight. A termite swarm acts like a magnet upon the bird population of its neighbourhood. Caste and creed are forgotten and every species hastens to the repast; no quarter is given, the insects being chased and captured on the ground as well as in the air. The agile and graceful gliding swoops of the swallows and swifts contrast strangely with the ponderous, ungainly efforts of crows making unaccustomed aerial sallies in the pursuit. Kites, kestrels, crows, owlets, mynas and bulbuls, sparrows, bayas and munias, tree pies, drongos and orioles, tailor birds and wren-warblers all join in the massacre, while even woodpeckers and barbets can seldom resist the temptation.

Nesting birds provide much important material for the study of animal behaviour. These can best be studied from a ' hide ' erected in the proximity of their nests. A portable ' hide ' is easily made with a few iron rods or bamboo poles and some canvas, or one of straw and leafy branches can usually be rigged up on the spot without difficulty. The birds soon get inured to its presence and can be watched from within in comparative comfort and at close quarters. Bird photography adds enormously to the zest of bird watching. Many facts of far-reaching significance concerning nesting habits and sexual behaviour have been brought to light by the careful observations and pictorial evidence of bird photographers. There is no pleasanter way of prolonged and intensive watching than in pursuit of bird photography, and there can be no success in bird photography without patient and intensive watching. Camera studies of birds in their natural surroundings and busy at their normal occupations are a joy not only to their maker, but also to others who have not been fortunate enough to share in his watching. The several attractive photographs reproduced in these pages will bear this out. No one interested in this fascinating pastime should miss the late Lieut.-Col. R. S. P. Bates's informative article on 'Bird Photography in India' published in Volume 40 of the *Journal of the Bombay Natural History Society* (May, 1939).

Useful suggestions for various types of hides and their construction, and other hints for bird photographers will also be found in Book 2 of the BIRDS OF CEYLON by W. W. A. Phillips (1952). Entirely new ground in the photography of birds in India has recently been broken by Loke Wan Tho. By the use of high speed flash equipment he has obtained remarkable action pictures at 1/3000 to 1/5000 of a second. The technique is described by him in the *Journal of the Bombay Natural History Society*, Vol. 50(4) — August 1952. The photograph of the hoopoe (Plate 87) is an example of his high speed flash work.

A north Indian jheel in winter is a veritable paradise for the bird watcher. Every species of water bird, as well as those that live about the margins and in the marshy reed-beds, may be met here, and an unique opportunity is afforded of getting acquainted with them. It is an exhilarating experience, even for one who is not a shikari to drift along in a punt over the placid water on a cold morning with the din of honking, quacking and trumpeting on every hand, and the fluttering and swishing of wings of countless wildfowl overhead. The multitudes of the birds, apart from their great variety, leave a picture on the mind that is not easily lost.

It must not be supposed that this list exhausts the possibilities for bird watching in India. Indeed pleasure can be derived from the most everyday birds in the most humdrum surroundings, and even the jaded city dweller can regale his leisure hours without the necessity of going far afield in search of special opportunities. Birds can be attracted to our homes and gardens without any great difficulty by the provision of suitable feeding trays, baths, and nesting boxes. These simple and inexpensive appliances not only add charm and ornament to the garden but they soon engender that friendliness and confidence in the bird visitors which is so essential for their enjoyment at close quarters.

An excellent pamphlet — Field Guide No. 3: Nestboxes — has recently been published by the British Trust for Ornithology, Oxford. It gives particulars and diagrams of many types of nestboxes, and all relevant information concerning their use. (Price 40 p.)

Everyone who watches birds intelligently enough to enjoy them, and who carries with him a note book and pencil, should be in a position to contribute in some measure to our store of knowledge. The essentials are Patience, plus the ability to observe accurately and to record faithfully, even though the observations may sometimes disagree with the books or the observer himself may sometimes wish things to happen differently!

Above all it is important that sentimentality be kept in check and to remember at all times that the behaviour of birds cannot be interpreted entirely by human analogy. Birds do not possess the power of reasoning; therefore their actions, however intelligent they may seem, are essentially little more than instinctive reflexes.

All unusual or original field observations are worthy of permanent record since they are the bricks of which ornithological structures are built. To test the value of your notes they should be offered for publication to the *Newsletter for Birdwatchers*, the monthly bulletin of the recently formed Birdwatchers' Field Club of India (address: Dodda Gubbi Post, Via Vidyanagar, Bangalore 562 134) or—if of a more tech-

nical character—to the *Journal of the Bombay Natural History Society*.
Amateur bird watchers as well as seasoned ornithologists will find it
profitable in many practical ways to belong to either or both these
separate organizations. Membership terms can be obtained from the
respective honorary secretaries.

Books to read:

(1) A GUIDE TO BIRD WATCHING. By Joseph J. Hickey. (Oxford
University Press, 1943)

(2) HOW TO STUDY BIRDS. By Stuart Smith. (Collins, 1945)

(3) WATCHING BIRDS. By James Fisher. (Pelican Books, 1946)

(4) BIRD WATCHING AS A HOBBY. By W. D. Campbell. (Stanley Paul,
London, 1959)

(5) ABOUT INDIAN BIRDS. By Laeeq Futehally and Sálim Ali.
(Blackie, Bombay, 1959)

(6) WATCHING BIRDS. By Jamal Ara. (National Book Trust, India,
1970).

INDEX OF SPECIES

(Italics indicate that the species is only partially described)

INDEX OF SPECIES

INDEX OF SPECIES

INDEX OF SPECIES

INDEX OF SPECIES

APPENDIX

HOW TO RECOGNIZE BIRDS IN THE FIELD

1. Birds with prominent Tails

Size*	Species	Length of Tail	Prominent colours of Bird	Page
D ±	Haircrested Drongo (6a)	6½"; slightly forked; upcurling at end	Glossy blue-black	146
C−	Greenbilled Malkoha (6d)	9½"; broad, graduated, white-tipped	Greenish ashy grey	147

2. Birds with prominent Bills

Size*	Species	Shape, colour and length of bill	Predominant colours of Bird	Page
F+	Caspian Tern (6b)	2¼"; stout; coral red	White; pale grey	146
G-H	Kora or Watercock ♂ (6a)	Bright red with fleshy 'horn' on forehead	Bright red legs and eyes	143
J	Great Stone Plover (6e)	3"; stout, upcurved black-&-yellow	Greyish sandy; black; white	143

* See Key on p. vii.

5. Bright coloured Birds
a. *Chiefly GREEN or BLUE*

Size*	Species	Associated colours	Page
D+	Small Yellownaped Woodpecker	Yellowish green; crimson; yellow	148
E—	Greyfronted Green Pigeon ♂	Chestnut; grey; yellow	145

c. *Chiefly or largely RED*

D±	Southern Trogon ♂	Crimson; blackish; yellowish brown; white	147

6. Sober coloured Birds
a. *General effect more or less wholly BLACK*

Size*	Species	Page
D±	Haircrested Drongo (1)	146
F+	Kora or Watercock ♂	143

b. *General effect more or less wholly WHITE*

G-H	Caspian Tern (2)	146

c. *General effect PIED BLACK AND WHITE*

A+	Heartspotted Woodpecker	148
H—	Pied Harrier ♂	142

* See Key on p. vii.

6. Sober coloured Birds — *contd.*

d. *General effect largely ASHY GREY, BLUE-GREY or SLATY*

Size*	Species	Associated colours	Page
G—	Greenbilled Malkoha (1)	Greenish ashy grey	147

e. *General effect more or less BROWN (all shades)*

Size*	Species	Associated colours	Page
B	Baillon's Crake	Rufescent; grey	144
D+	Southern Trogon ♀	Yellowish brown; orange brown; blackish	147
E	Brown Hawk-Owl	White	141
F—	Slatylegged Banded Crake	Rufous; black-barred white	144
G+	Maroonbacked Imperial Pigeon	Grey	145
H—	Pied Harrier ♀	White	142
H	Mottled Wood Owl	White; yellowish buff	141
H+	Greyheaded Fishing Eagle	White	142
J	Great Stone Plover (2)	White; black	143

* See Key on p. vii.

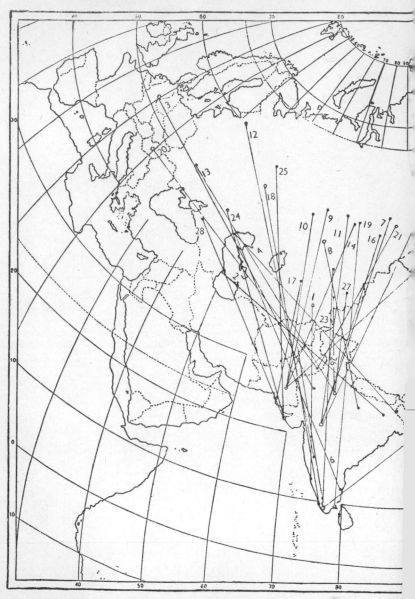

Map showing some significant Ring Recoveries.